PLACELESS

W0114416

PLACE LESS

Homelessness in the New Gilded Age

PATRICK MARKEE

MELVILLE HOUSE
BROOKLYN · LONDON

Placeless : Homelessness in the New Gilded Age

First published in 2025 by Melville House
Copyright © 2025 by Patrick Markee
All rights reserved
First Melville House Printing: October 2025

Distributed by Penguin Random House LLC,
1745 Broadway, New York, NY 10019 USA.
www.penguinrandomhouse.com

Melville House Publishing
46 John Street
Brooklyn, NY 11201

and

Melville House UK
Suite 2000
16/18 Woodford Road
London E7 0HA

mhpbooks.com
@melvillehouse

ISBN: 978-1-68589-167-1
ISBN: 978-1-68589-168-8 (eBook)

Library of Congress Control Number: 2025943960

Designed by Beste M. Doğan

Printed in the United States of America
10 9 8 7 6 5 4 3 2 1

A catalog record for this book is available from the Library of Congress

The authorized representative in the EU for product safety and compliance is
Easy Access System Europe, Mustamäe tee 50, 10621 Tallinn, Estonia.
gpsr.requests@easproject.com

In memory of my mother,
Kathleen Hayes Markee

H.G. Wells once said, coming out of a political meeting where they had been discussing social change, that this great towering city was a measure of the obstacle, of how much must be moved if there was to be any change. I have known this feeling, looking up at great buildings that are the centres of power, but I find I do not say 'There is your city, your great bourgeois monument, your towering structure of this still precarious civilisation' or I do not only say that; I say also 'This is what men have built, so often magnificently, and is not everything then possible?'

RAYMOND WILLIAMS
The Country and the City

While we do our good works let us not forget that the real solution lies in a world in which charity will have become unnecessary.

CHINUA ACHEBE
Anthills of the Savannah

INTRODUCTION:
PLACES AND SPACES

In a more profound way homelessness is very much a product of the idea of "home" as a particular kind of place. In the Western world "home" is an ideal as well as a place—a spatially constructed ideology usually correlated with housing. At its most basic level homelessness denotes a lack of housing. But homelessness also signifies "displacement"—an existential lack that is perhaps even more fundamental than being without shelter.

Tim Cresswell
Place: An Introduction

THE NEW GILDED AGE

It was an era marked by rampant inequality and urban poverty. Industrial tycoons owned more than half the nation's wealth, wielded monopoly power, and corrupted the political system. Municipal leaders deployed militias and police on behalf of moneyed elites, brutally suppressing the revolts of restive laborers. A white backlash, often violent, grew amid even minimal signs of Black progress. Immigrants flooded into teeming cities, crowding tenements while landlords demanded ever higher rents. Underlying it all, massive shifts were transforming an economy in which manufacturing and industry prevailed.

This was the first Gilded Age of the late nineteenth century, and its echoes and reverberations have grown louder and more insistent over a century later. Unaccountably, we've arrived at another Gilded Age, but this one brought with it something new—a decades-long crisis of mass homelessness.

With this book, I've set out to explore the phenomenon of modern mass homelessness in our New Gilded Age, an era defined, like its late nineteenth-century namesake, by exploding inequality and seismic shifts in the economic and urban landscape. In these pages, I have attempted to offer a wide view of mass homelessness and displacement informed by historical analysis, urban theory, the latest policy research, and my own frontline experiences from more than two decades working as a homeless advocate. In short, I have tried to show that modern homelessness is both antecedent and symptom of the neoliberal era—and that far from being yet another urban malady, it has been instead a harbinger of wider forms of displacement in this New Gilded Age.

Too many accounts of homelessness have treated it as a special case—a social work problem, a matter of personal pathology and dysfunction, or some peculiar subspecies of urban poverty. Worse still, homelessness has too often been portrayed as an intractable problem that will "always be with us." I've chosen instead to consider modern homelessness as the inevitable consequence of structural shifts in the capitalist economy, worsening inequality, systemic racism, and neoliberal government policies. What emerged was a loss of place—not only the loss of home and shelter, but also the loss of identity and security, as well as community and a role in our economic and civic life. I've then analyzed how the historical and economic forces of this unequal era accelerated the widening problem of displacement, with homelessness being only the most visible and tragic symptom.

In tracing the history of mass homelessness, I've also relied on the experiences of countless homeless people whom I have met over the years—people who struggled against overwhelming odds, facing government hostility and harassment, to survive day after day and ultimately escape homelessness and find a home. In this book, I've tried to tell some of their stories—above all, to show that the enormity of the crisis was, in the end, about real individuals.*

Writing about modern mass homelessness, I knew I could never do justice to those who have lived through the crisis, nor those lost to it. So I've chosen to root the story in some historical, visible urban landmarks—places that offered refuge to homeless people but were also sites of displacement. In one chapter, I examine the harsh crackdowns on homeless people in Madison Square Park, part of the ruthless and racist policing tactics that helped fuel the lucrative hypergentrification of the surrounding neighborhood. In another chapter, I tell the story of the threatened eviction of dozens of homeless people from a train tunnel beneath Riverside Park, and how politicians, the news media, and others sought to pathologize the tunnel dwellers as well as other homeless people. In a later chapter, I explore the history of armories, the vast, fortresslike buildings used to shelter tens of thousands of homeless New Yorkers, many of whom were low-wage laborers—the same armories that were built in the first Gilded Age to quarter militias deployed by wealthy elites to suppress worker uprisings.

Modern homelessness was also a consequence of harsh, deliberate policies crafted and implemented by a series of New York mayors and public officials, and by their counterparts in DC and nationwide. It was impossible to understand the modern homelessness crisis in places like Boston, San Diego, Austin, and Washington, DC, without grappling with the history of the crisis in the nation's largest city. I've therefore tried to show how the recent history of New York's experience with homelessness and displacement could both explain the national phenomenon and illuminate the debate about how to handle the crisis.

----

* I've changed the names of homeless individuals whose stories I've recounted in this book, unless those people appeared in news reports.

MODERN MASS HOMELESSNESS

While homelessness has existed in various ways throughout American history, the past century has seen just two extended periods of mass displacement: the Great Depression of the 1930s and the contemporary period of modern mass homelessness, which began in the late 1970s and has not ended after more than four decades. Historians have estimated that, on any given night during the worst years of the 1930s, there were well over a million homeless Americans, and millions of people experienced homelessness annually.[1] The mass homelessness of the Great Depression, when the nation's total population was about a third of what it became in the early twenty-first century, was undoubtedly more acute on a night-to-night basis than in the modern era. But it was also of far shorter duration, lasting for only a decade or so.

It has become nearly impossible to reckon with the scale of modern mass homelessness.** In 2024, the federal government estimated that some 771,000 people experienced homelessness on a single night—that is, they slept in shelters, on the streets, or in other public spaces. This estimate was almost certainly an undercount, and it obscured the fact that, over the course of a year, as many as 3.5 million different people actually *experienced* homelessness. These measures also overlooked the much larger "hidden homeless" population of people living in doubled-up arrangements or severely overcrowded dwellings. One study found that, during the same period, there were 3.7 million people living in doubled-up housing—meaning that, by the 2020s, more than two in every hundred people in the United States was without a stable home.

** Throughout this book, I've used the term "homeless" to describe this phenomenon. The word has deep historic roots, dating to the nineteenth century, and it came to be the nearly universal term for the crisis by at least the 1970s. Throughout American history many words, some quite offensive, have been used to label people without homes: "vagrants," "bums," hobos," "tramps," "derelicts." By the early twenty-first century some advocates and researchers preferred to use the (unfortunately clunky) term "people experiencing homelessness," and by the 2010s many other advocates began to use the word "unhoused" (even though most city-dwellers lived in apartments, not houses). Throughout the period covered in this book, "homeless" was the most commonly used term.

The scale of the modern homelessness crisis in New York, the nation's largest city, was almost harder to fathom. By the year 2025, more than 130,000 people were homeless each night in New York City, an astounding figure, and the highest ever recorded in the forty-plus years of modern mass homelessness. This was five times greater than the size of the nightly homeless population at the beginning of the twenty-first century, and eleven times larger than that in the early 1980s, during the first years of the modern crisis.

The large majority of New York City's homeless population slept in shelters, thanks to legal "right to shelter" protections (see chapter 2). Among the 130,000 people homeless in New York City each night, around three-quarters of those in shelters were in families, including some forty-five thousand children. Thousands more individuals slept rough each night on the streets, in the subway system, in parks, or in other outdoor places. Because of the legacy of systemic racism and inequality, Black and Latino New Yorkers made up nearly 90 percent of the homeless population, despite constituting only half of New York City's total population. Indeed, according to a 2015 research study I wrote, one in every seventeen Black children in New York City had experienced homelessness over the course of a single year.[2]

New York City's "hidden homeless" population—the growing number of New York households forced to double up with relatives or friends or to live in severely overcrowded or illegal dwellings—was even larger. One stark sign of this invisible homeless population was that, over the course of the 2023–24 school year, more than 146,000 students in the New York public school system—a remarkable one in every eight students—had experienced homelessness.[3] Researchers and advocates estimated that well over two hundred thousand people made up the hidden homeless population. This meant that, a quarter of the way through the twenty-first century, as many as four in every hundred New Yorkers lacked a stable home on any given night.

MUSICAL CHAIRS

How did the modern homelessness crisis evolve, and why has it persisted for so long? The most elegant illustration I ever heard of the dynamics of modern homelessness was found, oddly enough, in a children's game—musical chairs. In each round of the game, a chair was removed before the next began. Children would walk in a circle around the chairs, and, when the music stopped playing, the players would race to sit down in the remaining chairs. Each chair, in the metaphor, was an affordable home—or, as happened in the era of modern mass homelessness, one of the thousands of affordable or government-assisted apartments that were removed each year. And the rounds would continue, of course, as more chairs—or more housing units—were taken away.

So, who got the remaining chairs? Well, as I remembered it from my childhood, the winners were the bigger, stronger, and more ruthless kids. The weaker kids got pushed out of the game and wound up chairless. In the homelessness scenario, the poorest and "weakest" people were the ones pushed aside. Those who most swiftly lost their homes included people living with disabilities, the unemployed, poor families, individuals struggling with mental illness, and women fleeing domestic violence. Over time, as new rounds of the game began and the music started up and then was silenced again, the number of homeless people continued to grow.

It was a neat metaphor that helped show the problem wasn't the players—it was the force removing the chairs. In this book, I've attempted to work out *how* and *why* the chairs—or, rather, the homes—were taken away, and what economic and political forces were responsible. I've also tried to show what happened to those who were removed and displaced, who became part of a growing surplus population of discarded people. Finally, I've attempted to illustrate how homelessness was only one way that displacement became so widespread in the New Gilded Age.

PLACE
LESS

CHAPTER 1

THE TRAIN TUNNEL: PATHOLOGIZING HOMELESSNESS

The press routinely treated the homeless not as victims but menaces. Some papers defined "tramp" in racial terms—as an urban Indian—or, in the words of one professional, "a lazy, incorrigible, cowardly, utterly depraved savage." The Times suggested that readers worried about tramps "procure a large dog who understands how to insert his teeth where it will do the most good." . . . Reformers believed that more coordinated action was needed to bring down vagrancy and beggary. . . . Almost all of those present [at an 1877 meeting of charitable organizations] agreed that tramps were socially defective beings.

Edwin G. Burrows and Mike Wallace
Gotham: A History of New York City to 1898

THE TUNNEL

The train tunnel ran for fifty city blocks, nearly three miles, under Manhattan streets and parkland. It stretched along the island's far west side, near the Hudson River, from West 72nd Street uptown to West 122nd Street in West Harlem. It was one of those rare New York City places that made one feel both inside and utterly outside the city, as if, for a few moments, a visitor who'd ventured far enough into its recesses could convince themselves that they'd fled the chaos and noise of the city without ever leaving.

The first time I walked deep into the tunnel, one autumn afternoon in 1995, I felt myself steadily, step by step, wrapped in darkness. The pallid October sunlight from the southern entrance faded, and I could feel my pupils dilating to capture the available light, allowing me to glimpse the grime-streaked concrete walls, the graffiti, and the railroad tracks with their battered wooden ties. I was instantly aware of the descending silence, as if the volume knob on an old stereo were turning down the usual background thrum and clatter of New York City. But then, gradually, imperceptibly, other sounds intruded: rats skittering on the gravel and rails, water dripping from the two-story-high tunnel ceiling or a ventilation grate, the echo of someone shouting from the tunnel mouth behind me. And, all at once, I was reminded that the dark, muted tunnel was merely another manufactured creation in the thoroughly artificial environment of New York City—and, most startling of all, one that became, for many years, a last-resort home for dozens of desperate New Yorkers seeking refuge.

In the mid-1990s, early in my career as an advocate with the Coalition for the Homeless, I spent several months helping to resettle the last of several dozen homeless people soon to be expelled from a train tunnel on the west side of Manhattan. Beginning in October 1995, I trekked a few days each month to a derelict lot not far from the Hudson River. There, a once-disused rail line disappeared into a vast tunnel that stretched northwards under Riverside Park, surfaced in West Harlem, and continued on to Albany and points upstate.

During those few chilly months in a changing, embattled New York City—where Mayor Rudy Giuliani's brutal, racist, and overtly antihomeless policies were being hailed by many elites as having "saved" New York—I met some remarkable people who'd managed to survive some unimaginably trying circumstances. Even more, I came to learn some crucial lessons about the enduring, and pernicious, myths surrounding homelessness in the New Gilded Age.

"WEST SIDE IMPROVEMENT"

The Riverside Park tunnel wasn't excavated. Instead, like the park above, it was built over some existing railroad tracks at the direction of urban autocrat and master builder Robert Moses. The original, narrower Riverside Park dated to 1875, during the first Gilded Age. It had been planned, in part, by Frederick Law Olmsted and Calvert Vaux, the legendary landscape architects who had also designed Central Park, Prospect Park, and a host of other elegant green spaces.

The original park was delimited and cut off from the river by the Hudson River Railroad lines, which connected New York City to Albany. But Robert Moses ultimately had a grander vision for the narrow greenway. Robert Caro's legendary biography *The Power Broker* described Moses in 1912, then a young student of municipal bureaucracy—a bureaucracy he'd later come to master and rule as arguably the most powerful New York public official of the twentieth century—looking down from the "high bluff that was Riverside Drive":

> Below him, along the edge of the river, was a wasteland. . . . The
> wasteland was named Riverside Park, but the "park" was nothing
> but a vast, low-lying mass of dirt and mud. Running through
> its length was the four-track bed of the New York Central. . . .
> Unpainted, rusting, jagged wire fences along the tracks barred
> the city from its waterfront. . . . Walking in the park was an
> adventure; the walker sank at intervals into the landfill of which
> it had been constructed, for water had eaten away much of the fill
> from below. . . . Other solid spots held human refuse: derelicts
> who had built tar-paper shanty towns considered so dangerous
> that the police stayed away from them. At night, the open fires
> over which the derelicts cooked flickered in the darkness below
> the Drive.[1]

Even as a mere trainee working in a city government office, Moses conceived a grand plan he later dubbed West Side Improvement. Two decades later, after he'd cemented his control of several New York government agencies and authorities in the 1930s, Moses marshaled more than $100 million in spending to make his dream a reality. He eventually created the Henry Hudson Parkway, expanded Riverside Park to the river and uptown, and constructed the tunnel over the New York Central's railroad.

The tracks of the West Side Line, as it was then called, had once served the slaughterhouses of downtown Manhattan and were later used for freight trains hauling goods to and from the manufacturing zones in Chelsea and the Garment District. But over the coming decades, the trains fell victim to competing railyards in New Jersey and the Bronx, as well as the expanding freight-trucking industry. Factories and workshops in Chelsea and other parts of Manhattan's west side shuttered as manufacturing firms moved their operations, and jobs, to cheaper locales outside the city. Train traffic on the West Side Line was halted. The rail tracks, and the tunnel, were essentially abandoned by the late 1970s—the same period that witnessed the emergence of modern mass homelessness in New York.

TUNNEL DWELLERS

No one knows precisely when the first homeless people began sleeping in the Riverside Park tunnel. But the population of tunnel dwellers grew sharply in the 1980s, as the number of homeless New Yorkers began to soar. And, historically, when the shelter population of homeless "single adults" (those not part of families) was growing, the unsheltered population was also rising. In the city's ballooning shelter system, the number of homeless single adults bedding down each night nearly tripled. It rose to eleven thousand people per night by 1989—a figure that didn't even account for the eighteen thousand homeless kids and parents also sleeping nightly in family shelters by the end of that decade.

By the late 1980s, there was no doubt that there were thousands of people sleeping rough each night on the streets, in parks, and in transportation terminals. As homelessness in New York worsened, some desperate people turned to increasingly remote places to find makeshift shelter, including the subway network, bridge abutments, and train tunnels. By the early 1990s, there were dozens of homeless people sleeping each night in the Riverside Park tunnel, and many had built shanties and other ramshackle dwellings in different areas, most of them crowded near the southern entrance. Though many felt safer there than on the streets, the tunnel remained a treacherous place. Rats and other vermin roamed free, garbage accumulated, there was no running water, and the winter cold and damp still threatened death or severe injury by hypothermia or frostbite. But with train traffic virtually halted for a decade, many desperate people chose the hazards of the tunnel over those of the subways or of the vast, warehouse-like municipal shelters that the city government had hastily created in the first decade of the homelessness crisis.

Some folks ended up living in the tunnel for years at a time. Joe, a Vietnam War veteran, called the tunnel home for more than twenty years; for much of that time, he lived with his partner, Cathy, in a sturdy plywood shack, with a mattress propped up on plastic milk crates. José, who had lost the last of a series of low-wage jobs when a garment factory closed, stayed in the tunnel for thirteen years. Bernard, dubbed the Mayor of the Tunnel, lived there for more than a decade in a ramshackle camp he'd fashioned deep underground.

Tales of the homeless people in the Riverside Park tunnel were recounted in numerous news articles, nonfiction books, films, and at least one novel. Perhaps the best accounts came from photographer Margaret Morton's 1995 book *The Tunnel*, which included direct recollections of the tunnel dwellers she knew so well, alongside her austere and luminous photographs.[2] Marc Singer's documentary film *Dark Days*, shot over several years on black-and-white 16 mm film and memorably set to the music of the hip-hop artist and turntablist DJ Shadow, was a moving and gritty portrait of life in the tunnel. The Dutch anthropologist Teun Voeten's book *Tunnel People* offered a garrulous, sympathetic portrait of the tunnel residents and concluded by tracking them down more than a decade after they had left.[3] Colum McCann's acclaimed early novel *This Side of Brightness* told the story of a homeless man who was descended from a "sandhog," one of the Irish immigrant workers who, during the Gilded Age, dug the massive rail tunnels under the East River as well as the subway system.[4]

The tunnel also became famous for its jumble of graffiti as early as the 1970s. Over time, many New Yorkers came to call it the Freedom Tunnel, after the graffiti artist Chris "Freedom" Pape, whose best work—including a portrait of "Mayor" Bernard and versions of the *Venus de Milo* and Francisco Goya's *The Third of May 1808*—could still be seen well into the twenty-first century. Indeed, many years later, during the height of the Michael Bloomberg era, the Riverside Park tunnel became a curiosity and unlikely tourist destination. It was marketed to "urban explorers" as a place where young hipsters could see decades-old graffiti and witness some relics of the "bad old days" of a lost, irretrievable New York.

In similar fashion, some of the stories and accounts of the people living in the tunnel morphed into urban folklore, or even something worse. Jennifer Toth's 1993 book *The Mole People* became perhaps the most well-known account and remained in print for years, unlike similar ethnographic studies.[5] But its stigmatizing title would outlive the text of the book itself, and the term "mole people"—indeed, the idea of some alien species of homeless tunnel dwellers—came to permeate the popular culture of the era.

THE "HARDCORE" HOMELESS

For more than a decade, the Riverside Park tunnel was a refuge as well as a last resort, but eventually, it ceased to be even that. In 1991, a rail extension was built to allow nondiesel cars, like Amtrak's passenger trains, to travel to Pennsylvania Station. Amtrak announced that it would begin passenger train service through the tunnel, and in 1995, after the trains had started to run again, the agency prepared to expel the homeless people from the tunnel for good.[6]

Hearing from tunnel residents about the impending eviction, a group of neighbors and activists on Manhattan's Upper West Side—including the filmmaker Marc Singer and the photographer Margaret Morton—raised a ruckus and contacted the Coalition for the Homeless. Coalition staff investigated and, among other things, discovered that during the previous year, in November 1994, Secretary of the US Department of Housing and Urban Development Henry Cisneros had set aside an obscure allocation of some 250 federal housing vouchers for homeless people living in train tunnels. He had taken this unprecedented action when, on a visit to New York, he had witnessed firsthand dozens of homeless people sleeping rough in the subway system.[7] However, many months after Cisneros's pledge, only two of those vouchers had actually been issued, leaving the rest unused. The Coalition urged federal officials to halt the tunnel evictions while it worked with another local nonprofit organization to utilize the special allotment of vouchers to help move the tunnel dwellers to their own homes.

This plan was considered audacious. Even after more than a decade of modern mass homelessness, there was a widespread notion that there existed a group of "hardcore" homeless people who simply could not live in homes of their own—that these folks were somehow too sick, too unready, too broken. And the "mole people" of the tunnels were seen as prime examples of that mythical hardcore homeless group. But to anyone who'd talked with the Riverside Park tunnel dwellers, it was also clear that merely offering them a worse alternative—a cot in the shelter system or some other cold public space—would never succeed. What they needed and wanted was real housing.

When I first visited in late 1995, the work of relocating the tunnel dwellers to their own homes was underway. A young caseworker from our partner organization, Project Renewal, had done an incredible job navigating the byzantine bureaucracy of obtaining ID and other necessary documents for people who'd long lost them or never had them at all, and then completing paperwork for the federal housing vouchers. My Coalition colleague Mike had begun rounding up the last holdouts—a handful of tunnel residents who were fearful of leaving the only home they'd known for years, or didn't believe the looming threat of Amtrak's expulsion order.

At the same time, long-standing tunnel dwellers like José, Bernard, Joe, and Cathy, who were all in the process of moving to apartments, had been joined—and in some cases replaced—by a group of recent immigrants from Mexico, Central America, and the Caribbean, many of them day laborers who had fallen on hard times. My focus, as a passable Spanish speaker, was to work with the Latino immigrants to obtain the required paperwork and ease their fears about moving from the familiar tunnel to an unfamiliar home. But I was also lucky enough to get to know, even if only briefly, Bernard and other longtime tunnel residents and learn some vital lessons.

SUPPORTIVE HOUSING

Our work with the Riverside Park tunnel dwellers was, in most ways, a success. By the time Amtrak fully fenced off the tunnel in 1996, we had helped some forty homeless people who'd lived underground—including some of the Latino immigrants who'd arrived during the last year—move into real housing. Almost none of them ever returned to homelessness.

The tunnel dwellers were helped by the federal rental vouchers that advocates had managed to pry loose from the housing agency. After moving into their new homes, most were also assisted by social workers and received mental health treatment, sometimes for a brief, transitional period, and sometimes for years afterward. This combination of subsidized housing aid and social services, aimed at ensuring stability, had become known as supportive housing.

One of the first supportive housing programs, a rehabilitated Washington Heights building for once-homeless men living with mental illness, and poor families, was created by Ellen Baxter. She was a brilliant woman who, as noted in chapter 2, had cowritten—alongside the equally brilliant anthropologist Kim Hopper—one of the first studies of modern-day Bowery homelessness, and who later cofounded the Coalition for the Homeless. Baxter's pioneering program, like another created by two Franciscan monks in midtown Manhattan, provided subsidized housing along with supportive services for people living with mental illness and other disabilities, rather than leaving them to fend for themselves.

By the 1990s, the supportive housing model really took hold and began to be replicated throughout the country. As detailed in chapter 2, it started with the 1990 signing of the New York / New York Agreement, a joint initiative of the city and state governments that created more than 3,600 supportive housing apartments targeted at homeless people living with serious mental illnesses like schizophrenia and bipolar disorder. The state-city accord not only helped thousands of the most vulnerable people in New York move from shelters and the streets into their own homes; it also literally transformed and reshaped the lives of people who'd been abandoned, left without treatment to self-medicate with alcohol or drugs while struggling on the streets or in the labyrinthine shelter system. More important, the agreement—at the time, the largest supportive housing initiative ever attempted nationwide—helped catalyze an unprecedented decline in New York's unsheltered homeless population. As the decade progressed, everyone, from street outreach workers to everyday New Yorkers, could see the difference on city streets.

PATHOLOGY

In the early to mid-1990s, the idea that "hardcore" homeless people could be successfully housed was considered outlandish for two major reasons. First, there was a growing "compassion fatigue," a public sense of futility driven by the persistence of the homelessness crisis and government failure to address the problem, followed by outright hostility generated during the "backlash era" (see chapter 4). Second, antihomeless and right-wing notions had begun to permeate both government policymaking and the philosophy and approach of mainstream homeless service providers.

My months trekking to the tunnels occurred during the height of Giuliani's harsh attacks on what he and the hysterical tabloid press cynically portrayed as a chaotic, dysfunctional, dystopian New York City. This meant that if one were homeless, or a young Black or Latino man, or a single mother, or a welfare recipient, or anyone else whom Giuliani and his allies demonized on a regular basis, one became a target—of the perpetually enraged mayor's verbal attacks, of aggressive police tactics, and of a city bureaucracy aimed at cutting off most forms of assistance.

The "mole people" of the tunnel were thus another distorted signifier of the "bad old days" of the 1980s. But the rise in homelessness during that time was rarely discussed in terms of actual causes and real solutions. Instead, the tabloid newspapers spilled thousands of gallons of ink writing about the "squeegee men" gathering near the entrance of the Lincoln Tunnel and other commuter corridors; "Billie Boggs" (née Joyce Brown), an erratic homeless woman struggling with mental illness and addiction, who had slept on the streets of the wealthy Upper East Side and resisted efforts to be forcibly committed to a state hospital; or Larry Hogue, a homeless veteran who'd suffered a traumatic brain injury during his military service and was prone to aggressive, sometimes violent behavior—the *New York Daily News* and others dubbed him the Wild Man and sought to have the authorities remove him from the gentrifying neighborhood around West 96th Street.

In the ranting world of the tabloids and Giuliani's rhetoric, it was as if these few individuals stood in for all homeless and poor New Yorkers. Thus, a hyperbolic, cartoonish, menacing picture of homelessness was woven into a cultivated narrative about New York City's decline and crisis. This was the city of the "backlash era" as it existed in the *New York Post*, the local TV news, and the popular imagination: the Times Square of porn palaces and drug bazaars—already primed for a real estate industry–led makeover; the rising crime rate that was similarly rising in cities around the country, and would soon begin a nationwide decline; the emergence of crack cocaine addiction and the violence attached to the illicit drug trade—reminiscent of Prohibition-era gang violence; the random acts of horrific violence that the media selected for endless dissection, like the Central Park jogger case—though, as some observers noted, two equally horrendous but virtually unreported stranger rapes occurred within a week of the Central Park incident, but those victims were Black women and the crimes happened in the outer boroughs, so the media ignored them; and the relentless defense by the press and politicians of the historically hostile and racist tactics of the New York Police Department (NYPD)—typified by the jogger case and the wrongfully convicted, and later exonerated, "Central Park Five." Into this fever-dream version of New York City arrived Giuliani and his determination to "clean up" the city. The tunnel's "mole people" thus became early, collateral damage. The mayor, as detailed in chapter 3, prioritized harsh police enforcement, meaning arrests and harassment, of homeless people citywide, culminating in his 1999 order to arrest *all* homeless people sleeping on city streets.

This was the reason the title of Toth's otherwise well-intentioned book, *The Mole People*, remained so troubling and has proved damaging over the years. Toth wrote an author's note in which she questioned her use of the title but ultimately chose to keep it because some homeless people used the term.[8] But this hyperbolic title helped perpetuate an image of the Riverside Park tunnel dwellers as animalistic, alien, and *other*. Over time, the term "mole people," with all its pejorative connotations, has carried over to other homeless people living in other train tunnels or in the subway system.

During my decades of work as an advocate, I fielded countless inquiries about "mole people": news reporters looking to interview or film the "underground homeless"; policymakers convinced that vast numbers of homeless people dwelled under city streets; students and others entranced by the absurd idea of tribal communities, with their own exotic rituals, living in near isolation amid a sprawling metropolis. The name "mole people" conjured up the image of a separate race of beings, like H. G. Wells's Morlocks or the villainous Mole Man's blind minions from the *Fantastic Four* comic books—a race far removed from regular New Yorkers.

This was the same rhetorical weapon wielded by the tabloids, right-wing pundits, and Giuliani against "Billie Boggs," Larry Hogue, and countless other homeless people. Homeless New Yorkers were routinely depicted as pathological, crazy, drug-addicted, or dangerous and violent, even though it was obvious that homeless people were far more likely to be victims of violence than to commit it and were victimized at far higher rates than nonhomeless people. Likewise, Giuliani, his aides, and their right-wing allies would effectively blame homeless people for their homelessness. They'd portray homeless people as lazy, resistant to work, and lacking "personal responsibility," and would then craft policies supposedly designed to instill these ineffable qualities but that were really designed to deny or cut off safety-net benefits. The overwhelming fact that the vast majority of homeless New Yorkers were Black or Latino only made these stereotypes more pernicious, demonstrating how rooted they were in the wider American legacy of racism and the specific white-backlash politics that Giuliani and his ilk practiced.

"TRAMPS" OF THE GILDED AGE

Efforts to pathologize homeless people had their roots in the first Gilded Age. The global economic crisis of the 1870s (see chapter 2) created the first major wave of homelessness in a rapidly growing and industrializing New York City. Tens of thousands of people lost their jobs and homes and sought aid in police precinct houses—then the only form of municipal shelter, and a dismal one at that—and from local charities. Amid the expansion of a nationwide railroad network, the United States also witnessed the emergence of large groups of itinerant, poor laborers, mostly men, riding the rails from town to town in search of work and aid. They came to be labeled "bums"—after "bummers," a term for mercenary soldiers—or more commonly "tramps," a pejorative name also derived from military lingo.[9]

The elites of the period, along with their compliant allies in the press, portrayed these homeless wanderers in the most vicious terms imaginable. Foreshadowing the right-wing discourse that would reign a century later, the "tramps" were depicted as lazy, shiftless, unwilling to work, and desirous of handouts and charity. The remedies proposed by the wealthy, the newspapers, and even charitable organizations, at that time largely run by the same civic elites, also presaged the harsh policies of the modern age: cutting off and denying aid entirely. "Charity rages like an epidemic," declared the *New York World*, and such charity encouraged "idleness and dependence in the lower classes."[10]

But there also existed a more poisonous strain of thought about early American homelessness. Historian Tim Cresswell has written that "reactions to tramps, whether male or female, tended to define this new social type as an 'other'—as a marginal character whose unsavory characteristics served to help define what constituted health and normality. . . . It is a characteristic technique of 'othering' to define a category of people or forms of behavior as 'pathological.' Words such as *pathological, deviant, normal,* and *abnormal* haunt the early days of social investigation, and all of them swirl around the new figure of the tramp."[11] Early social researchers focused on the supposedly aberrant nomadic nature of the homeless men, ignoring both the mass joblessness of the period and the absence of any genuine social safety net.

More disturbing, the "tramps" became an early focus of the emerging field of eugenics. Charles Davenport, a leading figure in the American eugenics movement, conducted research on "nomadism" in the late years of the Gilded Age, concluding, according to Cresswell, that "the urge to wander was associated with a whole litany of psychoses, including suicide, temper, migraine, epilepsy, hysteria, 'sprees' and 'sexual outbreaks.' All of these could lead to a paralysis of the inhibitions that are normally relied on to prevent nomadism in civilized people. These 'nomadics' were, in Davenport's view, a product of their genetic makeup and thus were members of a special nomadic race."[12]

Such notions about the pathology of homeless people persisted, albeit in more muted form, decades later in the New Gilded Age. They shaped the racist and brutal policies around policing and the systematic denial of government assistance to homeless and poor New Yorkers, the large majority of whom were Black and Latino. And they formed the substructure for an approach to homeless people that assumed they were irreparably broken and in need of repair, fundamentally unready to take control over their own lives.

NO WAY HOME

Perhaps more troubling than the flagrant antihomeless, right-wing attacks was the second factor undergirding the myth of the "hardcore" homeless people. This was the notion that many, even most, homeless people were simply not "housing-ready," and before they could be provided with housing aid, they needed to undergo therapeutic programs of one type or another. Over years, it even came to be widely accepted within the otherwise liberal homeless services community.

One of the principal exponents of this view, and the person who did more than anyone to enshrine it in public policy, was future Governor Andrew Cuomo. Ironically, his efforts had their roots during the otherwise progressive administration of David Dinkins, New York City's first Black mayor. In 1991, his second year at City Hall, Dinkins had crafted a five-year homeless plan, titled "A Shelter Is Not a Home." The plan called for the creation of more housing, more "transitional housing" (i.e., improved shelters with enhanced social services), and the replacement of large, warehouse-style facilities, located in armories, with smaller shelters. However, an early version of the document leaked to a Staten Island newspaper, which spotlighted the notion of opening new shelters, triggering fierce opposition. The backlash spread citywide as local communities, NIMBY neighborhood associations, and other rabble-rousers lambasted the plan to create new shelters.[13]

Seeking to undo the political damage, in the autumn of 1991 Dinkins and his top officials discarded their homelessness plan and resorted to a time-tested, albeit somewhat cynical tactic: the creation of a "blue-ribbon" commission. Unfortunately, the person Dinkins appointed to head the homelessness commission had an agenda of his own. Andrew Cuomo, who had previously worked for his father, Governor Mario Cuomo, as an adviser and political enforcer, had started a nonprofit organization called HELP USA that opened a family shelter in Brooklyn.[14] Cuomo had really created the group as a springboard for his return to politics, and Dinkins's unwitting invitation offered an opportunity for him to make that transition more expeditiously than as a mere shelter operator.

Upon taking over the commission, Cuomo immediately rejected all the liberal provisions of the earlier Dinkins plan. He partnered with a little-known Republican businessman and self-styled homeless advocate, George McDonald, to write the commission's final recommendations. Extravagantly titled "The Way Home: A New Direction in Social Policy," the report was suffused with Cuomo's right-wing views on homelessness and poverty. It called for wholesale privatization of the homeless shelter system, eligibility reviews for people seeking shelter (an inspiration for Giuliani's shelter-denial policies, as detailed in chapter 6), and, most of all, the implementation of programs that would instill "personal responsibility."[15] The report explicitly claimed that homelessness was caused by the failings of homeless people themselves: "The commission found that 'homelessness' is frequently a symptom of some underlying problem, such as lack of job skills or education, a substance-abuse problem, or mental illness."[16] It also bluntly recommended that the city government not provide housing aid to homeless people until they had undergone treatment or engaged in training programs.[17]

Moreover, the report overtly criticized many of the Dinkins administration's policies, including its most successful one: the allocation of public housing apartments, federal housing vouchers, and city-subsidized apartments to homeless families. Right-wing ideologues like Cuomo, along with other critics of Dinkins, claimed, without any evidence, that poor families were flooding the shelter system in order to obtain housing aid, not because they were genuinely homeless.[18] This myth of the "Dinkins deluge" remained an article of faith among city government officials, and even some homeless service providers, long after it had been disproven, and it later inspired Mayor Michael Bloomberg's most disastrous policies.

McDonald recounted a conversation with Cuomo at City Hall before the report became public: "Andrew and I walked out together and I said I knew Dinkins would not like what we would propose: fire all the union people and contract out the services of about three thousand people to not-for-profits. We're walking down the steps, and I say, 'What if he won't do it?' Andrew gave me a piercing look: 'We go to war.'"[19] As it was, Cuomo appeared to use a trick he would continue to use throughout his political career. In January 1992, before Dinkins had reviewed the full report and a month before its official release, it was leaked to the news media, garnering some tabloid support and fully airing the criticisms of Dinkins's homelessness record. Dinkins tried to ignore the rogue commission's recommendations for months, but by September 1992, the administration was forced to embrace some elements of the report, particularly the creation of shelters operated by nonprofit organizations.[20]

But the main legacy of the Cuomo commission was its right-wing philosophy, which went on to inform New York City's approach to homeless policy for another two decades. As political scientist Thomas J. Main summarized this worldview in his history of homeless policymaking in New York, "The two key assumptions of this philosophy would be, first, the belief that there was 'something wrong' with homeless people, an 'underlying cause' that was crucial to their being homeless. The second assumption was that this underlying cause must be addressed through a quid pro quo of shelter for self-help in the form of enrollment in some form of rehabilitation."[21]

Main described Cuomo's (and, later, Giuliani's) approach to homelessness as "paternalism." While this would have been bad enough, the philosophy behind the policies was far more pernicious and destructive. It was essentially a combination of classic "blame the poor for their own poverty" conservatism and a behaviorist model that took it as a given that homeless New Yorkers were somehow broken and had to be retrained, remodeled, and repaired—with the way to do that being through punitive policies.

Building on Cuomo's right-wing policy recommendations, Giuliani went on to impose a conservative "personal responsibility" ideology on the homeless shelter system, drawing from his own antigovernment philosophy, which, at the time, was radically dismantling the welfare system (see chapter 8). Giuliani moved forward rapidly with the privatization of most municipal shelters, including the creation of new shelter-based programs and rules. Over the space of several years, the city government "privatized"—or, more precisely, contracted out the operation of—dozens of municipal homeless shelters, most particularly in the adult shelter system. In 1992, only seven shelters for homeless single adults were operated by nonprofit organizations. But, by 1997, only three years into Giuliani's mayoralty, thirty-three of the forty shelters for homeless adults had been "privatized."[22]

Many groups that took on contracts significantly improved services and conditions, which had been poor in city-operated facilities, and a few shelters were exceptionally well run. But what emerged was a far more complicated, less coherent system, with arbitrary rules that often misaligned services with residents. Even well-meaning nonprofit service providers became too focused on the management of shelters and programs, and less on the worsening housing landscape confronting their clients and the cutbacks in government housing aid and safety-net benefits. Ultimately, even improved shelters remained shelters, not homes, and the privatization campaign did nothing to create more housing resources.

In 1993, President Bill Clinton appointed Andrew Cuomo an assistant secretary of the US Department of Housing and Urban Development, and four years later made him head of the agency. One of Cuomo's principal duties was to administer homelessness assistance grants to cities and states established by the first major federal homelessness legislation, the McKinney–Vento Homelessness Assistance Act of 1987. Cuomo helped to ensure that a part of that act, which primarily funded homeless services—known as the "continuum of care"—became a centerpiece of national and local policy. That is, he encouraged communities to adopt policies that would essentially require homeless people to engage in treatment, rehabilitation, or training programs before they could get help, and especially before they could obtain housing aid. As longtime legal advocate Maria Foscarinis wrote:

> Implementing the model relied on their *being* housing—and without adequate funding there wouldn't be. And the assumption that people had to enter the shelter system and then "graduate" was contrary to what was known even at the time about offering permanent housing as a necessary first step, not a final one. Even worse, it was not only patronizing, but it also suggested that homelessness was a personal failure instead of a structural one.[23]

Starting with the fundamental notion that many, if not most, homeless people were not "housing-ready," the continuum of care became a philosophy and framework that guided homeless policy at both the national and local level for many years. It directed localities to craft a range of service programs that did little to alleviate homelessness, often diverting resources from actual housing aid. In the end, the continuum, and its mandated programs and services, essentially became a way of rationing a dwindling supply of affordable housing.

TUNNEL TO HOME

Since the early days of the modern crisis, advocates and homeless people themselves had long argued that subsidized housing combined with support services could create stable homes, even for people with long or repeated episodes of homelessness, including those struggling with severe mental illness and addiction disorders. In the 1990s, those supposedly utopian notions came to be buttressed by a growing body of empirical research and evidence. Academic researchers confirmed that the "success rate" of supportive housing—the share of formerly homeless people living with disabilities who remained in their homes—was extraordinarily high.

By the early part of the following decade, the first of many studies also found that supportive housing was in fact *cheaper* for taxpayers than leaving homeless people with health problems to cycle between shelters, hospitals, and jails. A landmark evaluation of the New York / New York Agreement by the University of Pennsylvania researcher Dennis Culhane and his colleagues found that the cost of a supportive housing apartment was actually *less* than leaving a person homeless.[24] The researchers did something that no one else had attempted before: They tallied the spending by every level of government on people who were left homeless, but who, out of necessity or because of government policies like criminalization, spent significant time in costly institutions like hospitals, jails, and shelters. They then compared those government expenditures with those on supportive housing and discovered that providing housing cost the same or less. The title of an influential 2006 *New Yorker* article by Malcolm Gladwell also did the math, calculating the cost to Nevada taxpayers of one homeless man in Las Vegas who'd spent years in and out of various kinds of costly institutional care: "Million-Dollar Murray."[25]

The other breakthrough from the 1990s came from the pioneering work of a community psychologist and supportive housing operator named Sam Tsemberis. In talking to homeless men on New York City streets, he realized that many often refused to go to large municipal shelters and would rather move into an apartment immediately, contrary to the prevalent myth of the "housing-resistant" homeless person. So, he tried exactly that, and with his nonprofit organization he organized support services—visits from social workers, access to medication and treatment, and more—to help the men keep their homes.[26] The logic behind this approach was blindingly obvious, confirming what homeless people themselves had long experienced—it was far more difficult to engage in mental health treatment or recover from addiction while homeless (whether sleeping in a shelter or on the streets) than to do so while living in an apartment.

Tsemberis called this approach Housing First, and over time, it was replicated by other groups in New York and across the country. In the twenty-first century, several US cities embraced such policies with resounding success. Houston, Texas, managed to reduce its homeless population by more than half in the twenty-first century by utilizing Housing First programs.[27] Salt Lake City, Utah, cut its population of long-term homeless people by more than 90 percent with Housing First assistance.[28] And several research studies found that homeless people who were helped via such programs had greater housing stability than those who went through a "treatment first" model—specifically, those who followed the right-wing "continuum-of-care" approach championed by Andrew Cuomo and Rudy Giuliani.

One of the major controversies surrounding our work with the Riverside Park tunnel residents was the then-radical idea that we helped them move directly from the tunnel to real housing without first requiring them to stay in shelters or undergo "rehabilitation" before being deemed "housing-ready." The system had been purposefully designed to force desperate people to jump through bureaucratic hoops and wait long periods in order—*maybe*—to secure housing aid. It reflected, at its root, the poisonous notion that homeless people were somehow different, *incomplete* as individuals, and not yet ready for a home. But during my months visiting the Riverside Park tunnel, this philosophy seemed more absurd than ever; all I could see were people who could make a home literally anywhere.

THE MEMORIAL

Many of the former Riverside Park tunnel dwellers ended up in supportive housing, including Bob, a longtime resident of the tunnel who stopped using drugs after moving into a former SRO hotel in Hell's Kitchen that had been converted into housing with on-site social services. Others, like Joe and Cathy, who lived in an East Harlem walk-up apartment, and Bernard, who moved in with his father in Harlem, were finally able to afford their own homes and avoid returning to the streets.

I saw some of the former tunnel folks in 1999 at the funeral for one of the original tunnel dwellers. José had lived for four years in an apartment in the Morrisania neighborhood in the Bronx, with the help of a federal housing voucher, and stayed there until his death. Seeing the old faces from the tunnel at the memorial—and over the years, from time to time, at the Coalition's offices—I remembered thinking they looked different: calmer, healthier, less gaunt and desperate. But still, and I may have been imagining this, they also looked haunted, as if the years in the tunnel would never leave them.

Our work in the tunnel was not without its failures. My colleagues and I were able to help a few of the newer Latino tunnel residents get the required paperwork. But some were undocumented or had long ago lost their immigration papers. Some drifted away before we could help them. By winter's end in 1996, Amtrak had erected a colossal, almost impenetrable fence around the southern entrance, and virtually all the tunnel dwellers were gone.

THE RENTAL

The danger of the "mole people" myth, along with the enduring efforts to pathologize homeless people, was that it made them seem fundamentally different—either broken or weirdly romanticized. Perhaps the most peculiar structure in the tunnel was a two-story shanty near the south end, adjacent to the western tunnel wall. It seemed unlikely that anyone lived on the "second floor" of this dwelling—I assumed it stored someone's belongings—and even less likely that it could support the weight of a person. But sure enough, on my third or fourth visit, I met the occupant of this precarious attic, a Honduran immigrant who'd only been staying in the tunnel for a few weeks. And remarkably, he told me that he was *renting* the space, for five dollars a week, from the homeless man who'd built the two-story shack.

I used to tell colleagues and friends this story as a sort of joke, saying that it proved that even in the harshest, bleakest environs, capitalism found a way to endure. But it occurred to me, over time, that it was only half a joke. One thing I was reminded of while working in the tunnel, a lesson that I encountered repeatedly during my many years as an advocate, was that homeless people were just people—no more, no less, and no different. Moreover, attempts to stereotype, denigrate, pathologize, or romanticize them were always suspect—and often damaging.

RAYS OF LIGHT

It has always been difficult to describe the tunnel without making it seem either too grim or, strange to say, too beautiful—and it could, indeed, be very beautiful. During the autumn and winter when I made my periodic visits, the Riverside Park tunnel grew bitterly, bitingly cold. By December, patches of snow lay on the tracks under the few rusty grates, and icicles hung overhead. But even in October, when I first ventured north, past the sunlit southernmost entrance, the tunnel felt at least a dozen degrees colder than the rest of the city.

At the south end, where most of the shanties were gathered, the smell—of food, of refuse, of urine, and what I came to think of over the coming years of my work as a mixture of masculine sweat and despair—was overwhelming. Garbage and rubble, railroad ties and rusted metal, and the usual urban detritus—plastic bags, fast-food wrappers, and soda bottles—were strewn amid the shacks.

But heading north, into the darkness, all that changed. There, the most unforgettable part of the tunnel was the unexpected light—diffuse, hazy, and breathtaking. The unaccountable delicacy of the light could be found in Morton's shimmering black-and-white photographs and Singer's *Dark Days* film.

One early winter day, around the time he left the tunnel for good, "Mayor" Bernard took me on a walk deep into its depths. We continued past the sprawling settlement, complete with a campfire and makeshift benches, that Bernard had built for himself on the west side of the tracks at a spot where the tunnel's edge widened away from the rails. We talked as we walked, with me asking a dozen undoubtedly naive questions about daily survival underground, and Bernard answering in his laconic, patient fashion, until we gradually lapsed into silence.

But most remarkable of all were the enormous, slanting shafts of light, descending slowly, if one could say that about beams of light, from the checkerboard grates in the tunnel ceiling. The light was, in a word, breathtaking. And probably sensing my wonder, Bernard paused alongside me and said something like, "I really will miss this place. Sometimes, it's just so beautiful."

Thinking back on that moment, as I have many times in the years since, it struck me that one of the truths about the people in the tunnel was not that they were broken or lost, but rather that they *had* lost. They'd lost jobs and money, they'd lost family, they'd lost countless belongings, they'd certainly lost homes. And then, being expelled from the tunnel, many to safer and more secure dwellings, they lost something else again.

THE LOWER EAST SIDE AND TOMPKINS SQUARE PARK: THE ORIGINS OF MODERN MASS HOMELESSNESS

The Bowery today is chiefly given over to pawnshops, restaurant equipment houses, beer saloons, and miscellaneous small retail shops. Here flophouses offer a bug-infested bed in an unventilated pigeonhole for twenty-five cents a night. . . . Thousands of the nation's unemployed drift to this section and may be seen sleeping in all-night restaurants, in doorways, and on loading platforms, furtively begging, or waiting with hopeless faces for some bread line or free lodging house to open. No agency, at present (1939), provides adequate food, shelter, and clothing for these wanderers. Missions furnish food and lodging for a few, and try by sermon and song to touch the souls of the down-and-outers.

Federal Writers Project
The WPA Guide to New York City

THE NEIGHBORHOOD

In the East Village, my longtime New York City neighborhood—itself a remnant of an older, historic community called the Lower East Side—there was a man who slept on a Second Avenue sidewalk near St. Mark's Place, in a cramped recess behind a standpipe, a space measuring no more than three feet wide and two feet tall. Small and slight, with straggly, shoulder-length black hair, he had a face as wrinkled as crumpled tin foil. At night, he'd coil himself up into the fetal position and recede into the tiny, occluded space behind the pipe, and sleep through another homeless night.

I spoke to him several times back in the 1990s, early in my decades of work as a homeless advocate. I repeatedly offered him help, which he gently, if somewhat distractedly, declined. The workers at the nearby bodega where I shopped said that he was an "Eskimo" (as they put it) from Alaska, and that he drank a lot. I saw him curled up in that tiny place behind the standpipe during every season, even on the coldest nights and mornings of winter. Over time, he appeared to be in increasingly worse shape—his frame grew skinnier, his hair became thinner, and his face looked even more gaunt and deeply lined.

Eventually, in the early years of the twenty-first century, the Second Avenue building with the standpipe recess underwent a renovation—one of so many in yet another wave of gentrification in the East Village and Lower East Side, and, indeed, throughout much of New York City. Construction barricades kept him from his regular sleeping space. When the fences were eventually taken down, the three-by-two-foot space where the man had slept had been filled in by cinder blocks.

Not long after that, I heard he'd died on the streets, on an unseasonably cold night. He joined the ranks of the thousands of homeless people who had perished unsheltered, in New York City's public places and spaces, since modern homelessness emerged in the late 1970s.

A couple of blocks downtown from the standpipe, there was a limestone church—dating from 1892, during the first Gilded Age—on whose steps homeless people routinely sat or panhandled before a fire gutted the structure in 2020. Next door was a Greek Revival townhouse where the filmmakers Joel and Ethan Coen shot scenes in 2012 for one of their signature films, *Inside Llewyn Davis*. The townhouse was converted a year later into a women's shelter in response to the growing homeless population of that period. A few blocks to the south were the Catholic Worker Houses, founded during the Great Depression by the legendary activist Dorothy Day, who offered shelter, meals, and fellowship to poor people during an earlier era of mass homelessness; the remaining houses continued to offer temporary lodging and food to neighborhood residents in need.

Further downtown and over toward the East River, below Houston Street, was the Urban Family Center, one of the oldest and largest municipal shelters for homeless families and children, whose bland, institutional exterior blended in with the public housing projects surrounding it. Nearby, on the north side of Houston, was Public School 188, better known as the Island School, which had one of the highest concentrations of homeless students in New York City; in the early 2020s, around half of P.S. 188's elementary school students were homeless.

More than half a dozen other homeless shelters were scattered across the East Village, from Avenue D to the Bowery, from East 2nd Street to right across the street from Tompkins Square Park. The ten-acre park itself continued to have a sizable homeless population, depending on the season, though not as large as just before the terrible summer night in 1988, when the NYPD launched a brutal, military-style assault to remove dozens of homeless people who'd created makeshift encampments in the park. Across the street from the park, a disused Catholic school building became, in 2024, the "processing center" for thousands of homeless immigrants, most of them from Latin America and Africa, who were seeking shelter and asylum.

On East 3rd Street, just off the Bowery, sat the largest shelter in the East Village. Once known as the notorious Muni, or Municipal Men's Shelter, it was the city's main homeless facility in the late 1970s. The anthropologist Kim Hopper, who conducted some of the earliest fieldwork of that era, described the horrendous conditions and casual brutality of the place in those days. Shelter staff routinely beat homeless men and then crowded them to sleep on the filthy floors of the infamous Big Room, the last resort for those seeking shelter on a cold night.[1]

In the late 1970s, on the sidewalks and alleyways of the Bowery, the first unmistakable signs of the modern homelessness crisis were observed. Each night, hundreds of men could be found sleeping rough on the streets of what was then New York City's most notorious "skid row." Many died there, too, like the man who slept behind the standpipe. Dozens perished on the streets in each of those early winters. Before long, modern homelessness spread beyond the Bowery and the city's other poor precincts to become part of the fabric of an increasingly stratified, unequal New York City.

Well over four decades after mass homelessness spread beyond the shabby precincts of the Bowery, there were still homeless people sleeping on the streets of the East Village and Lower East Side. As I'd pick up my young son at his local public school in Alphabet City, I'd see them throughout the neighborhood hunched in storefront doorways, huddled under scaffolding, or curled up on a bare stretch of sidewalk, under an awning or ledge, seeking shelter from the elements. More than anywhere else, one encountered homeless people in Tompkins Square Park, which has been, for more than a century, both a site of respite for poor and homeless people, and a place of conflict over their very presence.

TOMPKINS SQUARE IN THE GILDED AGE

The first of the two historic police riots in Tompkins Square happened in the early years of the Gilded Age. In 1873, the US and European economies were struck by a severe financial crisis that was largely triggered by speculative investments in railroads and other industries, sparking a yearslong, deep economic recession. In New York, tens of thousands of workers lost jobs, and wages in construction, garment factories, and railroads were cut by as much as 40 percent.[2]

The 1873 economic crisis also triggered the first substantial wave of homelessness in an urbanizing New York. Some ninety thousand people sought shelter in police stations and almshouses, and communities of shanty dwellers grew on Manhattan's west side.[3] By the winter of 1873–74, a quarter of the city's workforce had lost their jobs, and the widespread devastation affected both men and women. One official of a charity commented, "Formerly [we had confined] relief to women. Now the men come to us hungry with hollow cheeks. . . . It is terrible, terrible."[4]

Over many months, as the visible poverty and misery in New York worsened, the city's elites waged a backlash that would echo, a century later, in equally venomous public discourse around urban inequality. Civic leaders, politicians, and the press blamed poor New Yorkers for their condition, portraying them as lazy and immoral. Most of all, though, the elites feared rising labor unrest and mobilized the police department to quash any rallies and marches.[5]

This set the stage for the events of early 1874. Labor organizers planned a mass public gathering of workers, and Tompkins Square was chosen as the protest site because of its historical links to the movement. In the late 1850s, rallies there had led to the creation of a public works program for unemployed workers, and in more recent years, radical labor groups had gathered in the square. Despite the freezing cold, thousands of men, women, and children assembled on January 13, 1874. Soon, the gathering crowd became one of the largest labor protests in the city's history. But the police response was immediate, furious, and strikingly violent. As *The New York Herald* reported, "On horseback and on foot, [the police] immediately launched into the crowd and began a terrifying assault, blocking the square's exits." Another news account reported, "Women and children ran screaming in all directions. Many of them were trampled underfoot in the stampede for the gates." Samuel Gompers, the legendary labor leader and later president of the American Federation of Labor, was present in Tompkins Square that day and later described it as "an orgy of brutality."[6]

The city's leaders viewed the police force's violent suppression of workers in Tompkins Square as nothing short of a victory, and even celebrated it. Mayor William Havemeyer declared, "Nothing better could have happened." The police commissioner said, "It was the most glorious sight I ever saw the way the police broke and drove that crowd. Their order was perfect as they charged with their clubs uplifted."[7] The *Herald* ventriloquized for the elites and capital when it delivered a stern, condescending sermon to the city's workers: "He shares in the prosperity and when a season of difficulty arises he must be prepared to bear patiently the suffering incidental to hard times."[8]

The 1874 police riot at Tompkins Square was a triumph for the city's political leaders and business community. Private employers and the city government spent the following year putting down strikes and dismantling labor organizations, while also laying off more workers. And they prepared to wield more state-sanctioned violence to suppress worker unrest, just as inequality in New York was on the rise.

THE ERA BEFORE MODERN HOMELESSNESS

Decades later, in the period between the Great Depression and the 1970s, homelessness existed in New York City, but in a limited fashion. The vast majority of homeless people were older men; in the 1950s, the median age of homeless men was the mid-fifties, and women and children made up only a small fraction of the homeless population.[9] While the popular image of the homeless man was that of an alcoholic "vagrant," a "layabout," and a "bum," the reality was more complicated. Multiple studies of poor districts in New York and other cities from the period found that most of the men living there worked or had worked in the past year, or otherwise had some steady, if meager, source of income, like a veteran's pension. As Columbia University researcher George Nash concluded in a 1964 survey of the Bowery, "Contrary to commonly held stereotypes, the appearance of many homeless men differed little from that of other poor workmen."[10]

Most homeless New Yorkers were crowded into "skid row" districts, typically located within or adjacent to "slums" or "ghettos," where the poorest city dwellers resided. These were, by and large, the only places in the city where visible signs of homelessness—people sleeping on sidewalks or lingering in parks—could be found. In New York City, the largest and oldest of these skid row districts was the Bowery, an avenue stretching over a mile through the Lower East Side. The area was dominated by run-down buildings and cheap, single-room housing, including residential hotels and the notorious Bowery lodging houses, which rented by the night and whose "rooms" were in actuality minuscule cubicles with chicken-wire ceilings. Another, less famous—or infamous—district was located in central Harlem, where poor men lived in SRO hotels and basement rooms of apartment buildings. In keeping with the racial segregation of the city, most of the poor men in the Bowery were white, while nearly all of the poor men in the Harlem skid row were Black; a 1964 survey found that Black New Yorkers made up 31 percent of total skid row residents but only 16 percent of those on the Bowery, by far the city's largest district.[11]

What kept homelessness so limited in size and scope in the period between World War II and the late 1970s? There were several key factors. The era was marked by rapid economic growth, rooted in industry and manufacturing. Government programs, particularly those emerging from the New Deal and labor struggles, played an essential role in muting income inequality. Benefits for unemployed workers and poor families and the Social Security pension for seniors created a vital safety net. But housing aid was also a critical factor, and in this realm, New York had a singular legacy to build on.

The earliest and most progressive housing movements in the nation had begun on the Lower East Side during the Gilded Age. In the late nineteenth century, immense numbers of immigrants, mostly from southern and central Europe, had arrived in New York to pack into already overcrowded, unsafe dwellings. The Lower East Side was the chief destination of the immigrants, and most of the neighborhood's housing stock was comprised of tenements—typically six-story buildings with a "dumbbell" design, utilizing minimal windows and ventilation and crafted to maximize the number of units per lot. In the 1880s, the Lower East Side was the most densely populated place on the planet, and by 1900, approximately eighty thousand tenements housed nearly half a million people, out of a total city population of 3.4 million.[12]

In response to the tenements' perilous levels of overcrowding, a movement grew among Lower East Side dwellers to improve housing conditions. The pioneering journalist and activist Jacob Riis, himself an immigrant who had experienced homelessness, brought national attention to the issue with his landmark exposé *How the Other Half Lives*. Over time, several major reforms of New York housing law and tenement design were won.[13]

But other housing problems persisted, among them the rising rents triggered by New York's rapidly growing population and the unscrupulous, rapacious behavior of property owners. In 1904, landlords threatened to raise rents by as much as 30 percent. Tenants on the Lower East Side, many of them Jewish garment workers from eastern Europe who had experience with socialist labor movements, organized a successful "rent strike," which spread as far uptown as Harlem.[14]

A far more widespread and radical series of rent strikes occurred between 1917 and 1920, beginning on the Lower East Side but eventually spreading citywide.[15] Tenants unions were formed in neighborhoods across the city, and the housing activists began to work closely with the Socialist Party and labor organizers. Over the three years of active rent strikes, thousands of families participated and withheld rent. City elites were terrified of the growing tenant-labor alliance, and landlords began to organize themselves into some of the first real estate associations in the country. Ultimately, however, and in fits and starts, government officials bowed to pressure from tenants and organizers.

In 1920, the New York State Legislature passed the Emergency Rent Laws, the first major rent-regulation statute in the United States. Crucially, it limited annual rent increases imposed by landlords, and protected the tenancy of renter households, who could renew leases and not be evicted arbitrarily. The 1920 law became the basis for later rent-regulation laws in New York, and it even inspired a short-lived federal rent control law during World War II. In the 1960s, however, under pressure from the real estate industry, the state government allowed some apartments to charge unregulated rents. Thousands of units became deregulated, and New York City's rental housing vacancy rate plummeted. Finally, the state legislature passed the Emergency Tenant Protection Act of 1974, creating the modern rent-regulation system. Under the law, tenants of privately owned rental apartment buildings were permitted to renew their leases automatically (absent some violation), protecting them from arbitrary eviction and preserving stability. In addition, landlords could only raise rents each year by a limited percentage, set by a public board.

Rent regulation, born out of a housing crisis and immigrant-led movements on the Lower East Side, played a critical role not only in protecting tenants, but also in preserving the stock of low- and modest-cost rental housing, which was still in the hands of private property owners. But during the Great Depression, there was also a movement to create publicly owned housing. On East 3rd Street on the Lower East Side, the first public housing in the United States, a block of dark brick buildings called First Houses, was opened in 1936. The following year saw the passage of the landmark United States Housing Act, which created the national public housing system.

Public housing, which was created for working-class and poor renters and which limited rents based on a tenant's income, expanded throughout New York City. By the twenty-first century, there were approximately 335 public housing developments, with about 178,000 apartments citywide. However, many of the earliest public housing developments, in New York and elsewhere, were racially segregated and refused to accept Black tenants. Many also initially excluded the lowest-income renters, and over the following decades, civil rights activists, public housing residents, and legal advocates fought to desegregate the system.[16]

One other major government program helped to add to New York City's affordable housing stock in the post–World War II period. In 1955, the state government launched an ambitious initiative called the Mitchell–Lama program—named for the two state legislators who sponsored the enacting law—to create subsidized apartment buildings. While it was primarily aimed at middle-class households, the initiative also built thousands of housing units for low-income renters. The Mitchell–Lama program eventually created some 105,000 apartments citywide.

In sum, government action—much of it rooted in the housing movements born on the Lower East Side—played a central role in maintaining housing affordability and preventing mass homelessness before the 1970s.

THE 1970S AND THE BIRTH OF MODERN HOMELESSNESS

The capitalist crises of the 1970s transformed the economic and political life of New York City. Over the course of the decade, the city lost more than six hundred thousand jobs, nearly half of them in manufacturing, and the service-sector jobs that eventually came to replace them paid far lower wages.[17] New York City's population fell by more than 10 percent, or more than eight hundred thousand people, to the lowest levels since the Great Depression. Hundreds of thousands of New Yorkers left the city, many of them to surrounding suburbs, in a wave of "white flight." This, in turn, triggered a surge in housing abandonment and even insurance-scam arson, which resulted in the loss of tens of thousands of housing units.

The local economic downturn generated a severe fiscal crisis for New York's municipal government, which had, over the preceding decades of relative prosperity, implemented a nascent welfare-state apparatus that provided medical, housing, educational, and income assistance to millions of poor and working-class residents. The response to the fiscal crisis was guided largely by creditor banks and right-wing politicians, both in New York and Washington, DC. What emerged were harsh austerity policies and the dismantling of the safety net for the poorest New Yorkers. These policies later became the template for both national and global neoliberal policies that shaped subsequent decades.[18]

By the latter half of the 1970s, the conditions for what was to become modern mass homelessness were unmistakable. The first evidence was the visibility of unsheltered homeless New Yorkers, mostly men, outside the traditional skid row precincts. Homeless people were seen sleeping in parks and subway stations across the city, but most of all in large transportation facilities, like Grand Central Terminal, Pennsylvania Station, and the Port Authority Bus Terminal, all in midtown Manhattan. As early as August 1976, *The New York Times* published an article titled "Vagrants and Panhandlers Appearing in New Haunts," which opened with the following paragraph: "The Bowery scene has spread. In the late hours vagrants now can be found singly and in twos and threes in the triangles on Broadway from Herald Square to 72nd Street, along the southern edge of Central Park, in the side streets off Times Square, around the fountained plats of the Avenue of the Americas, along Lexington Avenue above 42nd Street, in the small parks of the Lower East Side and in Trinity Place."[19]

The article went on to describe emerging and expanding groups of homeless people in many parts of Manhattan, from the theater district to the southern edge of Central Park. In 1977, the veteran *Times* reporter Ralph Blumenthal rode the subways for most of four consecutive days and wrote a diary-style chronicle. He found many homeless people sleeping on trains and in stations throughout the city, including "a one-eyed man on crutches who pulls out a black sleepmask to aid his slumbers, an elderly woman who promptly goes to sleep sitting down" at the Woodlawn Terminal—as well as panhandlers and "decoy policemen disguised as derelicts."[20]

The first comprehensive overview of the emerging homelessness crisis was published in 1981 by the Community Service Society. "Private Lives / Public Spaces" was the result of nearly two years of intensive fieldwork and research conducted by Kim Hopper and Ellen Baxter.[21] The duo conducted interviews with some two hundred street homeless New Yorkers, on sidewalks, in Grand Central Terminal and on an East River pier. They also highlighted the deplorable conditions of the city government's then makeshift, haphazard, and wildly inadequate system of providing homeless New Yorkers with shelter from the elements. This included the flophouses of the Bowery, for which many homeless men, dubbed "ticketmen," were given vouchers for temporary stays, as well as the notorious Municipal Shelter just off the Bowery, and an annex facility called the Keener Building, an old hospital facility located on Wards Island in the East River.[22]

The Bowery and the Muni shelter would factor heavily in the landmark battle around the legal rights of homeless New Yorkers that launched in the late 1970s and continued for decades. Baxter and Hopper began to work with Robert Hayes, an attorney then volunteering with the Legal Aid Society. The trio documented how homeless men were systematically denied help at the Muni, which was then considered the so-called front door, or intake point, for the nascent shelter system, and how they were forced to languish on the streets. During those years, Hopper once told me, hundreds of homeless men would die on the streets, mostly, but not exclusively, during the winter months, while others suffered injuries due to exposure or frostbite.

Hayes developed a legal theory based on Article XVII of the New York State Constitution. This vital amendment had been added to the charter in 1938, during the depths of the Great Depression, and was supported by the populist New York Mayor Fiorello La Guardia, among others.[23] It stated, "The aid, care and support of the needy are public concerns and shall be provided by the state and by such of its subdivisions." In 1979 Hayes, on behalf of several homeless plaintiffs, brought a class action lawsuit, *Callahan v. Carey*, in the New York State Supreme Court. The lead plaintiff of the case was Robert Callahan, a homeless military veteran and short-order cook. Some years later, Hayes fondly recalled Callahan as a wily character and a survivor:

> He became my guide to the Bowery. . . . There were tricks to
> learn. If one sneaked into a mission at the right time, you could
> get a bowl of soup and avoid the sermon. He knew about the
> bathrooms in the courthouses. He knew which grates blew dry
> heat; he knew park benches that were, well, pretty safe. He had
> the pride and the sense, back there in 1979, to avoid the Men's
> Shelter except in the dead of winter. He liked to be called the
> mayor of the Bowery, though to most of his friends he was
> Callahan.[24]

How did Hayes put together his argument that Callahan and others deserved shelter? The case asserted that Article XVII amounted to a "right to shelter" for homeless men, and furthermore, that the shelter provided by the city and state governments must meet minimum basic standards of decency. In an interview with *The New Yorker* thirty years later, Hayes paraphrased the key provision from Article XVII:

> "The aid, care and support of the needy etc. SHALL be
> provided." . . . In our presentation before the judge, we simply
> argued that "shall" means "shall." I dug around in the N.Y.U. law-
> library basement and found speeches given by the amendment's
> supporters and drafters back in 1938 that showed the intent. . . .
> These proved that the amendment was supposed to apply in
> hard times as well as in good. I kept the story simple because I'd
> never tried a case before and didn't really know what I was doing.
> Sometimes the judge had to instruct me in the rules of evidence.[25]

On December 5, 1979, the court ruled preliminarily in favor of the homeless plaintiffs, and mandated that the city and state governments provide shelter to all homeless men who requested it. In August 1981, after nearly two years of ongoing litigation and intensive negotiation, Hayes and the homeless men reached a historic settlement with city and state officials.[26] The result was a consent decree, a binding contract of sorts, that established a right to shelter for all homeless men in New York City: "The City defendants shall provide shelter and board to each homeless man who applies for it provided that (a) the man meets the need standard to qualify for the home relief program established in New York State [i.e., each man who is poor enough to qualify for welfare benefits]; or (b) the man by reason to physical, mental or social dysfunction is in need of temporary shelter."[27]

The *Callahan* consent decree gave the Coalition for the Homeless, which had been formally established the previous year, the ability to monitor health and safety conditions in the shelter system, with the understanding that the plaintiffs could return to court to seek enforcement of the decree if the government was failing to live up to its obligations—and sure enough, this was something we had to do numerous times over the following decades.[28] While the *Callahan* decree only protected homeless men, who then made up the large majority of unsheltered homeless New Yorkers, a follow-up case brought in 1982 by Hayes and the Coalition, *Eldredge v. Koch*, extended the right to shelter to homeless women, who were later covered by the consent decree.[29]

The primary impetus behind the *Callahan* case—and the principle of the right to shelter for homeless individuals—was to save lives. Death from exposure, hypothermia, and other cold-related injuries, as well as by violence, had always been alarmingly commonplace among unsheltered homeless people. Even Robert Callahan died while sleeping on Mott Street in the Lower East Side—only months before the consent decree that bore his name was signed.

DEINSTITUTIONALIZATION AND THE LOSS OF SINGLE-ROOM HOUSING

In concert with the wider structural economic shifts of the 1970s, there were two additional, critical factors that triggered the rapid growth in homelessness in the early years of the crisis. The first had to do with dramatic changes in the way people living with mental illness were treated and housed, a phenomenon that came to be labeled "deinstitutionalization." This process (described in more detail in chapter 7) began in the 1950s with the development of new medications and therapeutic models to treat some of the most severe mental illnesses. Journalistic exposés of the horrific conditions in some state facilities, along with a growing movement—inspired by the civil rights movement of the same era—to promote community care, also drove the mental health system away from mass institutionalization.

Thus, instead of consigning people living with chronic mental illness to state psychiatric facilities, as had been the practice for decades, state governments—and particularly New York's—began downsizing or shuttering state hospitals and discharging resident patients to the community. Between the 1960s and the end of the 1970s, the number of patients residing in New York psychiatric hospitals fell by more than two-thirds.[30] The problem, however, was that New York's government failed to invest the enormous budget savings from the elimination of state hospital beds in adequate community-based care—and, most crucially, in housing. Thus, tens of thousands of New Yorkers living with mental illness were effectively dumped into the community with little or no support.

The second, related factor behind the early rise in New York City homelessness was the rapidly diminishing number of single-room housing units. For most of the twentieth century, single-room housing— which included the "flophouses" and lodging houses of the Bowery, SRO units, and residential hotels, typified by shared kitchen and bathroom facilities—had played a vital role in providing cheap housing for low-income single adults and childless couples.[31] In 1960, the single-room housing stock comprised nearly 130,000 units citywide, and throughout the 1970s, it was the main source of housing for the poorest residents in New York City.[32] However, changes in housing and zoning codes essentially outlawed the creation of new single-room housing, and by the 1960s, the number of single-room units had reached a maximum limit, meaning that the gradual erosion of this housing was only a matter of time.

In the 1970s, the single-room housing stock began to shrink rapidly due to conversion and demolition, falling to just twenty-five thousand units by the end of that decade. Changes in municipal tax policy caused much of the loss, in particular a property tax abatement program that had been created to encourage developers to renovate and upgrade deteriorating buildings, such as warehouses, and convert them into residential buildings. Because most SRO buildings were located in gentrifying neighborhoods like the Upper West Side, owners exploited the tax break to convert single-room housing into higher-cost rental apartments, cooperatives, or condominiums. By the 1980s, most of New York City's single-room housing stock had vanished, and with it, the "housing of last resort" for the poorest New Yorkers.[33]

THE FIRST DECADE OF MODERN MASS HOMELESSNESS

The impact of mass homelessness on families and children lagged behind the worsening conditions for poor individuals. But family homelessness began to reach crisis levels by the early 1980s. For most of the previous decade, the number of New York families who were homeless was relatively modest—typically a few hundred families per night—and episodes of homelessness were short-lived. One reason was that the gap between the cost of rental housing and the incomes, and crucially the government income supports, of poor families was not so wide. In 1975, the median monthly rent for a New York City apartment was $171, while a poor family receiving welfare benefits received up to $194 per month as a "housing allowance."[34] Likewise, throughout the 1970s, the federal government was expanding federal housing assistance for low-income households, although it remained insufficient to reach all needy families. Finally, the federal minimum wage, which at the time determined New York's wage standard, nearly doubled over the course of the decade, which meant low-income workers had a better chance of competing in New York's tight housing market.

The city government's response to family homelessness was rudimentary; families were sheltered primarily in cheap commercial SRO hotels, which were commonly referred to as "welfare hotels." Conditions were often horrible, with children and adults getting sick due to the close quarters, shared kitchens and bathrooms, and vermin infestation. A lone exception was found on the Lower East Side, just south of Houston Street, where the Henry Street Settlement, a century-old charitable organization, had opened the Urban Family Center in 1972. Located in an old residential building, it was the nation's first genuine shelter for families, complete with apartment-style units and social services.

The severe economic recession of the early 1980s—aptly called the "Reagan recession"—led to a national unemployment rate of 11 percent and caused a surge in family homelessness.[35] In New York, the impact of the downturn was compounded by the legacy of austerity policies adopted during the fiscal crisis—which had crippled the safety net and were largely maintained by Ed Koch throughout his three terms as mayor. On top of that, Reagan implemented his own brutal austerity regime, with a particular ideological focus on cutting back assistance for poor families. Between 1979 and 1989, federal housing budget authorizations were slashed by a remarkable 78 percent, with a heavy impact on cities like New York. As a result, the number of homeless families in municipal shelters soared in the early 1980s. In early 1983, there were some 1,500 families, with nearly five thousand children, sleeping in the shelter system, but by the end of 1984—less than two years later—the number of families had more than doubled, to 3,300 families and 7,700 children.

The rise in family homelessness, and the city government's failed response, led to more legal challenges by advocates. In 1983, Steve Banks, a young attorney with the Legal Aid Society, brought a class action lawsuit against the city and state governments on behalf of his client, Yvonne McCain, a homeless mother, and other families. McCain, a survivor of domestic violence, had been evicted from her Brooklyn apartment in 1982. After requesting help from the city government, she and her children were sent to a rundown welfare hotel in midtown Manhattan, which she described in an interview years later:

"They put us in a room on the 11th floor," she said, adding that both sides of the mattresses were stained with urine. "I remember calling my mother and asking if she could bring me newspapers to put over the mattresses. I stayed up worrying that the kids didn't climb out the windows, because there were no bars." Ms. McCain, a battered woman, spent four years in that hotel. As the case crawled through the courts, she bounced from shelter to city-supported apartment and back. Her estranged husband once found her and broke her nose.[36]

The case bearing her name, *McCain v. Koch*, sought the same right-to-shelter protections for homeless families that the *Callahan* and *Eldredge* cases had secured for homeless single men and women. It also challenged the horrendous conditions that McCain and other families had endured in welfare hotels and city-operated facilities. Ultimately Koch, who had come to regret signing the *Callahan* consent decree, refused to agree to a similar settlement for homeless families, and the litigation continued in various forms for twenty-five more years. But in 1986, the plaintiffs in the *McCain* case won a major victory. The New York State Supreme Court's Appellate Division issued an order "barring the denial of emergency shelter to homeless families." This created an effective right to shelter for homeless families with children.[37]

New York City's homelessness crisis continued to deteriorate through the 1980s. The main municipal shelter population nearly tripled, growing to a peak of more than twenty-eight thousand residents per night in 1988. The number of homeless single adults in city shelters more than doubled, to more than ten thousand men and women, and the number of families in shelter more than tripled, to include nearly eleven thousand children. These tallies did not include thousands of homeless New Yorkers sheltered by other city agencies—such as domestic violence survivors or "runaway youth"—or by churches and synagogues. Most important, they did not include the thousands of homeless individuals sleeping on the streets, in parks, in the subway system, or in other public spaces. There has never been an accurate measurement of unsheltered homelessness in New York City, but there was little debate that the unsheltered homeless population soared to historic levels in the late 1980s and early 1990s. Indeed, the decennial US Census from 1990 estimated an unsheltered population of more than 10,400 homeless people in New York City—which, remarkably, represented 21 percent of the total national unsheltered homeless population.[38]

Despite the legal guarantee of shelter, one reason so many homeless New Yorkers remained on the streets was the deplorable state of the still-ramshackle municipal shelter system. The Koch administration's initial response to the rising number of single men and women in need of shelter, particularly in the wake of the mandate under the *Callahan* decree, was rapidly and arbitrarily to open immense shelters in vacant government-controlled facilities. These included a dozen armories (see chapter 9); former hospital buildings (like the former psychiatric unit at Bellevue Hospital, described in chapter 7); and even shuttered school buildings, like the Brooklyn Women's Shelter in the East New York section of Brooklyn. Many of the shelters were hard to reach, even by public transportation, and far from the commercial districts where, by necessity, most unsheltered homeless people congregated.

The two largest adult facilities were the least accessible of all. The Wards Island shelter complex, located on an island in the East River, centered around a former hospital building and eventually grew to encompass more than 1,200 beds.[39] And the Camp LaGuardia shelter, which expanded to more than one thousand beds, was located sixty miles north of the city in Orange County, at the site of a former women's prison, on a property so large that it straddled two separate towns.

Municipal shelters routinely failed to meet even the most basic standards of health and safety. Advocates and homeless people fought for improved conditions in shelters, as well as additional legal protections. In the early 1990s, advocates challenged the use of some of the massively dangerous, warehouse-style shelters. For around a decade, the city government had lined the drill floors of armories with hundreds of cots for homeless men. The Fort Washington armory in the Washington Heights neighborhood of Manhattan, for instance, infamously had some 1,200 men sleeping on its drill floor. Long-standing state regulations limited the size of shelter facilities to no more than two hundred beds, but officials did nothing to enforce the code. Finally, legal advocates brought two class action lawsuits that ultimately required several shelters, including the Fort Washington, Sumner, and Franklin armories, to reduce their size to two hundred beds, and over time, city officials phased out the use of drill floors as sleeping areas.[40]

In 1984, the Coalition for the Homeless won a major victory in federal court in *Pitts v. Black*, which successfully challenged the refusal of local boards of elections to register people to vote when they lacked a fixed address—a case that essentially secured the right to vote for homeless people.[41] In 1985, the Legal Aid Society won a state court decision prohibiting city and state governments from removing children from their families and placing them in foster care merely because the family lacked housing. In early 1989, years into the AIDS epidemic, the Coalition won a case finally requiring the city and state to provide medically appropriate shelter to homeless people living with AIDS.[42]

These victories secured basic rights for homeless New Yorkers and challenged dangerous conditions in the shelter system, leading to significant reforms. But ultimately, the advocacy community's focus on litigation reached an impasse with respect to housing. In targeted, strategically designed cases brought by the Coalition and other groups, advocates filed lawsuits to secure housing resources for vulnerable subpopulations of homeless people, such as individuals living with chronic mental illness and people diagnosed with AIDS. But in every case, the courts refused to take the logical step of ordering the government to provide housing aid—even when presented with overwhelming evidence of need, as well as the persistent refusal of every level of government to make adequate investments in housing resources.

While the courts and government failed to act, the housing affordability gap widened enormously. Even by 1983, a US Census Bureau survey of New York City housing found that, over the previous three years alone, the city had lost more than thirty-five thousand rental apartments, and that apartment rents had increased by 25 percent.[43] Between 1975 and 1991, median rents and utility costs for New York City apartments rose by 18 percent in real, inflation-adjusted terms, while median renter incomes actually fell in real terms by nearly 1 percent. By 1991, there were actually 225,000 *fewer* low-rent apartments than there were poor renters citywide. And this gap would only widen further over the following decades.

HOMELESS HOUSING POLICY IN THE 1980S

Throughout the first decade of the New Gilded Age, every level of government cut back sharply on both investments in affordable housing creation and housing aid for poor New Yorkers. In 1978, the federal housing agency's budget accounted for 8 percent of the total federal budget, but by 1983, it accounted for only 2 percent. The effects of federal cutbacks on New York City's low-income renters were staggering. Between 1981 and 1991, federal capital funds for maintenance and repairs of public housing fell from $3 billion to $1 billion per year, triggering decades of neglect and disinvestment in a vital housing stock for nearly four hundred thousand poor and working-class people.[44] Likewise, the sharp Reagan cutbacks in federal rental vouchers, the largest federal housing program, contributed to rising family homelessness.

New York's state government mimicked the neoliberal austerity policies of the Reagan era. In Albany, Governor Mario Cuomo governed as a fiscal conservative during his dozen years in office (1983–94), in stark contrast with his carefully cultivated national reputation as a liberal stalwart. Cuomo and New York State lawmakers, for instance, refused to renew the Mitchell–Lama program. In New York City, more than sixty-five thousand units of subsidized rental housing had been created under the program, but the subsidies were limited to twenty-year terms. Beginning in the 1980s, many of the private owners of Mitchell–Lama developments began to opt out of the program, taking their buildings into the private market and raising rents. The number of Mitchell–Lama "opt-outs" accelerated in the 1990s, with more than 40 percent lost to the private market by the end of the decade.[45]

But one Albany policy failure contributed to the affordability crisis for poor and homeless families as much as any specific housing policy, and it involved welfare. Since 1975, the New York State welfare benefit had been divided into two parts: cash assistance, meant to pay (however inadequately) for food, clothing, and other necessities; and the welfare housing allowance, or "shelter allowance," meant to pay for rent. State legislators and regulators had the power to increase the value of the allowances to reflect rising rents and prices, but they stubbornly refused to do so.[46] In 1975, the welfare housing allowance for a New York City family of three people (the average household size) was $194 per month, enough to rent a modest apartment. However, over the next two decades, state officials increased the welfare housing allowance only twice, while housing costs soared. From 1975 to 1991, welfare housing allowances actually *lost* more than 40 percent of their value in real, inflation-adjusted terms, while median rents grew by 18 percent in real terms. Meanwhile, for poor single individuals in New York City, including those who were homeless, Albany set the welfare housing allowance at only $215 per month—and refused to increase it again for more than thirty years.[47]

The eroding value of such housing allowances was one of the cornerstones of neoliberal policymaking in New York—part of the right-wing project to shred the social safety net—and remained one of the key factors driving modern mass homelessness during the New Gilded Age. Advocates challenged these heartless policies in court but won only partial victories. One class action lawsuit brought by the Coalition for the Homeless led to enhanced housing allowances for poor people living with AIDS; the number of households receiving this aid soared by more than 800 percent over the following decade, reaching a total of twenty-two thousand recipients by 1999.[48] But the far more consequential case involved poor families with children. In 1987, the Legal Aid Society filed the landmark *Jiggetts v. Grinker* lawsuit, arguing that welfare housing allowances were too low to permit families to find and keep stable, safe housing, as required by New York law. As with many epochal legal cases involving homelessness, such as the *McCain* litigation over shelter rights, the *Jiggetts* case stretched on for more than two decades as a succession of neoliberal policymakers refused to provide adequate housing assistance. But as the case progressed, the New York State Supreme Court ordered an interim program colloquially known as "*Jiggetts* relief." Although it was only a stopgap measure, the larger housing allowance helped prevent homelessness for tens of thousands of vulnerable families over many years.[49]

HOUSING NEW YORK

Another legacy of the Koch era was that New York City's municipal government assumed the role of "landlord of last resort" for tens of thousands of poor and working-class households. During the 1970s, New York

City experienced a wave of housing abandonment due to factors such as "white flight," "redlining," and bank disinvestment amid population loss. Throughout the decade, New York City lost nearly three hundred thousand housing units.[50]

Aiming to prevent the further abandonment and the loss of thousands more buildings, the city government began to assume ownership and management of tax-delinquent properties through so-called in rem proceedings. City officials initially anticipated that the public ownership of the buildings would be temporary, expecting that suitable owners would be quickly found. But there was little interest in the properties, and the local government's inventory skyrocketed. By 1986, there were more than ninety-five thousand housing units in the in rem portfolio, with nearly fifty-six thousand vacant. By that point, New York City's municipal government effectively owned and managed the second-largest stock of publicly owned housing in the United States, with the largest being the nearly 180,000 public housing units administered by the New York City Housing Authority.

The policy quagmire of the in rem housing stock marked a critical turning point in municipal housing policy during the Koch era, as well as afterward. New York City had the chance to build a genuine European or Canadian-style "social housing" system. Ultimately, however, Koch's neoliberal, free market ideology, combined with the city's fiscal challenges and reduced aid from Albany and Washington, DC, thwarted those efforts. Nevertheless, the city government's administration of such a large swath of New York's affordable rental housing set the stage for perhaps the only example of progressive housing policymaking during the first decade of the modern homelessness crisis. The administrations of Ed Koch and his successor, David Dinkins, took two significant steps that not only addressed the housing affordability crisis, but also contributed for the first time ever to reductions in the city's homeless population.

The first program was the largest in scale. In 1986, Koch announced the Housing New York initiative, a ten-year plan to invest in the creation and preservation of affordable housing citywide—at the time, the largest such local housing initiative in the nation.[51] The Housing New York program ultimately built or preserved 151,000 units of affordable housing over a decade. And while it only created approximately fifteen thousand new units of housing—so-called new construction—much of the program involved the rehabilitation of in rem buildings, many long-sitting vacant or dilapidated due to mismanagement. Therefore, the "preservation" part of the program actually added to the city's housing supply. Finally, fully 10 percent of the apartments created under the Housing New York initiative, or fifteen thousand units, went to homeless families and individuals.[52]

Koch's ambitious housing plan, and its role rescuing and reshaping neighborhoods, became perhaps the signature legacy of his twelve years as mayor, something he grudgingly came to acknowledge. In a 2003 *New Yorker* interview, Robert Hayes related a conversation he had with the aging, but still cantankerous, former mayor:

> After a while, the subject moved to our old disputes over
> homeless issues and the right to shelter. Koch said that if it
> hadn't been for the pressure from us advocates to do something
> about housing for the homeless he might not have been forced to
> undertake his *in rem* [Housing New York] program. Now he was
> an old man, and he knew that the *in rem* housing was going to be
> his legacy. He told me he knew that, and then he did a very un-
> Kochlike thing. . . . He thanked me.[53]

THE NEW YORK / NEW YORK AGREEMENT

The Housing New York initiative not only added to the city's dwindling stock of affordable rental housing, but also catalyzed another successful program aimed exclusively at assisting homeless New Yorkers. In 1990, as noted in chapter 1, Dinkins and Mario Cuomo signed a joint city-state accord, the New York / New York Agreement, to create thousands of units of housing specifically for homeless individuals living with mental illness—a belated response, in part, to the legacy of deinstitutionalization. Most of the apartments were in rehabilitated structures, such as former SRO hotels, with both housing and services administered by nonprofit organizations. The accord ultimately created more than 3,600 units of supportive housing, at the time the largest such initiative in the nation.[54]

The twin investments in housing led to significant reductions in homelessness. The number of homeless single adults in the municipal shelter system had soared to nearly 10,800 people per night in 1989. But only five years after the New York / New York Agreement was ratified, the nightly census of homeless single adults fell to approximately six thousand, marking a historic decline of 44 percent. What's more, the number of homeless people sleeping on city streets and other public spaces, which peaked in the early 1990s, began a steady decline for the remainder of the decade.

For the homeless family population, the impact was also striking. During the 1980s, the number of homeless families in the traditional shelter system peaked at 5,200, with nearly eleven thousand children, in 1988. The number of homeless families then fell to only 3,200 families per night by the summer of 1990, a remarkable 38 percent drop, largely due to the new city-funded housing resources. Another cause of this decline was the Dinkins administration's successful policy of prioritizing homeless families for federal housing programs—that is, allocating a significant share of scarce federal housing vouchers and public housing apartments to homeless families, bypassing multiyear waiting lists.

Unfortunately, the success of that policy was undermined by the impact of the early 1990s economic downturn, which hit New York City particularly hard; combined with the aftermath of the 1987 stock market crash, total employment in the city fell by nearly 10 percent by 1992. Thousands of families lost their housing and sought shelter, driving up the family shelter population. But some Dinkins officials, influenced by right-wing critics, mistakenly thought that housing aid was drawing more families to the shelter system. So, the Dinkins administration instituted a policy called Alternative Pathways, which diverted some federal housing vouchers away from homeless families to other, nonhomeless poor families. As a consequence, the number of homeless families shot up, and the stress on the poorly managed system increased. After some months, Dinkins abandoned Alternative Pathways and returned to the previous, far more effective policy.[55] Nonetheless, the distorted policy debate around providing federal housing aid to homeless families would linger well into the twenty-first century.

TOMPKINS SQUARE IN THE NEW GILDED AGE

In the late 1980s, as modern homelessness entered its second decade, the neoliberal governance of the Koch era dovetailed with the sharper right-wing politics of Reagan and the resurgent conservative movement. What emerged was a significant backlash against homeless New Yorkers, a gradual but marked shift from the general sympathy with which homeless people had been treated at the beginning of the 1980s. As detailed in chapter 3, the NYPD was at the forefront of the backlash, but it was abetted by the reactionary "populism" of the tabloids, which exploited the increased visibility of homeless people and panhandlers in flagrant, often explicitly racist language to call for a police crackdown.

The August 1988 "Tompkins Square Park riot"—like its predecessor a century earlier, during the first Gilded Age—was a full-blown police offensive, a military-style incursion waged against homeless people and neighborhood protesters. And like the many police crackdowns on homeless people in decades to come, it involved the confluence of gentrification, the real estate industry, and the forced displacement of Black and Latino New Yorkers.

In the months preceding the police riot, much of Tompkins Square Park had become a rough dwelling place for dozens of homeless people. But the park remained the scruffy heart of the still-bohemian neighborhood, a gathering place for Black and Puerto Rican families, older Ukrainian men sitting around chess boards, teens playing basketball, and community activists. The Koch administration and real estate interests, aiming to accelerate the gentrification of the neighborhood, planned to renovate the park and impose a previously unenforced curfew dating from the nineteenth century. Similar gentrification-spurring renovations had already occurred in Washington Square Park and Union Square Park, where a major real estate developer had pushed for their "clean-up."[56]

The surrounding East Village neighborhood had been gentrifying for years—the name "East Village" itself had been invented by real estate brokers to evoke the tonier Greenwich Village to its west and attract white residents—but still carried the scars of housing abandonment and disinvestment. Residents were divided in their response to the homeless encampments in the park. Recent arrivals and local merchants, mostly white and representing the more gentrified areas west of the park, pushed for the removal of homeless people and the "new" park curfew, while lower-income, longtime neighborhood residents of Alphabet City called for no curfew and more social services.[57]

Despite the opposition of many neighborhood residents, the Koch administration decided to impose the park curfew on the night of August 6, 1988. An enormous phalanx of NYPD officers, some mounted on horses, others on foot, carrying truncheons, night sticks, and wearing riot gear, erected barricades around the park hours before the scheduled 1:00 a.m. deadline. A small group of protesters, carrying signs reading, "Gentrification Equals Class War," had gathered on Avenue A. Before midnight, well in advance of the curfew hour, the police entered the park, corralling and evicting those inside. After the park was cleared, the NYPD attacked the protesters, swinging batons and chasing down those who tried to flee. Ultimately, about seventy people were injured, nearly all by the police, and nine were arrested.[58]

By dawn of August 7, the police had left the area, and over the following weeks and months, neighborhood parkgoers, including homeless people, returned to Tompkins Square. But the larger battle continued, for the park and for the further gentrification of the East Village and the Lower East Side. In the spring of 1989, police crackdowns on the park's homeless encampments ramped up again, and the NYPD expanded its enforcement to include squatters in the surrounding area. That year, I joined with friends at a homelessness legal clinic to help excavate a squat in an abandoned, city-owned building in Alphabet City. A few of the squatters were white artists and urban hipsters, but most were poor Puerto Rican families displaced from their homes elsewhere in the neighborhood. The vacant, rundown tenement building, like the park, offered a makeshift refuge in a gentrifying, pricier, less welcoming neighborhood.

Finally, in December 1989, after Koch had lost his reelection bid, but before Dinkins took office, the NYPD officially closed down Tompkins Square Park, surrounding it with fences and multiple garbage trucks, and the police expelled all the homeless people.[59] The park remained fenced-in and empty for years, and did not reopen until 1994, the same year that newly elected Mayor Rudy Giuliani fully ushered in the backlash era.

CHAPTER 3

MADISON SQUARE PARK: CRIMINALIZING HOMELESSNESS

In New York City there are three centers for people living on the street: Central Park, Grand Central Terminal, and Central Booking.

This last is the city's own private purgatory. A timeless void between apprehension and judgement. When you finally emerge—ragged, unwashed, and hungry—into the crisp, efficient courtroom, you can easily see why everyone there treats you like a less evolved life-form.

The cops hardly need a reason to put street people in this place these days. But I gave them one anyway. I tried to swing a free ride on the subway by slipping through the turnstiles without paying.

It was "sweep" day.

I was swept.

Lee Stringer
Grand Central Winter: Stories from the Street

SWEPT AWAY

The first thing I noticed about James was that he talked like a train whistle. We first met on a balmy spring night back in 1996, on a sidewalk a couple of blocks north of Madison Square Park in Manhattan. Even though he slept on the streets most nights, alongside a few dozen other homeless men and women bedding down on sidewalks near the park, James was always neatly dressed, usually sporting a polo shirt, khaki slacks, crisp navy-blue windbreaker, and ivy cap with a snap brim. And then there was the whistle in his voice, high-pitched, present one moment and gone the next, reminding me of the Gopher character in the *Winnie the Pooh* cartoons I had treasured on the old *Wonderful World of Disney* TV show, during my childhood.

Early in Rudy Giuliani's third year as mayor, I trekked over to Madison Square Park and met James. Homeless people sleeping in the area had reported a sharp increase in harassment by the police, including what sounded like targeted "sweeps." The Coalition for the Homeless operated a long-standing program that fed homeless and hungry people on the streets, sending food-laden vans out every night to a couple dozen locations in Manhattan to distribute sandwiches, hot stew, fruit, and milk. The staff and volunteers working the vans had begun to hear reports of aggressive police activity citywide—which was not surprising, given Giuliani's public statements about aggressively targeting "quality of life" problems. Madison Square Park seemed to be one of the hot spots.

For homeless people seeking a safe, out-of-sight place to bed down for the night, Madison Square Park had certain clear advantages. It was surrounded by low, knee-high fences, had a curfew that was only nominally enforced, and had a reputation for being safer than the larger parks. Even more important, up and down the surrounding blocks were plenty of vacant storefronts and scaffolding—this was commonplace in the mid-1990s, before the hypergentrification of the neighborhood, which was soon to arrive—providing makeshift shelter from the elements on rainy or snowy nights. At the time, two sizable groups of homeless people were sleeping on 27th and 28th Streets, just west of Fifth Avenue, and for many weeks, the Coalition's feeding vans stopped there to hand out food to more than fifty individuals each night.

It was on one of these blocks that I first got to know James, and he soon introduced me to many other homeless people who had experienced harassment by the police. Over dozens of interviews, a clear pattern emerged from their stories. Late in the night, a squad of NYPD officers would descend on the park and arrest, or threaten to arrest, the people sleeping there. They issued summonses for various minor offenses and ordered the homeless folks to vacate the area. The police raids initially focused on Madison Square itself, with teams of officers sweeping the park to eject any homeless person they could find. In fact, one of the reasons I first encountered James and the large group of homeless people a couple of blocks north of the park was that they had been pushed there by the NYPD sweeps.

The mid-1990s police crackdown on homeless New Yorkers, which continued for months, was in no way isolated to Madison Square Park. The NYPD conducted similar sweeps in every other Manhattan park, Times Square, midtown, Wall Street, and various parts of the outer boroughs, which represented only the most visible part of a larger strategy.

The crackdown on homeless people in Madison Square Park was thus only one skirmish, though a singularly harsh and brutal one, within the broader campaign that Giuliani launched against homeless and poor New Yorkers in the "backlash era." That effort was itself a part of the wider, relentless war that Giuliani, and later Michael Bloomberg, waged on Black and Latino New Yorkers for two decades. And the outcome of that ongoing onslaught, for its wealthy beneficiaries and poor victims, unalterably reshaped entire neighborhoods and the economic and civic life of the city.

MADISON SQUARE

Madison Square Park's history was a parable, at least from the perspective of the city's gilded elites and their chroniclers, for the rise, fall, and revival of New York.

The six-acre park sits at the intersection of Fifth Avenue and Broadway, bordered on the east side by Madison Avenue and on the south and north by East 23rd and 26th Streets. Named for James Madison, the nation's fourth president, it was opened to the public in 1847 on a part of Manhattan Island that had been, in the era before European colonization, a swampy wetland inhabited by the Lenape. Later, with the arrival of the Dutch and English and the expulsion of indigenous communities, it became a hunting ground and potter's field. In the early nineteenth century, the area near the park was home to a juvenile detention home, and then, beginning in 1839, a farmhouse called Madison Cottage that was converted into a roadhouse, the first of many lodging houses and hotels that would dot the neighborhood over the coming decades.[1]

During this period, the park itself was a simple affair, little more than an open field surrounded by the early residential and commercial buildings in the area, although over the coming decades, benches and promenades were added. During the draft riots of 1863, some ten thousand troops were quartered in Madison Square in order to suppress the unrest. Madison Square was also the site of a massive rally the following year in support of General George McClellan's campaign to unseat Abraham Lincoln, one sign of New York City's financial and commercial ties to the slaveholding states of the Confederacy.[2]

Before and especially after the Civil War, during the Gilded Age, the amenities of Madison Square Park helped trigger a wave of residential development in the neighborhood for the aristocratic elite. The grand Fifth Avenue Hotel straddled the entire block between 23rd and 24th Streets, overlooking the park. With eight hundred rooms, it was the first hotel in the nation with elevators, and ten US presidents visited during its half century of existence. More luxury hotels sprang up on the surrounding blocks, as did exclusive private clubs, fancy restaurants like Delmonico's, and boutique shops that were part of the famed Ladies' Mile retail district.[3]

Throughout the Gilded Age, Madison Square Park remained the gravitational center of the neighborhood and the site of multiple attractions.

Statues were erected depicting President Chester Arthur and Secretary of State William Seward, as well as a memorial to Civil War Admiral David Farragut. From 1876 to 1882, the park even displayed the torch and arm of the Statue of Liberty as part of an effort to raise money for the construction of the monument's pedestal.[4]

By the peak of the Gilded Age, then, Madison Square Park and its environs were established as not only a comfortably fashionable and affluent district, but also as a thriving commercial hub. Over time, this legacy, and the nostalgia it engendered, became decisive in shaping its later history.

QUALITY OF LIFE

A century later, Madison Square Park also served as a laboratory for a prolonged and relentless campaign to criminalize homelessness. Giuliani, in his second and ultimately successful 1993 campaign for mayor and throughout his eight years in office, made no secret of the central goal driving his mayoralty: to "clean up" New York. His vision of cleansing the city required not only an underlying and unremitting assault on Black and Latino communities, but also the erasure of visible signs of poverty from affluent, white precincts of the city. While this sanitation of New York was in some ways an end in itself, it was also undertaken to advance the neoliberal project of "reviving the city," which emerged as code for unleashing real estate development, further cutting back on government spending and regulations, dismantling social welfare programs, and ultimately benefiting the city's elite classes.

Targeted police crackdowns on homeless people had certainly preceded Giuliani, beginning with the emergence of modern homelessness in the late 1970s and early 1980s. Mayor Ed Koch and his administration had directed the NYPD to clear homeless people from certain parks and transportation hubs, like Grand Central Terminal and the Port Authority Bus Terminal. But those antihomeless salvos had been tempered until the public mood began to shift in the late 1980s. As Benjamin Holtzman noted in his history of the rise of neoliberalism in New York, "Though Koch wanted to take more aggressive steps against the homeless, for much of the 1980s, public opinion largely remained sympathetic toward them. . . . But over the next few years, public opinion began to shift. With little being done to address root causes, the problem seemed increasingly intractable to casual observers. Public sympathy waned: journalists and scholars would label this 'compassion fatigue.'"[5]

The Koch administration then engaged in various targeted crackdowns on street homelessness, the most flagrant of which was the Tompkins Square Park police riot of 1988 (see chapter 2). The Dinkins administration was less aggressive in its antihomeless policing schemes. However, in response to rising rates of violent crime citywide, which paralleled national trends, Dinkins significantly expanded the size of the police force. And amid a surge in visible street homelessness in the early 1990s, Dinkins bowed to pressure from city elites and the tabloid press to address the problem.

But nothing that came before compared to the harsh and relentless Giuliani antihomelessness crusade. Upon taking office in 1994, Giuliani and his first NYPD commissioner, Bill Bratton, declared an aggressive campaign against urban "disorder," typified in their view by so-called quality-of-life violations. In this, they received full-throated support from the city's two major tabloids, the extreme right-wing *New York Post* (owned by the reactionary billionaire Rupert Murdoch) and the mostly right-wing *New York Daily News*, both of which had an outsize influence on New York politics in the era before digital media. Inevitably, these "violations" of New Yorkers' quality of life, far from being abstract or merely about behavior and actions, turned out to be other New Yorkers. What's more, they were some of the poorest, most vulnerable residents of the city: panhandlers, many of them not homeless, who asked passersby for spare change on sidewalks and at ATM kiosks; the "squeegee men" who lingered at bridge and tunnel entrances, asking for money to clean the car windshields of commuters, and who were flagrantly demonized by the tabloids; indigent turnstile jumpers in the subway system; and, of course, homeless people.

The NYPD's quality-of-life campaign quickly evolved into a broader push to criminalize homelessness. In the summer of 1996, my colleagues and I obtained an NYPD operations document, blandly titled "Quality of Life Enforcement Options: A Reference Guide," that had been issued to police officers citywide.[6] The first eight of its seventeen pages detailed exclusively the statutes and regulations on the books that officers were supposed to exploit in order to target the behavior of homeless people: lying on park benches; panhandling; illegal "camping"; keeping boxes, mattresses, or other belongings in public places; public urination; street vending; and on and on. The guide focused special attention on a host of vaguely worded rules (e.g., "conduct himself or herself in any manner which may cause or tend to cause annoyance, alarm, or inconvenience"), written decades earlier about activities in transit facilities and public parks, which officers could weaponize in almost any circumstance to round up homeless people.

To make matters worse, the police enforced these ordinances in a wildly unjust and unequal manner. In those years, it went without saying that if, say, a young white professional in office attire exited a nightclub and urinated in a doorway, or a well-dressed white tourist lay down on a Central Park bench, they were at virtually zero risk of receiving a ticket from the NYPD—much less being arrested. But a homeless person, especially a Black or Latino man dressed in shabby clothes, who engaged in exactly the same behavior was targeted by the police. He then either faced a fine that he could never afford or was taken into custody.

While the police were harassing the homeless folks at Madison Square

Park, the Giuliani administration also launched a full-scale effort to abolish every homeless encampment in Manhattan. Squads of NYPD officers, often accompanied by garbage trucks and demolition equipment, descended on homeless people who were sleeping in groups—some with shacks or other makeshift structures, often under bridges, near vacant lots or construction sites, or along the waterfront. The police would bulldoze whatever structures existed and, like they did at Madison Square Park, throw away the homeless people's meager belongings, including clothes and bedding. Around midnight on a bitterly cold February night in 1997, police used axes and bulldozers to demolish the last of the large Manhattan encampments. The group of a few dozen homeless people had been sleeping in some abandoned coal bins near the Hudson River at West 66th Street, adjacent to a site where the real estate heir and developer Donald Trump was erecting the Riverside South apartment complex. *The New York Times* quoted Trump proudly defending the removal of the homeless people: "Some things have to be done that are going to be ultimately very good for the city."[7]

Midway through his second mayoral term, Giuliani made explicit what had always been lurking under the surface of his antihomeless policing tactics—every homeless person on the streets was subject to arrest. In November 1999, a man in midtown Manhattan struck a woman over the head with a paving stone, and it was instantly assumed, without any evidence, that the attacker was homeless. The next day, a front-page *Daily News* headline screamed, "Get the Violent Crazies Off Our Streets." Giuliani and his second NYPD commissioner, Howard Safir, announced that the police would immediately begin arresting all homeless people in New York City, except those who obeyed an order to go to a municipal shelter, which many were afraid to do. Over the following weeks, the number of people arrested on city streets rose sharply, driving many homeless New Yorkers even deeper into the shadows.

It turned out that the man charged with assaulting the woman in midtown had never spent a night on the streets or in a homeless shelter (though he had lacked a stable address for some time). But this revelation failed to dampen the tabloid hysteria or cause the administration to rescind its blanket arrest policy. Giuliani's entire approach to street homelessness—rooted in his "zero tolerance" and "quality of life" policing strategies, and signaled early on with his aggressive campaign against the "squeegee men"—was premised on efforts to demonize and pathologize homeless New Yorkers. Even in his January 2000 State of the City address, when he was attempting both to defend and manage the fallout from his policy of arresting the homeless, Giuliani couldn't help but resort to vitriolic language: "Some of the people lying on the streets are predatory criminals who kill other people lying on the streets, rape them, rob them, or try to kill you."[8] Even in 2015, more than a decade after he'd left City Hall, Giuliani summarized his homelessness strategy this way: "You chase 'em and you chase 'em and you chase 'em and you chase 'em, and they either get the treatment that they need or you chase 'em out of the city."[9]

THE NEW CENTURY

In the early decades of the twentieth century, before its coming decline, Madison Square Park rested comfortably in a zone of wealth and gentility. Visiting New York in 1915, the novelist Willa Cather described it this way: "Madison Square was then at the parting of the ways; had a double personality, half commercial, half social, with shops to the south and residences to the north. It seemed to me so neat, after the raggedness of our Western cities; so, protected by good manners and courtesy—like an open-air drawing-room. I could well imagine a winter dancing party being given there, or a reception for some distinguished European visitor."[10]

During this period, Madison Square Park grew to be surrounded by three of Manhattan's archetypal buildings. The bizarre, triangular, unmistakable Flatiron Building was built in 1902. The Metropolitan Life Insurance Company Tower, completed in 1909, was adorned with its iconic clock, and was briefly the world's tallest building (until the Woolworth Building, located downtown, eclipsed it four years later). And the New York Life Building opened in 1928, crowned with a pyramid comprising twenty-five thousand gold leaf tiles. Furthermore, the first two venues named Madison Square Garden neighbored the park, until the famous arena was relocated to midtown in the late 1920s.

The Madison Square neighborhood also became home to clothing and toy manufacturing, including the Lionel Trains company, as well as printing and publishing. But as with the rest of the city, over the coming decades, these small industrial concerns began disappearing, as did the jobs that went with them. The Great Depression of the 1930s devastated the city's industrial base, and many firms never recovered. The number of manufacturing jobs in New York City stood at around one million in 1950, but continued to fall over the subsequent decades to just over 180,000 by the end of the century. Shops and other commercial businesses began to close, leaving many buildings surrounding the park half empty or altogether vacant. Madison Square Park and its environs took on a shabby gentility as New York City entered the 1960s and endured the crises of the following decades.

THE SWEEP

One late night in spring 1996, shortly after meeting James and hearing his reports of police harassment of homeless people in Madison Square Park, I witnessed the NYPD's crackdown firsthand. Around twenty officers poured into the park, rousting people from benches and other sleeping areas. The police made several arrests and issued tickets to other homeless people, which I knew would most likely result in bench warrants when the fines inevitably went unpaid, resulting in more arrests down the road. I interviewed as many of the homeless people as I could, urging them to visit the Coalition offices so we could connect them with legal aid.

The worst of the sweep was the wholesale destruction. NYPD personnel in canvas jumpsuits and uniforms roughly collected every item and threw them into the dump truck. The police threw all this away, including clothes and bags strewn around the makeshift dwellings, while some of the homeless men shouted at them. This remained my most enduring memory of that night, even decades later: Black men, weary and distressed, yelling as white officers methodically discarded their belongings.

BLOOMBERG AND STOP-AND-FRISK

Michael Bloomberg, the billionaire Republican who was elected New York's mayor in 2001, escalated the antihomeless policing strategies of the Giuliani era. Even more, Bloomberg intensified the systemic racism of the NYPD's wider approach to so-called public safety in New York through the deliberate expansion of tactics like "stop-and-frisk." During Bloomberg's mayoralty, the police conducted more than five million stops of city residents, with a peak of nearly seven hundred thousand stops in 2012 alone. The large majority of the people stopped and searched by the NYPD, often for the flimsiest of reasons, were young Black and Latino men—indeed, Black and Latino New Yorkers were nine times more likely to be stopped by police than white people. In 2013, a federal court ruled that the Bloomberg stop-and-frisk policy was unconstitutional and amounted to racial profiling.[11]

In every important way, Bloomberg subscribed to the same right-wing, antipoor philosophy and embraced the same approach to "zero tolerance" policing as Giuliani. During Bloomberg's twelve years as mayor, the NYPD, under Commissioner Ray Kelly, continued to target homeless people for arrests and summons in huge numbers, often as part of the department's ballooning stop-and-frisk program. Indeed, in January 2002, barely a week after taking office, Bloomberg and Kelly announced Operation Clean Sweep, which the *New York Post* described—glowingly, of course—as "the NYPD's quality-of-life crackdown that aims at wiping out public urination, prostitution and squeegee men."[12]

One example of the ideological continuity from Giuliani to Bloomberg involved the Fifth Avenue Presbyterian Church, a Gothic-spired monument that had opened in 1875, during the Gilded Age. The church had long operated a small shelter for homeless men in its basement, and, when the shelter's beds were full, church leaders permitted people to sleep outdoors on its steps. In November 2001, the NYPD began arresting the homeless people staying there. Some police officers reported that Giuliani's City Hall had directly ordered that the homeless individuals be swept from the steps to prevent luminaries like Vice President Dick Cheney, who often stayed in the nearby St. Regis Hotel, from seeing visible poverty.[13] The church argued in federal court that the arrests violated its First Amendment right as a religious institution to provide care and sanctuary. Nevertheless, after taking office in January 2002, Bloomberg pursued the case and continued to do so for years, until the church prevailed in the US Court of Appeals in 2006.

Another policy borrowed from the Giuliani playbook involved warrant sweeps in shelters. The Giuliani-era police harassment of homeless people was not limited to the unsheltered population. Over the years, the NYPD would routinely send officers into municipal shelters to arrest homeless people who had outstanding bench warrants—typically for unpaid fines or missed court appearances related to minor infractions, like public urination or turnstile jumping. On a single frigid night in January 2000, the NYPD arrested 125 homeless people in shelters, including a seventy-year-old man and eighteen homeless men at a shelter reserved for people diagnosed with mental illnesses.[14] Bloomberg continued and multiplied the NYPD shelter sweeps during his three terms as mayor.

Early in his mayoralty, during the winter of 2002–3, Bloomberg and the NYPD stepped up arrests of homeless people on the streets and in the subway system. The administration specifically utilized the NYPD's Homeless Outreach Unit to arrest and harass homeless people, even though the team had been primarily designed to coordinate with social service agencies to marshal assistance. In November 2002, an officer in that unit, Eduardo Delacruz, refused to arrest a homeless man sleeping in a parking garage near Manhattan's Union Square. Delacruz had previously informed superiors that he would not detain homeless individuals, citing his religious faith and his belief that there was no crime in not having a home. Nonetheless, the NYPD charged Delacruz with refusing an order from a superior officer, and, in 2004, he was punished with two years of probation.[15] While the courageous Delacruz was undergoing discipline, in late November 2002, a class action lawsuit accused the NYPD Homeless Outreach Unit of selective enforcement. The Bloomberg administration eventually settled the case and agreed to issue new policies stating that officers could not single out homeless people for arrest.[16]

There were other legal challenges to the antihomeless police policies of the Giuliani and Bloomberg years. In a 1995 federal court case, the Coalition for the Homeless successfully ended Amtrak's practice of targeting homeless people for expulsion from Penn Station.[17] In 1997, the Urban Justice Center challenged vague statutes that the NYPD had used to arrest dozens of homeless men; the lead plaintiff, a soft-spoken homeless man named Augustine Betancourt, said that the police officer who rousted him from a Lower Manhattan park bench told him, "Direct order from Giuliani. You're not supposed to be sleeping here."[18] And in 2005, the Bronx district attorney, responding to a class action lawsuit, admitted that his office had wrongfully prosecuted cases brought under an antipanhandling statute that had been deemed unconstitutional by federal courts more than two decades earlier—a law that the NYPD nevertheless continued to use to arrest homeless people and panhandlers.[19]

While the legal challenges minimized some harm, they were unable to stop the wider antihomeless policing campaign. One example of the pointlessness, wastefulness, and cruelty of this policing philosophy was the yearslong campaign to criminalize the homeless men residing at the enormous 1,200-bed shelter complex located on Wards Island. In order to reach the shelter, residents had to take the M35 municipal bus, which left from the corner of East 125th Street and Lexington Avenue in East Harlem. For obvious reasons, many, if not most, of the homeless men did not have the fare for the bus, which was two dollars in the mid-2000s, so some would not pay the fare—and in certain cases, sympathetic bus drivers would let them ride for free. Around 2004, my colleagues at the Coalition for the Homeless received multiple reports from Wards Island residents that the NYPD had set up what amounted to a sting operation on the M35 bus. Undercover cops often rode alongside the homeless men and arrested those who had not paid; the bus would frequently stop several blocks from its East 125th Street terminus as NYPD officers conducted raids, targeting alleged fare evaders.

A 2005 *New York Times* report captured the absurdity of the policy and the enormous waste of police and court resources that were devoted to the targeting of homeless people:

> As the cases have made their way into court, they have
> confounded judges. Some refuse to give any sentence and order
> the defendants released, once they have pleaded guilty to the
> typical charge a misdemeanor crime of theft of services. . . . In
> interviews, five criminal court judges who spoke on the condition
> of anonymity questioned the wisdom of the arrests, saying that
> they wasted judicial resources. A court system spokesman said he

could not quantify the cost of arraigning one defendant, a process that involves a judge, a prosecutor, court officers and a court stenographer. Most defendants also spend the night in jail, which costs $163, according to a breakdown by the city.[20]

Despite the obvious unfairness, absurdity, and wastefulness of the crackdown on homeless Wards Island bus riders, the Bloomberg administration continued the practice for years more, despite protests by us and other advocacy groups.

In one illustrative case, a Legal Aid Society attorney represented a homeless man accused of not paying the Wards Island bus fare. Just before trial, a colleague later told me, the bus driver, who had allowed the homeless man to board without paying, broke down in a nearby room, unable to reconcile the risk of job loss with the threat of perjury. At his union rep's urging, the judge dismissed the case.

In Madison Square Park, too, homeless people still reported harassment by the police well into the first decades of the twenty-first century, and many began to avoid the park altogether. In 2013, my coworkers and I surveyed more than a hundred homeless people who visited the Coalition's feeding vans and described their experiences with the NYPD, and the answers were depressing but unsurprising. More than half had been arrested at least once while homeless. Nearly half had received at least one summons or ticket while homeless. And most said that they'd had one or more "negative experiences" with the police while homeless. Nearly four out of five said they believed that the NYPD treated homeless people differently from nonhomeless people.[21]

PRIVATIZING MADISON SQUARE PARK

The economic turmoil and the fiscal crisis of the 1970s, which devastated New York City, took a huge toll on Madison Square Park and its surrounding neighborhood, which had already begun to lose its glamor in the postwar period. As the city's economy shifted from manufacturing employment to lower-wage service jobs, and as elites launched a fierce attack on the public sector, the city's budget suffered harsh cutbacks. From 1968 until 1975, when the city government faced virtual bankruptcy, the Parks Department lost nearly 40 percent of its workers, with *The New York Times* reporting in 1976 that "park maintenance is almost abandoned and corrective work impossible."[22] From 1975 to 1981, overall municipal spending was reduced by 20 percent in real terms, with harsh cutbacks in services at every city agency.[23] In 1979, the *Times* noted deteriorating conditions at Madison Square Park and—in some of the earliest reporting on the emergence of modern homelessness outside the traditional Bowery skid row districts—described the park as "the site of daytime drug dealing and a place where derelicts drink and sleep on the benches."[24]

That same year, a former Parks Department official named Donald Simon proposed what historian Benjamin Holtzman later described as "a radical plan to save Madison Square Park and—he hoped—parks across the city." Simon's proposal, which would essentially privatize the park, signified yet another element of the neoliberal governance philosophy that emerged in the post-fiscal-crisis era in New York City. He outlined a plan to have the local businesses and corporations whose offices surrounded Madison Square Park help to finance basic services like maintenance and security. In return, Simon proposed that a private entity should take over the management of the park, all with the aid of business donations and leadership. His pitch to corporations with headquarters near the park was that investments in the "reversal of the park's decline" would eventually be "mirrored in a stronger demand for rental space." Working with a former New York City Parks Department commissioner, Simon eventually got funding from the Ford Foundation to create an entity called the Urban Parks Plaza.[25]

In addition to seeking millions of dollars in private funding for city parks, the organization believed that park renovations would force out "the unwanted elements" by drawing neighborhood residents. "Large numbers of people," the group stated, "tend to drive away the drug dealers and derelicts who by their very presence give the site a dangerous appearance." The Urban Parks Plaza ultimately managed to raise nearly $65,000 toward efforts to clean up Madison Square Park. But this amount was far below its goal, and far less than what was requested of the corporations, and by the 1980s, the organization closed down.[26]

But Simon's idea lived on. A similar organization, funded by corporate and midtown business interests, was launched to help revive nearby Bryant Park, which had also suffered from years of budget cutbacks. The founder of that group, Dan Biederman, later went on to help pioneer the creation of "business improvement districts" (BIDs), which relied on corporate and private funding to provide street cleaning and other services in places like midtown Manhattan and Wall Street—services that had traditionally been provided by the city government and unionized municipal workers.

Central to the mission of BIDs was the removal of homeless people. Biederman went on to found and lead the Grand Central Partnership BID, which covered the east midtown area surrounding Grand Central Terminal. The group employed homeless and formerly homeless people as private security guards, forming so-called "thug squads" that were instructed to remove, even by force, homeless people and panhandlers from the neighborhood. To make matters worse, the Grand Central Partnership only paid the homeless workers one dollar per hour, a blatant violation of labor laws. The Coalition for the Homeless, in partnership with the Urban Justice Center and pro bono attorneys, brought a class action lawsuit, and, after years of appeals and legal battles, in October 2000, the 198 plaintiffs were awarded $816,000 in back wages. The initial federal court ruling was written by future Supreme Court Justice Sonia Soto-mayor, who found, according to *The New York Times*, "that the business districts had violated minimum wage laws, had used the cheap labor of so-called trainees to undercut competing companies, and had contributed the resulting profits to hefty executive salaries."[27]

Despite the scandals and controversies surrounding the activities of BIDs, business leaders and other local elites, as well as the news media, routinely praised them as vehicles for revitalizing New York's business districts and parks. The *Economist* magazine, for instance, lauded BIDs as "the best hope for getting parts of America's cash-strapped cities working again."[28] Moreover, in an era of increasingly neoliberal municipal governance—which dated back to the Ed Koch administration but reached its apotheosis in the two decades of Giuliani and Bloomberg's mayoralties—the BIDs offered a model of privatized services with less accountability to the public.

Another legacy of Madison Square Park, then, was as a workshop for the growing privatization of public space and services in the New York City of the New Gilded Age. That mixture of private control of urban space combined with aggressive policing would ultimately be the key, in the decades ahead, to the transformation of the Madison Square area.

"VANISHING" HOMELESSNESS

From the mid-1990s through the first decade of this century, many New Yorkers and nearly all of the news media, particularly the tabloid press, celebrated the long NYPD crackdown on street homelessness. If one ignored the wider context, to say nothing of the impact on homeless people themselves, it was not hard to see why. Public homelessness became far less visible. So-called encampments and large groups of homeless people were largely eliminated. And in Manhattan's most notable, and tourist-friendly, locales—Times Square, Grand Central Terminal, Central Park, Wall Street, the midtown shopping districts like Herald Square—the NYPD had swept clean virtually any evidence of street homelessness. The major local news outlets, which had always been friendly to media mogul Bloomberg, reinforced his administration's narrative about the successful "cleanup" of the city. In 2010, *The New York Times* even published an article claiming, in a way that barely seemed credible even at the time, that there was only one single homeless person left sleeping in Times Square.[29]

"Where did all of the homeless go?" Countless times during my decades working as a homeless advocate, I would get this question in one form or another—from news reporters, elected officials, columnists, students, academics, policymakers, and even occasionally other advocates. For the longest time, I found the question irritating, even enraging, since it often came from people who should have known better. It was obvious that homeless New Yorkers had not simply vanished. Indeed, during the first two decades of the twenty-first century, particularly amid the skyrocketing homeless population of the Bloomberg years, the question seemed to reflect a willful ignorance. New York City's homeless shelter population had increased 72 percent under Bloomberg, as the real-time, publicly available data clearly showed, and each night during the 2010s, there were well over fifty thousand people homeless in New York City. So how could anyone ask where the homeless people had gone?

But, having seen firsthand the abysmal conditions of New York street homelessness in the late 1980s and early 1990s, I also knew what the questioners were getting at. They were talking about something both very real—the large number of vulnerable, desperate homeless people so visible on Manhattan streets in that earlier period—but also something mythical, rooted in a fable about New York City. It was a narrative that aligned with the rise-and-fall-and-revival narrative arc so perfectly embodied in the history of Madison Square Park. And it was a tale whose reinforcing myths— two myths, in particular, crafted in different ways by politicians, the media, and ideologues advancing a right-wing agenda—were worth unraveling.

To begin, there was the sadly persistent notion that the police were the solution to homelessness—that there were fewer homeless people on New York streets primarily because of aggressive policing. This was a story that Giuliani and his supporters particularly liked to tell and continued to spin long after Giuliani left City Hall and morphed into a failed presidential candidate, reliable Fox News bloviator, Donald Trump attorney, and wild conspiracy theorist. Bloomberg and various NYPD commissioners also liked to spin this tale, as did the tabloids, which had never met a crackdown on street homelessness they didn't applaud. The problem was that there was no hard evidence to support this myth, only anecdotes and perception. And there was plenty of evidence to counter it.

First, the data overwhelmingly indicated that the 1990s-era decline in homelessness began *before* the Giuliani police crackdowns—indeed, it began well before Giuliani even became mayor. While there has never been a precise measurement of New York's unsheltered homeless population, its rise and fall have nearly always correlated with the number of homeless single adults in shelters. And that population, which had soared to nearly eleven thousand men and women per night by 1989, declined by a remarkable 44 percent by the end of 1993, to just over six thousand people per night, during Dinkins's last year as mayor and before Giuliani entered City Hall. As discussed in chapter 1, most of that decline was due to the historic 1990 New York / New York Agreement to create supportive housing for homeless individuals living with mental illness.

The reason, therefore, that homeless people were seen less often on New York streets in the years after the early 1990s was, simply put, *that there were actually fewer homeless individuals.* Instead of being left to languish on the streets or in shelters, they had been provided with decent, affordable homes with support services, thanks to effective government housing programs. While aggressive, even harsh police tactics certainly made homelessness less visible, at least temporarily, much of that was cosmetic and fleeting. As I learned from James and the other folks sleeping near Madison Square Park, the police could never make homeless people completely disappear; they just pushed them away and made them harder to see, harder to find, and harder to help.

The second foundational myth of the "Giuliani cleaned up New York" narrative was the notion that "zero-tolerance" or "quality-of-life" policing strategies were singularly successful not only in addressing homelessness, but also in reducing crime. Under its various labels and slogans through the years, the origin of these "broken windows" policing tactics in New York City and elsewhere was a seminal 1982 article by sociologists George Kelling and James Q. Wilson, which argued that crime rates correlated with evidence of disorder, such as broken windows in a building or in a neighborhood.[30] Hence, the article argued, police should focus on minor, quality-of-life offenses to drive down more serious crimes, a strategy also known as "order-maintenance" policing.

The first major police official fully to embrace the Kelling and Wilson approach was Bill Bratton, who, under Dinkins, was the head of the NYPD's Transit Bureau, the unit in charge of the subway system. Bratton ordered his squad to focus on enforcing low-level offenses, like turnstile jumping and graffiti. And, of course, Bratton directed his four thousand transit officers to target homeless people, leading to a spike in homeless arrests. When Giuliani was elected mayor, he elevated Bratton to NYPD commissioner and expanded the broken windows–inspired, order-maintenance policing strategy citywide. But Bratton remained focused on antihomeless tactics. Indeed, shortly after taking over the NYPD, he infamously said, "We are going to flush them [homeless people] off the street in the same successful manner in which we flushed them out of the subway system."[31]

The zero-tolerance policing strategy of the Giuliani years worsened under Bloomberg. As noted above, the hallmark of the Bloomberg era was the systemically racist "stop-and-frisk" policy which caught up hundreds of thousands of Black and Latino New Yorkers in harsh and humiliating enforcement actions, and which Bloomberg defended as necessary to keep crime rates down. But after federal courts ordered a halt to the discriminatory policy, the NYPD was forced to reduce dramatically the number of "stop-and-frisk" actions—from a high of nearly 700,000 stops in 2012 to only 9,500 stops in 2020. And even without the harsh "stop-and-frisk" tactics, crime rates citywide fell and remained at historic lows.[32]

By the early twenty-first century, it was clear that there was virtually no empirical evidence that broken windows policing was the major cause of crime reduction. As numerous books and research studies have documented, not only New York, but also nearly every city in the United States—including those that did not adopt a zero-tolerance policing strategy—experienced major drops in violent crimes, and, indeed, overall crime rates from the mid-1990s into the early decades of the twenty-first century.[33] The major causes were primarily economic and demographic (e.g., the aging of a cohort of young men with few job opportunities), and also involved the waning of the illicit crack cocaine trade.

Broken windows, quality-of-life, or zero-tolerance policing had little to do with falling crime rates, but instead inflicted incalculable harm on Black and Latino communities, as well as on homeless people. It also, as historian and criminologist Alex Vitale has written, reoriented urban politics away from addressing fundamental inequalities and problems such as homelessness, and instead replaced those goals with a valorization of order.[34] But despite the damage it caused and the overwhelming evidence disproving it, the broken windows myth retained a powerful hold on New York City elites and politicians. Indeed, even the putatively progressive Bill de Blasio, after he took office in 2014, championed the broken windows philosophy and appointed Bill Bratton as his first NYPD commissioner.

CRIMINALIZING THE "VAGRANTS"

The antihomeless and racist policing strategies of Giuliani and Bloomberg were also rooted in the long, brutal history of municipal police forces in American cities. After the Civil War–era draft riots and amid the labor unrest of the 1870s, the city's elites installed an official metropolitan police force, complete with uniforms and weapons. But the new squad's principal duties focused on the violent suppression of worker uprisings, Black communities, and even community protests, like the Tompkins Square gathering of 1874.

The NYPD's brutal history of racist policing persisted throughout the twentieth century, even before the more aggressive tactics of Giuliani and Bloomberg. As Black New Yorkers began to mobilize against racism and police brutality, the NYPD struck back violently, most notably during the 1964 uprisings in Harlem and Bedford-Stuyvesant. In his history of movements opposing police brutality in New York City, historian Clarence Taylor wrote that "false racialized narratives were a major impediment to struggles for change. Police officers, along with many in the general society, equated blackness with criminality and attempted to control black people through brutal force."[35]

Police harassment of homeless people was inextricably linked to the systemic racism of urban policing. For most of the twentieth century, particularly in the postwar decades, homelessness was criminalized under the broad rubric of so-called vagrancy laws. Nearly every city in the nation had laws allowing the police to imprison people for days merely for being in a public place, and homeless people were one of the primary targets, along with sex workers, civil rights organizers, gay people, and leftist activists. Historian Risa Goluboff has written that "the laws' breadth and ambiguity gave the police virtually unlimited discretion. Because it was almost always possible to justify a vagrancy arrest, the laws provided what one critic called 'an escape hatch' from the Fourth Amendment's protections against arrest without probable cause. As one Supreme Court justice would write in 1965, vagrancy-related laws made it legal to stand on a street corner 'only at the whim of any police officer.'"[36]

The United States Supreme Court finally found vagrancy laws to be unconstitutional in the landmark 1972 case *Papachristou v. City of Jacksonville*, which involved a white woman with blonde hair who'd been arrested in Florida while out on the town with a white friend and two Black men. But as modern mass homelessness spread nationwide a decade later and persisted into the twenty-first century, municipal police departments found other means to criminalize homelessness. And in New York City, during the Giuliani and Bloomberg eras but also beyond, the NYPD used every tool at its disposal to treat homelessness as a crime.

The apotheosis of this brutal approach to homelessness and "vagrancy," and the poisonous politics behind it, may be seen in two cases from the Bill de Blasio and Eric Adams mayoralties. In July 2014, a white NYPD officer named Daniel Pantaleo killed Eric Garner, a Black man who'd been selling "loosies" (individual cigarettes) on a street corner in the Tompkinsville neighborhood of Staten Island. Pantaleo placed Garner in an illegal chokehold, and continued to choke Garner, even as he gasped, "I can't breathe." NYPD Commissioner Bill Bratton and the right-wing police union defended Pantaleo and the other officers involved, blaming Garner for his own death. And de Blasio, after initially calling for NYPD reforms, ultimately bowed to pressure from the police leadership and pro-police tabloids and effectively abandoned such efforts.[37]

Nearly a decade later, in May 2023, a homeless Black man named Jordan Neely was also choked to death, this time by a civilian, a white former US Marine named Daniel Penny. Penny put Neely into a fatal chokehold, which he continued for a minute past the point when Neely had gone limp. Neely, who had struggled with mental illness for many years, entered an uptown-bound subway train in Manhattan and, by all accounts, began behaving erratically—but not violently—shouting that he was hungry and needed a job. Penny grabbed him from behind, took him to the floor, and held him in the chokehold even after the train stopped. Afterward, Penny was lauded as a hero by right-wing politicians and the tabloids. He was ultimately acquitted, despite widespread belief that the evidence showed he had killed Neely.[38]

Neely, on the other hand, was demonized and pathologized in the news media and by Penny's defenders in the same fashion that many homeless New Yorkers had been since the 1980s (see chapter 1). But to those who knew him, Neely was a gentle man, though his history of schizophrenia and posttraumatic stress disorder—related to the gruesome murder of his mother by an abusive partner during Neely's childhood—occasionally led to changeable moods and behavior. An accomplished street performer and expert Michael Jackson impersonator, he'd gone from foster care to repeated periods of homelessness without ever being offered supportive housing, despite multiple contacts with city-funded service providers.

Neely's killing occurred during a public campaign, led by Adams, a right-wing populist, and the conservative New York Governor Kathy Hochul, to stigmatize homeless people in the subway system, particularly those living with mental illness. Amid hyperbolic and false claims by the local news media that violent crime on the subways was rising and that "crazy" homeless people were the culprits, Adams and Hochul had ordered wholesale sweeps of homeless populations from the subway system beginning the year before Neely was killed. But despite PR spin by city and state officials, including the mayor and governor, neither mental health services nor supportive housing saw meaningful expansion. In fact, an evaluation of the antihomeless campaign by the city comptroller found that, of some 2,300 homeless people living with mental illness who were swept from the subway system and the streets, only three were placed in housing.[39]

THE AFTERMATH IN MADISON SQUARE

As the mid-to-late 1990s crackdown on homeless people continued in Madison Square Park, James became an invaluable on-the-ground informant, a role he seemed to relish, in part, for its hints of clandestine espionage. By day, he'd visit the Coalition's Chambers Street offices and sit in my cubicle, sipping coffee and narrating, in his whistling voice, the previous night's sweeps, telling me how this person or that had been arrested. Sometimes he'd bring along another homeless guy who had received a summons from the police, and needed legal advice.

In the early weeks of the police crackdown, James introduced me to an attorney at a fellow advocacy organization, the Urban Justice Center, whose offices were then located near the park. We eventually worked together to monitor the worsening situation in Madison Square Park and assist the homeless people caught up in the NYPD crackdown. With the help of volunteer lawyers and paralegals, we set up legal clinics to help homeless people challenge their arrests and summonses, many of which were patently invalid or even unconstitutional—for example, when issuing summonses, many police officers would merely write things like "Sleeping on park bench," where they were supposed to detail the actual local statute that had allegedly been violated.

But as the months wore on, the police crackdown took its toll. One by one, the homeless folks sleeping in Madison Square Park began to move on to more distant, harder-to-find locations, away from the constant police harassment. We found fewer and fewer people sleeping near the park, and the number of people visiting the feeding vans began to dwindle. In 1997, the Giuliani administration helped to create the Madison Square Park Conservancy, a private group backed by wealthy donors, to manage the park. The following year, renovations resumed on the north side, leading to the expulsion of virtually the last homeless people from the site.

By the late 1990s, I saw James far less frequently. He'd moved on from

Madison Square Park. I heard some time later that he'd passed away, which hardly surprised me, given his advanced age and the physical and emotional toll that homelessness takes on people. I remembered him sitting by my desk, preternaturally still in his cap and windbreaker, whistling his way through another tale of the NYPD forcibly removing homeless people who were simply trying to find a night's sleep.

ERASING PEOPLE

A question I used to ask myself repeatedly during my years working as a homeless advocate was: What happens when you erase people from a place? What becomes of the people? What changes in the place?

I met Nestor in the weeks after the NYPD crackdown on Madison Square Park was launched. The first thing I noticed was that he was covered, head to toe, in black soot, from his unkempt, frizzy crown of hair to his broken sandals and massive feet. He was wearing nothing more than an equally soot-stained, charcoal-dusted sack with a ragged neck hole and sloppily-cut-out armholes, paired with filthy sweatpants that had been scissored off at mid-shin. With the layer of grime and black dust covering every square inch of his skin and tattered clothes, the effect was not unlike that of Pig-Pen, the hygiene-averse character from the classic *Peanuts* comic strip, who seemed to trail a perpetual cloud of dust—but only if Pig-Pen had a scruffy beard, horn-rimmed glasses, and was the size of a sumo wrestler.

Nestor was only twenty-three when I met him, but he'd been homeless, on and off, since he was nineteen. He'd grown up in a Far Rockaway housing project and, when the first chaotic symptoms of his bipolar disorder began to manifest, his family kicked him out of their apartment. He couch-surfed, spent some time in municipal shelters (which terrified him), and slept for a few months in a derelict subway tunnel, where he began to accumulate much of his grit and grime.

From the instant he sat down in my suddenly cramped cubicle, I realized that Nestor was not just a hulking giant but one of the most gentle souls I'd ever met. That day began a long relationship with Nestor, and over the years, I did my best to help him with a series of problems he encountered—with the police, public benefits, the shelter system, and housing. I'd sometimes meet him in a park or on some street corner to buy him lunch and catch up. And at some point, he'd always say something like, "You always worry about me, don't you, Mister Patrick?" with an unselfconscious vulnerability that was heartbreaking.

On two occasions, I accidentally ran into Nestor on subway trains. There he was, massive and covered in soot and grime, silently asking passengers for spare change. Our eyes met, and I did my best not to break his rhythm—this was, for all intents and purposes, his work at that time, part of his survival routine—before he moved on to the next subway car.

With the help of my coworker Tony and several social workers from other nonprofit agencies, Nestor eventually received treatment and medication, and, by the early 2010s, he was living in a supportive housing apartment and talking about going back to school. But it was a rough road getting there. At one point, he'd stopped taking his meds, like so many people struggling with mental illness did, and he smashed a vending machine—and for some senseless reason, he was convicted of felony-level destruction of property and sent to an upstate prison for more than a year.

Another time, he was arrested for panhandling on a subway train, becoming one more statistic in the NYPD's zero-tolerance crackdown on homelessness, and he was sent to Rikers Island, New York City's notorious jail complex. I went to see him there, my first time on the island, riding the deeply depressing bus filled with sad and anxious women and children visiting their incarcerated loved ones, and navigating the long lines through metal detectors, X-ray machines, and institutional-gray corridors. I finally saw Nestor in his regulation-orange inmate apparel in the visitor area. He was so clearly scared, and he looked, for the first time in my memory, small.

SHELTER TO JAIL

The hopscotch-like circuit that Nestor traveled—subway tunnels to Rikers Island to shelter to streets to upstate prison to shelter and streets again—was much like the cycle in which so many thousands of homeless people got trapped, including the dozens and dozens of homeless people caught up in the Madison Square Park sweeps. Jail and prison were part of the revolving door that spun so many homeless New Yorkers from one form of institution to another—at tremendous, pointless cost to taxpayers—often leading back, over and over, to shelter and the streets.

Some of the earliest academic research on the use of homeless shelter services found that one cohort of shelter residents, those who experienced some of the longest stays in shelters, often cycled between the shelter system and other institutions, especially jails and prisons.[40] A later study by University of Pennsylvania researchers revealed that, among more than seven thousand homeless single adults surveyed in New York City shelters, nearly a quarter had spent time in jail or prison in the two years before entering the shelter system.[41] Another study by the same researchers found that, of more than forty-eight thousand people released from New York state prisons between 1995 and 1998, more than 11 percent wound up in homeless shelters and nearly a third were later reimprisoned.[42] And as noted in chapter 1, an influential *New Yorker* article by Malcolm Gladwell documented how a single homeless man in the Las Vegas area had cost the local government more than $1 million in public spending on jails, shelters, and other care.[43]

The findings of these studies jibed with what my colleagues and I witnessed firsthand in municipal shelters and on the streets. Homeless people were arrested for minor, nonviolent offenses on a routine basis, and when they received summonses instead, many couldn't pay the fine or appear in court. This often resulted in bench warrants, putting the homeless people at immediate risk of arrest and jail. By 2016, New York City had over 1.4 million outstanding bench warrants, most tied to low-level quality-of-life violations.[44]

The revolving door between incarceration and homelessness was, if anything, even more damaging to people living with mental illness. In fact, until the early 2000s, people released from Rikers Island who had been diagnosed with mental illnesses and received treatment there were routinely dumped on Queens Boulevard with nothing more than bus fare and, at best, minimal medication. Many, if not most, wound up homeless, struggling not only to find a place to sleep but also to obtain health insurance, social benefits, and treatment. A class action lawsuit brought by the Urban Justice Center, settled in 2003, largely ended this harsh practice, but Bloomberg administration officials still refused to enact wider reforms, including what was needed most: housing with support services.[45]

For decades, New York City's largest homeless shelter was not even located in the city. As noted in chapter 2, the Camp LaGuardia men's shelter was situated in Orange County, some sixty miles north of Manhattan. The main building was actually a former correctional facility, the Greycourt Women's Prison. The old cells were still used as sleeping quarters for the homeless men—meaning that, until the shelter was closed in 2007, thousands of homeless men from New York City had been sent upstate to sleep in old prison cells.

During the many years I visited and inspected municipal shelters, I regularly noticed a peculiar label affixed to the lockers and mattresses in virtually every facility throughout the vast system: Corcraft. It turned out that Corcraft was a public company operated by the New York State Department of Correctional Services, the state agency overseeing the prison system. Corcraft sold goods manufactured by prison laborers. Inmates at seventeen New York prisons were paid between seventeen and fifty cents per hour to produce clothing, furniture, road signs, and other goods. These included thousands of items used throughout the New York City shelter system, such as pillows and mattresses, made at the Eastern Correctional Facility in Ulster County, and lockers, which were manufactured at—of all places—the infamous Attica prison, the site of the largest prison uprising in US history.

Of course, many of those prison laborers who were paid pennies an hour had themselves been homeless. Given the thousands of Corcraft-made items in municipal shelters, it has always been likely, if not inevitable, that a formerly incarcerated person ended up sleeping on a mattress he once helped manufacture as a prison laborer.

MADISON SQUARE IN THE NEW GILDED AGE

Why were certain people removed, and who stood to benefit from their absence? In her classic essay "Sentimental Journeys," Joan Didion wrote that New Yorkers like to tell neat stories about their city—about the eternal verities ("If you can make it here . . .") and the supposed virtues of instability (the "creative destruction" of capitalism), all of which shaped a narrative romanticizing the changing urban landscape.[46] Likewise, the city's elites, and much of its middle class, spun a narrative of near reverse nostalgia about New York City's seemingly perpetual rise and revival from the "bad old days." For new residents of gentrified neighborhoods, this was a particularly popular tale to tell—how rough and gritty the area had been before things "got better."

Consider Madison Square Park in the quarter century after the mid-1990s antihomeless crackdown that James and his comrades weathered. As I've described here, for all its architectural splendor and gilded history, as the twentieth century drew to a close the park and its surroundings were marked by the scruffiness and dinginess encountered in much of downtown Manhattan during the post-fiscal-crisis period. To the west, the storefronts of Fifth Avenue south of the Empire State Building had long given way to discount electronics shops, bodegas, cheap clothing outlets, newsstands, and check-cashing establishments. The park itself had also fallen on hard times, with worn benches, litter-strewn lawns of patchy grass, rusting jungle gyms, and, inevitably, homeless people seeking refuge.

But the intensifying NYPD war on homelessness, coupled with the privatized refurbishment of the park and untold millions of dollars of real estate investment in the area, fueled the hypergentrification of an already largely bourgeois neighborhood. In 1997, inspired by the model proposed years earlier by Donald Simon, the Parks Department partnered with the private City Parks Foundation to raise funds for a "revitalization" of the park. The Campaign for a New Madison Square Park financed the renovation, including the addition of a dog run and other amenities. It also led to the creation of the Madison Square Park Conservancy, which, like its Central Park and Prospect Park counterparts, completed the evolution of privatized control over the park's services.

Madison Square Park's so-called revival triggered two decades of commercial and residential development in the surrounding area. In 2006, a BID called the Flatiron / 23rd Street Partnership was formed with its own "Clean Team" to service the neighborhood's streets. Gleaming, glass-and-steel skyscrapers—like the fifty-story One Madison condominium tower, which opened in 2013, and the sixty-four-story Madison Square Park Tower, completed in 2018—rose up over the park and the older architectural landmarks around it. City data on new building permits for residential units reflect this surge in new development. In the wider midtown area encompassing Madison Square Park and its district, from 2000 to 2007 the number of permits issued by the Department of

Buildings grew from six hundred to an astounding two thousand annual permits, before the global financial crisis hit the following year. But even during the so-called Great Recession, development surged again, with more than one thousand permits issued in 2018 alone.

By the end of the Bloomberg administration and continuing into the de Blasio era, nearly two decades after I met James and his companions, Madison Square Park and its surrounding residential and commercial districts—variously dubbed NoMad and the Flatiron District by real estate brokers and trade journals—had become the latest Manhattan zone of unapologetic affluence.

Madison Square Park began to host chic public art exhibits by art-world celebrities like Maya Lin. It also became home to the first Shake Shack, a high-end fast-food chain created by a fashionable restaurateur (and cofounder of the park's private conservancy), which served the white-collar lunchtime crowd. The park was now surrounded by luxury condos and gleaming towers, with wealthy celebrity residents like American football star Tom Brady and model Gisele Bündchen, actor Jennifer Lopez, and former "first daughter" Chelsea Clinton, along with scores of less-famous but equally rich hedge-fund managers, Wall Street financiers, tech executives, and corporate lawyers. In 2014 billionaire right-wing media titan Rupert Murdoch paid $57 million for a penthouse apartment in One Madison; a year later he put it on the market for $72 million. As historian Christiane Bird described it, "In many ways the overflowing wealth had returned Madison Square and its environs to their nineteenth-century splendor."[47]

Underlying all the glitter and celebrity shine was an essential reality: The hypergentrification of the Madison Square Park area had generated, over roughly two decades, untold hundreds of millions of dollars in wealth and profit for property owners, developers, real estate investors, and local businesses. Civic elites and their media echo chamber liked to call the kind of transformation that occurred around Madison Square Park a revival, a renaissance, and they treated it as an unmitigated success—a sign of unquestioned progress. The same story could be told about so many other parts of New York City during the New Gilded Age: Times Square, Bryant Park, Prospect Park, Tompkins Square Park, Morningside Heights, and Fort Greene—all of them places from which homeless people were forcibly, even violently, displaced. None of those stories acknowledged people like James. But every one of these stories of revival also included, and depended on, their removal and erasure.

CHAPTER 4

THE SOUTH BRONX:
THE BACKLASH ERA

The transformation of the quality of life in New York and many other American cities was more than the creation of some new policing tactics or the construction of a new philosophy of the socially marginal. Rather, it was the melding of the two into a coherent new approach toward social control. This "quality-of-life" paradigm emerged as a set of concrete social practices united by a political philosophy that explained the nature of homelessness and disorder as one of personal responsibility and established punitive methods for restoring social order and civility. . . .The quality-of-life paradigm is a way of reorienting the efforts of city government away from directly improving the lives of the disenfranchised and toward restoring social order in the city's public spaces.

Alex S. Vitale
City of Disorder

THE JAIL

It was one of those sweltering August days in 2002, with temperatures in the high eighties and humidity at nearly 100 percent. In the South Bronx, only a few blocks from Yankee Stadium, an unusual delegation of city officials and legal advocates toured a forbidding edifice surrounded by fences with coiled razor wire. This was the former Bronx House of Detention for Men, once known as the River (after its River Avenue address), which had served as a notorious municipal jail from 1938 until its closing in 2000. But a few days before the tour, Mayor Michael Bloomberg's administration had suddenly, and controversially, decided to reopen the jail—not as a correctional facility, but as a shelter for homeless children and their families.

Among the group were the billionaire mayor, along with top city officials, including his homeless services commissioner, Linda Gibbs, who'd been appointed to the job only six months earlier, as well as municipal attorneys. Alongside the city officials were some of my longtime colleagues from the Legal Aid Society, who were representing homeless families in class action litigation.

What also made this tour singular was the context. The city's long-standing mismanagement of the intake process for homeless families and kids had persisted for more than a decade, flaring up during the Koch, Dinkins, and Giuliani administrations. As detailed in chapter 6, the epicenter of the city-government-created crisis was the Emergency Assistance Unit (EAU), at that time the sole intake office for newly homeless families seeking shelter. The EAU was located in the South Bronx, a few blocks away from the reopened jail. City Hall's chronic failure to provide safe, decent shelter to families in a timely fashion had resulted in an ongoing crisis at the EAU. Dozens, and at times hundreds, of infants, children, and adults were forced to sleep on floors and benches of the facility's waiting rooms, often for multiple nights, while awaiting transport to shelter.

The intake crisis of the summer of 2002 was one of the worst on record, but it could have been foreseen and prevented with proper planning. The post-9/11 economic recession had driven more families into homelessness, but the same phenomenon had occurred in other cities and states. A national survey of twenty-seven cities found a 13 percent increase in the number of families seeking shelter, giving city officials ample warning of what was likely to happen.[1] Moreover, advocates had alerted city officials to the looming problem months in advance, but those officials took little to no action to add shelter capacity.

Families and children suffered through weeks of misery and sleeplessness—bedding down on the crowded, filthy floors of the EAU, or being shuttled in the middle of the night from the facility to single-night accommodations for a few hours of sleep, only to be forced to return to the EAU the next morning, an ordeal that, for some, lasted for days. On many nights I had witnessed hundreds of parents and children, including toddlers and infants, forced to sleep on floors and benches at the EAU in horrific conditions, and my Legal Aid colleagues had documented the ongoing catastrophe for years (as recounted in chapter 6). One particularly tragic episode occurred in early August, at a Harlem hotel where a teenager and his family had been shuttled for the night; the boy killed himself, fearful that he'd be sent back to the EAU.[2]

Legal Aid Society attorneys representing homeless families had little choice but to seek relief in the courts. This was far from the first time that mistreatment of families at the EAU had been litigated; in 1992, after months during which more than 350 people per night slept on the floors of the intake office, the New York State Supreme Court found four Dinkins administration officials—including a deputy mayor—in contempt of court, and ordered them to spend the night sleeping on the floor of the EAU.[3] (A state appellate court ultimately spared the officials from experiencing what thousands of children and families endured.) So, a decade later, in the weeks before the Bronx jail was reopened, Legal Aid lawyers had once again sought and won state court rulings that ordered the city government to end the mistreatment of homeless families at the EAU, but the Bloomberg administration still failed to act. Finally, in desperation and with no other legal avenues available, and as they had a decade earlier, the Legal Aid attorneys filed a motion to find Linda Gibbs, the homeless services commissioner, in contempt of court.

This was the setting as the delegation passed through razor wire and entered the facility, where officials had tried to mask its function for both the press and the families forced to stay there. As *The New York Times* reported at the time, "Yesterday the thick metal bars by the elevators were covered with white sheets, wooden dividers were put between the steel toilets in the bathrooms, and curtains were put on each shower. Movable plywood dividers were put in the barracks-like dorms for a little privacy, and gray metal lockers were placed by each bed. But the entrance is still covered in razor wire, and the windows are still covered with steel mesh."[4]

Even though the Giuliani administration had rejected earlier proposals to reopen the Bronx jail because of potential harm to children, Bloomberg's administration pushed forward—and without informing either the Legal Aid lawyers or a court-appointed referee assigned by the judge to mediate the litigation. Four days after the jail was reopened, lead paint—an extreme hazard to small children, which could cause permanent brain damage—was discovered, requiring city officials to end the placement of children under the age of seven.[5] After more litigation, the city government was eventually forced to end the use of the jail as a shelter.[6]

But on that August morning, as a city official later told me, while Bloomberg, Gibbs, and the lawyers toured the detention facility, walking past exhausted mothers and children sweating profusely in the unbearable heat, the billionaire mayor could think of only one thing to say to the lawyers representing the homeless families—and it wasn't to discuss better solutions to the immediate crisis, or to talk about plans to create more affordable housing, or to lament the tragedy of the homeless teen's suicide, or to express regret for forcing poor children and their families to sleep in a jail. Instead, Bloomberg pulled aside the Legal Aid attorneys and insisted, tersely and indignantly, that they apologize for trying to hold *his* aide, Linda Gibbs, in contempt.[7]

GIULIANI AND THE BACKLASH ERA

Entering the 1990s, the backlash era ushered in a dramatic shift in attitudes and—more important—treatment of homeless New Yorkers. Years before Bloomberg placed homeless children and their families in a jail and then repeatedly defended that callous act, Rudy Giuliani had firmly established himself as the era's most antagonistic politician toward homeless individuals.

In fact, there had been a sharp rightward shift in Giuliani's public and political stance between the time of his first, failed campaign for mayor and his narrow victory in 1993; the difference was especially conspicuous in his harsh views on homelessness and poverty. In 1989, while campaigning with a more liberal approach, Giuliani had toured shelters with homeless advocates, promised to create more housing for homeless New Yorkers, and stated that, unlike Mayor Koch, he would not need a court order to help homeless people. In a 1989 speech titled "A City That Cares," he promised "an agenda driven by compassion and commitment," acknowledging "government's crucial role in helping people over the pains and difficulties of life."[8] He went on to criticize the Koch administration's record on homelessness, saying, "Our city had to be sued to open emergency shelters for homeless men. And sued again to shelter homeless women. And sued once more to house homeless families. What kind of leadership leaves the governing of our city to the courts? Common decency, conscience, commitment compels us to do better. . . . I will face these problems as a challenge to my conscience and the conscience of our city to help our fellow human beings."[9]

The Giuliani who successfully ran for mayor in 1993 and governed for the next eight years—to say nothing of the far-right-wing persona who emerged in the twenty-first century—was a completely different political figure. By the time he entered City Hall, Giuliani had fully embraced the harsh conservative philosophies that would undergird his welfare and homeless policies as mayor. While campaigning, he pledged that he would cut back on services for homeless people, limit shelter stays to ninety days, eliminate housing options for homeless families, and end the legal right to shelter.[10]

There were three pillars to Giuliani's approach to homelessness: (1) aggressive criminalization of street homelessness (detailed in chapter 3); (2) radical reforms of the shelter system and welfare system that were undergirded by a right-wing philosophy and a pathologization of homeless people (see chapter 1); and (3) relentless attacks on the legal right to shelter, as well as other protections for homeless people.

ASSAULT ON THE RIGHT TO SHELTER, PART 1

Giuliani's furious assault on the right to shelter had its roots in a dangerous antihomeless regulation issued by another right-wing Republican, Governor George Pataki, in January 1996, during the early weeks of winter. Underneath its banal title, "Eligibility for Temporary Housing Assistance for Homeless Persons,"[11] lurked the worst full-frontal assault on the legal right to shelter since the *Callahan* and *McCain* cases were launched more than a decade earlier.

The new regulation created multiple grounds for summarily ejecting homeless families and individuals from shelter, including alleged failure to comply with an "independent living plan," alleged failure to seek or accept housing, and alleged disruptive or violent behavior. In every instance, localities, including New York City, were required to expel the adults and children from shelter and refuse them reentry for thirty days or more. Even more dangerous, the regulation required local officials to terminate homeless people from shelter for alleged failure to comply with welfare rules, including participation in workfare programs—at a time when tens of thousands of welfare recipients in New York City routinely had their benefits suspended or terminated for supposed infractions of bureaucratic welfare rules each year. To make the situation even worse, the regulation dictated that, when homeless families were ejected from shelter, the locality would have to evaluate them for child welfare services—meaning that, while parents and other adult family members were forced to sleep on the streets, their children would be taken from them into the foster care system.[12]

Those of us who worked on the front lines with homeless people knew well that the rule, especially as implemented by a zealous and brutal Giuliani administration, could potentially force thousands of vulnerable people out of shelter and onto the streets. Working with our colleagues at the Legal Aid Society, we sought to halt the implementation of the proposed regulation by filing court papers in the *Callahan* case for homeless adults and the *McCain* case for homeless families. City lawyers said they would hold off implementing the rules until the issue was litigated in court, and legal disputes thankfully kept the regulation from going into effect for the next three years.[13] Ultimately, however, the judge overseeing the *McCain* case refused to rule that the shelter-ejection rules violated the state constitution's right to shelter, and her decision was upheld by an appellate court.

Therefore, in October 1999, just as winter was approaching, Giuliani announced that he was moving forward with rules that required homeless people to perform workfare and to comply with other welfare requirements—and if they did not, they would be thrown out of shelters.[14] This was the moment we had feared ever since the shelter-ejection regulation was issued years earlier. The legacy of the right to shelter was at stake, and there was the very real possibility that homeless New Yorkers could be cast out onto the streets, where many would die.

In a matter of days, my colleagues and I mobilized a vigorous campaign to stop the Giuliani rules from going into effect, including legal challenges, outreach to nonprofit groups and other allies, a media strategy, and grassroots organizing. While the threat was enormous, we were helped by some tactical mistakes that Giuliani and his administration made. First, he announced that the rules would go into effect in December, during the coldest and most dangerous time for unsheltered homeless people—not to mention, in the midst of the Thanksgiving, Christmas, and Hanukkah holidays, when sympathy toward homeless and poor people was at its most potent.

Second, Giuliani administration officials were characteristically blunt, even callous, about the fact that when homeless families were ejected from shelter, the children would be forcibly taken from their parents and placed in foster care. One of Giuliani's senior advisers stated, "Ultimately, the city is asking parents to take responsibility for themselves and to take responsibility for their children. . . . But if parents are unable to take responsibility for themselves, then it raises a real question of whether they can take responsibility for their children." A city attorney who oversaw the homelessness cases was even more explicit, saying that "failure to comply with various regulations could result in children being taken away because the mother's actions would be tantamount to neglect."[15] The notion of removing children from their parents simply because the parents had no shelter, or merely because they had allegedly failed to follow a bureaucratic rule, was repulsive to many New Yorkers. The Coalition for the Homeless had commissioned a public opinion survey of Giuliani's homelessness policy, and 70 percent of those surveyed opposed it.[16]

Giuliani administration officials defended the shelter-ejection rules using the jargon of "personal responsibility" and other ideologically loaded language it had long wielded to defend harsh welfare policies.[17] But a singularly well-reported *New York Times* article from the time by journalist Nina Bernstein illustrated the real-world consequences for homeless people. She profiled Lisa T., a twenty-eight-year-old formerly homeless mother of a baby girl, whose story was depressingly commonplace. She had been forced to reapply for shelter three times before being admitted, and was then required to apply for welfare benefits to help pay for the cost of shelter, even though she had never received such assistance previously. However, the city welfare agency terminated her benefits when she did not receive a mailed notice to "recertify" her case: "Under the new rules, however, the results could have been more dire: residents who lose welfare eligibility are no longer entitled to shelter, and their children could be taken into foster care, the city says. 'Over my dead body,' said Ms. T., who found jobs as a home health attendant on her own. . . . She said she does not think the new city policy is fair: 'They kick me out of the shelter and the city take my daughter for something I got no control over? Thank God I'm out of that system.'"[18]

As detailed in chapter 3, in November 1999, amid public panic over a midtown attack reportedly committed by a homeless man, Giuliani announced a harsh new NYPD policy—arrest any homeless person found on the streets. Shortly afterward, a newly obtained police department memo made the situation clear—if homeless people did not accept some ambiguous offer of "help" from a police officer, including an order to go to a municipal shelter, arrest was the only option.[19] Howard Safir, the NYPD commissioner, stated bluntly that if homeless people "don't obey, we're going to arrest them."[20]

But what if the homeless person could *not* go to a municipal shelter? What if the homeless person had been ejected and barred from the shelter system for thirty days or more, as Giuliani proposed? The new homeless-arrest policy therefore collided with the shelter-ejection policy, and it essentially mandated that many unsheltered homeless people would have to be incarcerated merely for being homeless and without shelter options.

The public outcry against Giuliani's "arrest the homeless" policy, coming on top of his plan to toss homeless New Yorkers into the streets, was the most palpable, virulent reaction to an antihomeless policy I can remember during my time as a homeless advocate. Even the *New York Daily News* published results of a poll finding that "69 percent of respondents disapproved of arresting homeless people who refuse shelter, 54 percent disapproved of evicting people from shelters if they refuse to work, and 63 percent disapproved of putting homeless children in foster care because their parents refuse to work."[21]

To ramp up the public pressure against Giuliani's dangerous actions, my Coalition colleagues and I organized the largest protest rally we'd ever mounted. It was held in Manhattan's Union Square on December 5, 1999, the twentieth anniversary of the first court decision in *Callahan v. Carey* recognizing a right to shelter. The highlight of the rally was a fiery speech by the civil rights leader and minister, Rev. Al Sharpton, who rightly called out the racism inherent in Giuliani's policies and attacked the foster care threat of his shelter-ejection rules: "If you look at Mary's story," Sharpton said, "if Mary had lived in Bethlehem under Mayor Giuliani, they would have gave Jesus to a foster care program." Then, referring to the commissioner of the welfare agency, he continued, "If Jason Turner had come into the barn that night, he would have said to the baby Jesus: 'You have been born to two unwedded parents. They don't have an address. They don't have a job. We have to take you in custody and arrest your parents.'"[22]

Contemporary press accounts said we gathered around a thousand protesters, based on NYPD estimates (which historically undercounted crowds at demonstrations), but the true size was far larger, probably three thousand people or more. A week later, a coalition of nonprofit organizations that operated shelters for thousands of homeless families—normally an extremely cautious group when it came to challenging antihomeless policies—announced that it would not enforce the shelter-ejection rule because, according to a news report, "it would put children in foster care if their parents refused to work." Giuliani angrily responded by cutting off funding for the shelters, which relied on city contracts. Sister Barbara Lenninger, one of the leaders of the family shelter group, responded vividly to Giuliani's threat in a *New York Times* article. "To think that he would say that if you won't throw a mother out and take her kids away, 'I'll cut your funding,' I cannot believe that," she said. "I cannot believe that a person of his education and religious training would say that." According to the *Times*, "Sister Lenninger added that she considered it part of her ministry to provide shelter for the homeless, and that 'if someone says I have to choose between following Jesus Christ and Rudy Giuliani, I'll follow Jesus Christ. And I'm not exactly known as a religious fanatic.'"[23]

The most important battle to halt the shelter-ejection rules was ultimately fought in the New York State Supreme Court. In an unprecedented joint hearing in December before the judges overseeing both of the ongoing right-to-shelter cases, *Callahan* and *McCain*, the court granted an injunction blocking the rules from going into effect while they were litigated in the *Callahan* court. We were fortunate to have an incredible group of lawyers, led by Steve Banks, arguing on behalf of homeless New Yorkers, and presenting compelling affidavit testimony from medical experts identifying the risks of death and injury to unsheltered people on the streets, as well as a former state official who had negotiated the original *Callahan* consent decree and opposed the new rules.

Finally, in February 2000, Justice Stanley Sklar ruled in favor of homeless adults to block the shelter-ejection rules. The highlight of his decision was the following passage: "Bureaucratic error is as much a part of bureaucracy, as human error is a part of life. . . . The simple bureaucratic error which might send an individual out into the street, because he or she was unable to understand or to cooperate with these requirements, might be the error which results in that individual's death by exposure, death by violence, or death by sheer neglect. The risk is simply too great to take."[24]

While the court decision was a major victory to protect the right to shelter for homeless New Yorkers, the attacks would continue after Giuliani left City Hall. In December 2001, barely two months after the September 11 attacks—soon after Bloomberg's election as mayor and only three weeks before Giuliani left office—his administration announced it would lay the groundwork for an appeal of the February 2000 court decision, and thus permit Bloomberg to continue pursuing the fight for the shelter-ejection policy.[25]

HOMELESSNESS AND HOUSING POLICY

Throughout Giuliani's first term as mayor, from 1994 through 1997, New York City's nightly homeless shelter population hovered around twenty-three thousand people per night, and even dropped to twenty-one thousand per night in 1997, while the number of unsheltered homeless people on the streets and in the subway system also declined. For the most part, none of this was due to any policy initiatives implemented by Giuliani. Instead, he benefited from major homeless rehousing policies introduced by his predecessors, and from a homelessness prevention program secured by legal advocates.

As discussed in chapter 2, Giuliani's administration benefited from three initiatives launched by his predecessors: Koch's extended Housing New York plan; Dinkins's priority placements for homeless families in federal housing programs, which kept thousands stably housed; and the New York / New York Agreement, which delivered supportive housing through the late 1990s.[26] Additionally, *Jiggetts* rent subsidies prevented thousands of evictions, especially in the Bronx, where overcrowded housing courts and limited legal aid made tenants particularly vulnerable.

Unfortunately, by Giuliani's second term, from 1998 through 2001, the homeless population began to grow again. The nightly population of homeless single adults rose as funding for new supportive housing apartments dried up and existing units filled up. The vacancy rate in the city's stock of supportive housing fell from 15 percent in 1992 to less than 3 percent in 2001.[27] As a result, the nightly shelter population of homeless single adults rose to 7,700 by the end of Giuliani's mayoralty and kept growing. Advocates, homeless people, and formerly homeless tenants of supportive housing mobilized a grassroots campaign to press Giuliani and Pataki to renew the New York / New York Agreement. However, after months of rallies and protests, Giuliani and Pataki only agreed to a small New York / New York II Agreement, which produced a third of the housing units created under the first accord.[28]

Giuliani also slashed investments in affordable housing development, and the impact of these cutbacks was especially damaging to homeless and low-income families. From 1991, under Dinkins, to 1998, under Giuliani, the city government's capital budget for housing was cut by 66 percent, falling to $235 million, the lowest level since the austerity era of the 1980s.[29] Giuliani administration officials often claimed they were forced by fiscal constraints to implement tight budgets, but the mayor dramatically increased spending in areas that mattered to him; for instance, NYPD expenditures doubled during Giuliani's time in office, from $1.8 billion to $3.6 billion.[30]

The housing cutbacks had an immediate impact on family homelessness. Families were forced to remain in shelters for longer periods—from 1994 to 1997 alone, average stays rose by three months.[31] The number of homeless families who were moved from the shelter system to subsidized housing fell by 40 percent from 1994 to 1999.[32] In the three years before Giuliani left office, the number of homeless families in shelters soared by 57 percent. In February 2001, the total homeless shelter population exceeded twenty-five thousand people, and *The New York Times* published a front-page article headlined, "Homeless Shelters in New York Fill to Highest Level Since 80's."[33] By December, Giuliani's last month at City Hall, the shelter population soared to just over thirty thousand people per night.

Underlying the worsening homelessness crisis in New York City was an equally worsening housing affordability crisis. From 1991 to 1999, the city lost more than 510,000 apartments with gross rents under $500 per month, representing more than half of all low-rent units and a quarter of all rental apartments citywide. Black and Latino New Yorkers were the hardest hit by the widening affordability gap, experiencing far higher rates of severe rent burdens and substandard housing conditions than white renter households.[34] New York City had become a deeply more unaffordable and unequal city under eight years of Giuliani's leadership. And those trends would only worsen in the twelve years of Bloomberg's mayoralty that followed.

BLOOMBERG AND THE BACKLASH ERA

Michael Bloomberg, one of the wealthiest people in the world, was inaugurated as New York City mayor on January 1, 2002. As the city was still recovering from the 9/11 attacks, he also confronted a worsening homelessness crisis left to him by the outgoing Giuliani administration. Most immediate was a "capacity crisis"—a shortage of needed shelter beds—for both homeless families and individuals. And with winter approaching, homeless men and women at "intake shelters" were forced to sleep on floors and chairs in waiting rooms, due to a shortage of available beds.

Faced with this situation, to say nothing of dwindling housing resources for homeless New Yorkers, Bloomberg elected to highlight a different issue. Only five days after he took office, Bloomberg spoke about making shelters safer, claiming—with only anecdotal evidence—that this was a major reason homeless people remained on the streets. He said he ordered his new police commissioner, Raymond Kelly, to study the issue of shelter safety, claiming that "if we have to we'll post a police officer at each shelter."[35]

In retrospect, Bloomberg's brief foray into shelter safety—the issue disappeared for his remaining dozen years in office—was telling. It signaled that he was prone to highlight issues that distracted from the real problem—that is, the rapidly rising homeless population and the need for housing resources—but that sounded reasonable to the average New Yorker. Also, it showed that Bloomberg was willing to exaggerate issues, despite his carefully crafted persona as a technocratic, data-driven manager. Indeed, city officials at the time refused to release data on safety issues in municipal shelters.[36] Moreover, it put a spotlight on the alleged dysfunctional behavior of homeless people themselves, implying that shelters were unsafe due to chaotic, dangerous residents. Finally, as with Giuliani, it identified the NYPD as a principal tool to wield against the problem of homelessness.

There was ultimately tremendous continuity between the policies and the right-wing ideology of the Giuliani and Bloomberg administrations. Criminalization of unsheltered homelessness and the brutal policing of homeless people in public spaces were key features of this continuity. Even before taking office, Bloomberg pledged to continue Giuliani's focus on criminalizing minor offenses, particularly panhandling, saying in December 2001, "Quality-of-life crimes are something we are not going to back away from. . . . Right after the first of the year, Ray Kelly has that in his sights, to make a major effort."[37]

As detailed in chapter 3, the NYPD under Bloomberg continued to arrest and issue summonses to homeless New Yorkers in huge numbers. He boasted about his antihomeless policing strategy a 2006 speech, timed to the unveiling of a plan to clear dozens of encampments: "We're going to let them know that their days on the streets must come to an end. . . . And we'll secure and clean up the places where they've been bedding down, to make sure that they won't be occupied again."[38]

ASSAULT ON THE RIGHT TO SHELTER, PART 2

The other Giuliani-era battle that Bloomberg took up was the attack on the right to shelter for homeless New Yorkers. But in this area, Bloomberg was far more ambitious, zealous, and successful than his predecessor.

In June 2002, city lawyers informed the Coalition for the Homeless and the Legal Aid Society that the administration would appeal the ruling in *Callahan* that had blocked the same shelter-ejection regulation Giuliani had tried to impose. But the administration had learned from the mistakes of the Giuliani approach, particularly the public backlash against the "workfare for shelter" requirement. For instance, according to one news article, "Gibbs said that unlike the Giuliani administration, she would not seek to bar from shelter anyone who failed to meet work requirements and other welfare eligibility rules."[39] However, the truth was that by challenging the court order blocking the entirety of the shelter-termination regulation, there was nothing to bar Bloomberg (or future mayors) from pursuing a harsh, Giuliani-style plan involving workfare and welfare rules as conditions for losing shelter. Bloomberg and Gibbs also revealed, according to a *New York Times* account, that the legal move was part of a larger strategy: "The Bloomberg administration has said that it wants freedom from court oversight to achieve the goals of its new homeless policy."[40] This began a yearslong campaign to attack not only the concept of court involvement in the treatment of homeless New Yorkers, but also specific judges who oversaw the cases.

In the months leading up to the court appeal, the media-savvy Bloomberg administration spun the "new" rules to a gullible, right-leaning *New York Times* reporter and other local news organizations as less harsh than they really were: "The city's commissioner of homeless services, Linda I. Gibbs, is adamant that hers is a kinder, gentler version of the Giuliani proposal, which has been blocked by a ruling in State

Supreme Court in Manhattan since January 2000."[41] The *Times* account also claimed that, in contrast to the Giuliani plan, instead of children of ejected families being taken into foster care, they would go into a parallel program called "respite care," which sounded better than foster care. But all it really meant was that the kids would still be taken from their parents, something the article failed to spell out. Indeed, only months earlier, a mayoral spokesperson had acknowledged (to a different, more diligent *Times* reporter) that some ejected families would still have their children forcibly removed into foster care: "Megan Sheekey, a spokeswoman for the mayor, said if parents ejected from shelter refused to place their children voluntarily in such homes [i.e., respite care], the children might then have to be involuntarily taken from them on charges of neglect and officially placed in foster care. 'It's a protective measure, obviously, so children do not end up living on the streets or in a car,' Ms. Sheekey said."[42]

Early in Bloomberg's first year as mayor, he and Gibbs decided to seek the termination of all court oversight of the homeless services system— including the legal right to shelter. However, there were significant legal hurdles to achieving that goal. The *Callahan* case for homeless individuals had been settled as a consent decree, and historically, it required a major change in circumstance or law to undo such a decree—and the persistence of homelessness was an unchanging fact. But the *McCain* case rested on a series of trial and appellate court orders that the city government could seek to overturn.

In the autumn of 2002, the Bloomberg administration ramped up its legal strategy, threatening to implement the shelter-ejection rules on homeless families. It also wielded the press to wage attacks on Justice Freedman. In another example of Bloomberg's enormous sway over the local media, he and his administration used the *New York Daily News* and *The New York Times* to undermine and misrepresent Freedman.[43] The compliant *Times* reporter published an article about Freedman that had all the makings of a hit job. It quoted multiple Giuliani administration officials, who described her as overreaching, micromanaging, and easily manipulated by Legal Aid lawyers. Giuliani's former top lawyer delivered a particularly sexist comment, saying Freedman was "emotionally, even overly emotionally involved in the case" ("She would constantly say, 'Look at these poor, poor, poor children' . . .").[44] The only voices in the article defending Justice Freedman came from attorneys who had worked on the *McCain* case as "special masters," or court-appointed referees—and, tellingly, from former New York City mayors Ed Koch and David Dinkins.

Facing media pressure and the risk of the state shelter-ejection rules being implemented, in early 2003, the Legal Aid Society reached a temporary pause in active litigation. Under the terms of this agreement, a three-person panel would be established to review the homeless services system for families with children over two years, and then make recommendations to the court, which the plaintiffs or defendants could accept or reject. In the interim, the existing court orders would remain in place and city officials would not enforce the shelter-ejection regulation.[45]

The two-year "pause" in litigation around family homelessness certainly did not end the problems in the shelter system. From late 2002 through 2003, the Bloomberg administration continued to struggle with shelter capacity as the number of homeless families seeking shelter rose, driven by the post-9/11 economic recession. The administration pursued options to accommodate families that were risky or simply outlandish. First, both Bloomberg and Gibbs continued to defend the use of the South Bronx jail as an appropriate facility for families and children, even after it had been closed.[46] Then, in late 2002, Gibbs flew to the Bahamas—in Bloomberg's private jet, no less—to inspect three cruise ships as potential shelters for homeless families. About the cruise ships, Gibbs told *The New York Times*, "In many ways they are ideal." Bloomberg defended the idea on his weekly radio program: "If you think about a cruise ship, it's exactly what you need."[47] The idea was nevertheless so absurd that it made international headlines, and the plan was abandoned the following year.

At the South Bronx intake center, the horrendous treatment of homeless families and children also continued, but with one welcome change. Under pressure from the court and scrutiny from the local media, the Bloomberg administration managed to end the practice of homeless families sleeping overnight at the EAU. Then, the administration unveiled a plan to replace the EAU with a newly constructed facility at the same location on East 151st Street. To do so, it closed the old EAU in late 2002 and created a temporary intake center at the nearby Powers Avenue Family Shelter, also in the South Bronx. The Powers Avenue facility had previously been used for single-night placements of families still caught up in the "eligibility review" process at the EAU and therefore, unlike the old intake facility, had sleeping accommodations, however minimal, for applicant families.

But those families still suffered many of the same chronic and harmful problems accessing shelter, due to the bureaucratic barriers erected under Giuliani and fortified under Bloomberg (see chapter 6). Despite the ongoing economic downturn that increased demand and heightened the need for assistance, the Bloomberg administration denied shelter at an ever higher rate —declaring families "ineligible," in the bureaucratic jargon of the shelter system. In 2004, on average, roughly 1,800 families applied for shelter each month, but only around 750 families were deemed "eligible"—a denial rate of 58 percent, up from the previous year.[48] The "ineligible" families faced repeated denials, followed by multiple reapplications and additional denials—a bureaucratic ordeal that often lasted weeks or months and took a toll on exhausted parents and children.

I met countless families who were wrongfully denied shelter during the Bloomberg years, but one family, in particular, garnered the attention and sympathy of many New Yorkers. Nicole Goodwin was an Iraq War veteran who had just finished her three-year military service. She returned to New York with her baby daughter, Shylah, and became homeless when she was kicked out of her mother's already-overcrowded public housing apartment. After weeks of couch-surfing, she and her baby were thrown out of another overcrowded home belonging to a friend's mother. That, according to a moving article by *New York Times* columnist Dan Barry, was when her ordeal began:

> She pushed her stroller a few blocks to the Emergency Assistance Unit, the city's flawed point of entry for homeless families. She explained her situation to a staff member who, she says, yelled at her for not having the proper paperwork handy. "I killed her with kindness," she said. "I've been yelled at before by the best."
>
> "I got that attitude from Iraq," Ms. Goodwin added. "If this isn't life and death, it's not that serious."
>
> She filled out an application for transitional housing, and after a while a bus arrived to take the Goodwins and other families to a one-night shelter on Powers Avenue. She thinks it was about 4 a.m.; she knows that Shylah's eyes were wide open.
>
> For the next several days, the Goodwins rode the city bus of homelessness—two nights more at the Powers Avenue shelter, and then several nights at the Skyway Hotel in southeastern Queens—while the city determined whether she was eligible for housing. Her life became a blur of riding late-night buses, maneuvering the subway system, filling out forms and comforting Shylah.
>
> On April 17, the Department of Homeless Services denied housing to the Iraqi war veteran on the grounds that she could live with her mother. Beyond the overcrowding that such a

return would create (four women and two small children in a two-bedroom apartment), she says that the decision ignored the untenable situation between mother and daughter.[49]

Goodwin and her daughter continued the grueling cycle of reapplications and denials until a US Department of Veterans Affairs counselor sent her to the Coalition for the Homeless. We advocated for Goodwin while putting her up in a hotel for a few nights so she and Shylah could get some rest. We eventually found an available apartment in the Coalition's only building for formerly homeless families. Goodwin was later diagnosed with posttraumatic stress disorder, but nonetheless managed to find work and earn a degree from the City College of New York.[50]

Goodwin's story was one of the few to have such a positive resolution, in part because of the media coverage.[51] But thousands of other "ineligible" families remained out of the spotlight, trapped in the limbo of the South Bronx intake facilities, denied basic shelter and aid by the harsh, right-wing policies of the Giuliani and Bloomberg era.

CHAPTER 5

BEDFORD-STUYVESANT: RECORD HOMELESSNESS IN THE LUXURY CITY

You are a New Yorker when what was there before is more
real and solid than what is here now.

Colson Whitehead
The Colossus of New York

BED-STUY, DO OR DIE

Since the Great Depression, the Bedford-Stuyvesant neighborhood in
central Brooklyn has been, alongside Harlem, the heart of Black New
York. Fleeing the terror of the Jim Crow South, Black people arrived
there in the 1930s; by the close of that decade, the neighborhood was
already home to some thirty thousand Black residents. During World
War II, that migration accelerated, with many seeking jobs at the adjacent Brooklyn Navy Yards. By 1950, there were more than 150,000 Black
people living in Bedford-Stuyvesant, more than half the neighborhood's
population, and many began moving to adjacent neighborhoods of Crown
Heights, Fort Greene, Brownsville, and East New York—eventually creating one of the largest Black communities in the United States.[1]

Much of the attraction of the neighborhood came from its elegant
brownstones and townhouses, particularly those in the Stuyvesant
Heights section, which had been constructed during the Gilded Age.[2]
But by the 1950s, banks began redlining and engaging in blockbusting
within the neighborhood, making it nearly impossible for Black residents

to buy homes, while realtors pushed out white homeowners and brought in lower-income Black renters. By 1960, nearly nine in ten neighborhood residents were Black, and over the following two decades, the city government and banks continued to cut investments and services in the area, leading to higher rates of poverty and severe housing problems like overcrowding and health and safety hazards.

Throughout the 1960s, community activists like Shirley Chisolm—who became the nation's first Black Congresswoman—mobilized to tackle the rising rate of poverty, forming programs that later shaped the federal "War on Poverty" effort. But the neighborhood still suffered from neglect, disinvestment, and racist policing; in July 1964, responding to the police shooting of a Black teenager, Bed-Stuy was the site of one of the period's first urban uprisings.[3]

By the 1980s and 1990s, the first decades of the New Gilded Age, homelessness had also made its mark on the residents of Bedford-Stuyvesant. The neighborhood had some of the largest shelters in the city, from the fortresslike Sumner Avenue armory to the cavernous Bedford-Atlantic armory, poised across Atlantic Avenue on the edges of Crown Heights. A research study that tracked the neighborhoods where homeless families had lived before seeking shelter found that more than half came from just ten neighborhoods—with Bedford-Stuyvesant ranked number one on the list.[4]

But homelessness represented just the most glaring form of displacement that the neighborhood experienced during the New Gilded Age. Beginning in the 1990s, but accelerating in the twenty-first century, the neighborhood began to gentrify—first the westernmost stretches, which saw refurbished brownstones and upscale restaurants and retail shops, but over time, this transformation spread throughout the area. And like elsewhere during the Bloomberg era, what city elites and the media celebrated was the glamor and shine—spruced-up townhouses, hip new eateries, and luxury boutiques. The people who'd made Bed-Stuy the neighborhood it was, but were later displaced, rarely if ever made their way into the story.

THE LUXURY CITY AND THE BILLIONAIRE MAYOR

If Rudy Giuliani's singular goal as mayor was to "clean up" New York City, his successor Michael Bloomberg also had a mission. The billionaire mayor sought to remake New York as a luxury city, a beacon of comfort and affluence, a shiny, glittering destination for the wealthy, and, in its way, an opulent, extravagant commodity. Bloomberg's dozen years as mayor left behind a transformed city that reflected his vision: a Manhattan skyline dotted with super-tall skyscrapers (seven of the city's tallest buildings went up during his tenure as mayor); the shimmering but monotonous glass towers of Hudson Yards; tourist magnets like the High Line park and the renovated piers and parks along the Hudson River; and the flourishing of new corporate districts in downtown Brooklyn and western Queens.

Unsurprisingly, given Bloomberg's temperament and worldview as a product of Wall Street and the Upper East Side, nearly all this activity occurred in Manhattan, the most luxurious borough of the luxury city. But the spillover effects of Bloomberg's mission—and more important, the consequence of his politics and policies—drove the transformation and gentrification of wider swaths of the city, from Bedford-Stuyvesant in central Brooklyn to Greenpoint and Williamsburg in north Brooklyn, to Astoria and Long Island City in Queens, and Harlem and Washington Heights in uptown Manhattan.

Uncharacteristically, Bloomberg embraced the issue of homelessness during his first term, partly to cultivate a more liberal guise and balance the Republican CEO identity that had won him election as mayor. More characteristically, Bloomberg's approach to homelessness was a mix of fundamentally right-wing, blame-the-poor ideology with his persona as a technocratic manager. He acted simultaneously as if the problem of homelessness could be tackled with flowcharts and spreadsheets, management tweaks to city agencies, and, most of all, punitive policies that denied vital assistance to needy families and individuals. All the while Bloomberg claimed that such harsh tactics were to instill "personal responsibility" in homeless New Yorkers.

Bloomberg and his key homeless services official, Linda Gibbs, took steps that reshaped New York City's approach to homelessness—and ultimately their actions led to record growth in the city's homeless population. By the time Bloomberg entered his third year as mayor, he and Gibbs had eliminated federal housing assistance for homeless families and children in New York City; created a series of deeply flawed rent subsidy programs; and dumped homeless individuals and families into dangerous and inappropriate housing. Indeed, for almost a decade, Bloomberg and Gibbs conducted a massive and failed social experiment that damaged the lives of tens of thousands of vulnerable adults and children.

THE NO-HOUSING EXPERIMENT

In June 2004, Bloomberg announced, to much fanfare, a plan to reduce New York City's homeless population by two-thirds over five years. But even before the plan was released, it was clear that it was destined for failure.

The New York Times obtained an early version of the homeless plan, and from the outset, there was one warning sign: "A draft of the Bloomberg administration's new homeless plan suggests an end to the priority given to homeless families over other poor people seeking to receive a federal subsidized housing voucher."[5] While this language never appeared in the final plan, it was soon enshrined in city policy. In October, the Bloomberg administration made it official, announcing that homeless families would

no longer be prioritized for the two main federal housing programs—
public housing and federal housing vouchers—effectively cutting off access to those programs.[6]

With this ruinous action, New York City became the only large city
in the United States effectively to deny federal housing aid to homeless
people. The use of priority status for homeless applicants in federal housing programs had been an essential part of New York municipal homeless
policy since the 1980s, given that waiting lists for federal programs had
more than a hundred thousand households and wait times lasted years.
Therefore, previous mayors had provided priority access for homeless
families and other needy groups.

Between 1990 and the year before Bloomberg took office, the policy had successfully re-housed nearly 40,000 homeless families. Each
year, several thousand public housing apartments would become available, due to residents moving out, the death of tenants, evictions, and the
rate at which the Housing Authority repaired vacant apartments. When
Bloomberg took office, the number of available public housing apartments
averaged nearly 7,500 per year, from a total stock of 178,000. The number
of federal housing vouchers available each year varied significantly because it depended on annual budget appropriations made in Washington,
DC (see chapter 10). The number of available vouchers was thus a combination of turnover in New York City's existing allotment of vouchers and
new vouchers. From the late 1990s through early 2000s, the number of
vouchers available averaged 7,800 each year.[7]

Federal housing programs were therefore the primary housing resource
for moving homeless families out of the shelter system. This became even
truer after the expiration of the Koch administration's Housing New
York plan, which had created thousands of city-subsidized apartments
specifically for homeless families. In contrast, under the Giuliani and
Bloomberg administrations, only 260 homeless families, on average, were

moved each year into city-subsidized apartments.[8]

The net effect of Bloomberg's cutoff policy was nothing short of devastating. From 1994, the peak year of subsidized housing resources targeted to homeless families, to 2013, Bloomberg's last year in office, the number of homeless families moved from shelters to subsidized housing plummeted by 96 percent—to just 227.[9]

The Bloomberg administration's justification for the cutoff policy was based entirely on falsehoods and right-wing ideological myths about homeless families—in particular, the pernicious notion that families would "make themselves" homeless or "pretend" to be homeless to obtain housing aid. The *New York Daily News* reported that, in announcing the policy, Gibbs claimed that "families [were] deliberately going into the shelter system as a way to get to the front of the line on rental assistance."[10] Another news report quoted her saying, "We don't want people to think that the best way to get housing is to bundle their children up and take them to the E.A.U."[11] Both she and Bloomberg would repeat versions of this "fraud" myth for years to come.[12]

This falsehood had been thoroughly disproven by numerous research studies, including a landmark 1997 study by economists Michael Cragg and Brendan O'Flaherty.[13] O'Flaherty and another economist later confirmed the key finding—that providing subsidized housing to homeless families reduces the homeless population and has at best a minor "attractor" effect—in a follow-up study in 2006.[14] Adding to the mountain of evidence against this antihomeless myth, additional research and evidence—including a study commissioned by the Bloomberg administration itself—proved conclusively that the vast majority of poor families receiving federal housing assistance maintained stable housing and had few, if any, repeat episodes of homelessness.[15]

Bloomberg's decision to eliminate federal housing aid for homeless New Yorkers was not only a catastrophic policy failure. It was also deeply ironic, given that, for his first two years in City Hall, federal housing programs had actually helped stabilize the size of the family shelter population and ameliorate the capacity crisis. Indeed, a *New York Times* article from June 2002, titled "Bloomberg Plans More Housing Aid for the Homeless," spoke about his intention "to increase the number of government subsidies for apartments significantly," in "a clear departure from the policies of the Giuliani administration."[16] Another *Times* article from the same month was headlined, "Once Again, Trying Housing as a Cure for Homelessness: Mothers With Children Are Getting Preference in City Assignments for Subsidized Apartments."[17] The article contrasted the putatively "generous" Bloomberg approach with that of Giuliani, who had cut back on city-subsidized housing resources—but had not fully eliminated access to federal housing programs. As it turned out, as in many areas of homeless policy, from policing to housing aid, Bloomberg's approach evolved to become even more extreme than Giuliani's.

THE NO-HOUSING HOMELESS PLAN

Amid the elimination of federal housing aid for homeless families and children, Bloomberg's five-year homeless plan, called Uniting for Solutions Beyond Shelter, turned out to be mostly a series of vague goals with little detail about policies or budgets.[18] Moreover, the plan lacked any new or targeted housing resources for homeless New Yorkers. Bloomberg and Gibbs had begun drafting it in the autumn of 2003, and over the next nine months, my colleagues and I heard disturbing rumors about its contents.

In the late 1990s, I was one of the lead grassroots organizers of the Campaign for New York / New York Housing, which sought renewal of the initial and very successful 1990 city-state agreement. In 2002, the campaign relaunched, and amid worsening homelessness, we called for an even larger third agreement: nine thousand units of supportive housing over five years, or 1,800 units per year, on average. The campaign, which included supportive housing organizations, advocacy groups, and homeless and formerly homeless New Yorkers, staged rallies and demonstrations at City Hall and the governor's office and met with key city and state officials.

In mid-June, just over a week before Bloomberg announced his five-year homeless plan, we obtained a draft of the document. Fatally, it contained no commitment to create more supportive housing:

> Some advocates for the homeless argue that while its rhetoric is grand, the plan is far too vague, particularly when it comes to affordable housing and supportive housing.
>
> "It feels a little bit like the emperor has no clothes," said Maureen Friar, executive director of the Supportive Housing Network of New York, who sat on a coordinating committee that advised the city on the report. "The plan has a lot of words without any goals we can measure to see what we've done next year. How can we measure results? It is disappointing that it is this general and out of sync from how the mayor has approached work in education and other areas he cares about."[19]

The leak of the draft document to the *Times*, and the outraged response from us and our colleagues, had an enormous, and thankfully positive, impact on the final plan. At the last minute, the Bloomberg administration was forced to commit to creating twelve thousand units of supportive housing over ten years. That pledge, clearly added to avoid a public relations disaster for the mayor, came so late it didn't even appear in the written version of the plan, which had already been printed, but was instead highlighted by Bloomberg and city officials at a press conference.[20] This was a significant addition that, while it fell short of our campaign's goal, would still address an enormous need. After months of negotiations with state officials, the following year, the Bloomberg and Pataki administrations at last announced a New York / New York III Agreement that would create thousands of units of supportive housing over the next decade.[21]

ENDANGERING HOMELESS NEW YORKERS

After federal housing aid for homeless families was eliminated, Bloomberg and Gibbs came to realize that, without those programs, there was virtually no way to move families out of shelters. So, in 2005, they launched a new rent subsidy program called Housing Stability Plus (HSP). As detailed in chapter 10, the new program, which limited rent subsidies to a maximum of five years and gradually reduced the value of the subsidy each year, proved to be a disaster and was eliminated after just two years. But it reflected Bloomberg and Gibbs's technocratic fetishization of "innovative" approaches to urban problems—even when those policies were terribly designed and disconnected from reality.

Though the HSP program's flawed, time-limited design was bad enough, its true dangers only became clear months later. At the inception of the HSP program, Gibbs had promised that city administrators would bend over backward to attract landlords, telling *The New York Times*, "The program was intended to eliminate many of the requirements of the federal rent vouchers that landlords hated the most—like drawn-out application and inspection programs—and added incentives like three months' rent up front to sweeten the pot."[22]

The Bloomberg administration's decision to forego apartment inspections proved devastating to countless families and children. It also served to attract some of the worst slumlords in New York to the program. During the first year, we heard from dozens of families who had been forced to move into apartments with hazardous conditions. Over several months, my Coalition for the Homeless colleague Lindsey Davis researched and authored a comprehensive, damning report that analyzed some two thousand HSP apartments and matched them to records of housing code violations. The report found that hundreds of families had been placed in apartments with multiple dangerous violations, including "lead paint hazards, broken windows, collapsed ceilings and floors, non-working appliances and fixtures, as well as a lack of heat, hot water, and electricity. New York City law defines each of these violations as 'immediately hazardous' to the health and safety of tenants living in the apartment."[23]

One HSP family we met had a particularly heartbreaking story. Roslyn, a homeless mother of two young girls, was working toward her bachelor's degree at the time she and her family were placed in a South Bronx apartment with an HSP subsidy. Greeting her upon moving into the unit was a notice on the front door that stated in bold letters, "CAUTION: POISON. Lead hazard area; do not enter work area unless authorized; respirators and protective clothing required. No eating, drinking, or smoking permitted." When the housing agency finally conducted an inspection, it documented twenty-nine violations in her apartment alone, including lead paint hazards on nearly every wall.

Roslyn's youngest daughter eventually tested positive for lead poisoning and developmental delays. Tragically, her child wasn't the only one to suffer contamination in an HSP apartment. In January 2007, the front page of the *New York Daily News* proclaimed, "How City Is Poisoning Kids," and carried a damning investigation by reporter Tina Moore:

> Crawling across the wooden floor of his mother's Brooklyn apartment, Jaylin paused to lick his chubby hand, swallowing flecks of toxic lead paint. The boy's mother had no idea the poison lurked within the cracks of the baseboard.
>
> "I came out of the shelter to be secure and start my life,"

Jaylin's mom, Jasmine Taylor, 23, told the Daily News. "If there was problems, they should have fixed it. My son got poisoned."

Jaylin and his mom are among thousands of parents and children who were placed in apartments—often in lead-tainted buildings—by the city Department of Homeless Services in a push to clear city shelters, the News has learned.

An analysis of city data revealed the city cited about 900 apartment buildings for thousands of lead violations after placing families in the buildings through the Bloomberg administration's Housing Stability Plus program. About 700 buildings tested positive for lead paint.[24]

The damning press reports finally forced the Bloomberg administration to implement real inspections for its rent subsidy programs. But my colleagues and I couldn't get over our outrage and anger. I got to know Jasmine Taylor and her son Jaylin, as well as other families who suffered from the same neglect. The idea that those children suffered lead poisoning and potentially irreversible harm simply because Bloomberg and Gibbs were too cheap or too stubborn to put in place a basic inspection process—all while posing to the public and news media as consummate managers and administrators—was infuriating.

The administration also sent homeless adults into treacherous housing arrangements. As detailed in chapter 10, beginning around 2006, the administration began placing homeless individuals, many of them living with disabilities, into dangerously overcrowded and illegal boarding houses called "three-quarter houses." Most of them were concentrated in central Brooklyn townhouses built for a few families, now packed with dozens of individuals.

One of them was run by a fly-by-night group called Miracle House, which operated a couple of overcrowded dwellings, including its flagship home on Gates Avenue, in the heart of Bedford-Stuyvesant. When I visited one spring day with a coworker, we talked to the "house manager"—really, we later learned, a resident who was paid a few dollars to answer the door and, most of all, deny entry to inspectors and public officials. We told him that we were from the Coalition for the Homeless and worked with lots of people looking for housing—true as far as it went, though not the real reason we were there. He let us in and gave us a tour, showing us incredibly overcrowded rooms, all packed with dented bunk beds, laid out in mazelike fashion.

Finally, he showed us a windowless, narrow, pitch-black room with six bunk beds, reminiscent of the quarters on a submarine. This was the "twelve-man room," he explained, and every man who moved into Miracle House had to sleep there for the first four months of his stay. The operator of Miracle House demanded that residents give him all their food stamps, and he often threw men out on a whim. Nevertheless, for many years, Gibbs stubbornly insisted that Miracle House and similar places were suitable "permanent housing" for vulnerable homeless people.

ASSAULT ON THE RIGHT TO SHELTER, PART 3

When Bloomberg resumed his attack on the right to shelter, the assault took place on two fronts: new rules, modeled on the Giuliani policy, to eject homeless adults from shelter to the streets; and a campaign to eliminate all court orders protecting homeless families with children.

In June 2003, a panel of the New York State Supreme Court's Appellate Division overturned the *Callahan* ruling that had blocked the Pataki shelter-ejection regulation, and a few months later the state's highest court, the Court of Appeals, refused to hear the case on procedural grounds. Thus, in the final months of 2003, the Bloomberg administration prepared, for the first time since the signing of the *Callahan* decree in 1981, to expel some homeless adults from shelters to the streets for thirty days or more.

The new shelter-ejection rule was called, in polished public relations jargon that nevertheless announced the underlying right-wing philosophy, Client Responsibility. It required that homeless shelter residents comply with an "independent living plan," seek housing, and follow other rules—and if they were found to have failed to do one or more of these requirements, they would be ejected from the shelter system.[25] Fortunately, although the Coalition and the Legal Aid Society had lost the larger battle about the rules themselves, we won some important protections for threatened shelter residents.

First, the regulation itself included language exempting many individuals living with disabilities, including mental illness, from the ejection rules—and while we knew that, in practice, city officials would still target such individuals, we could organize legal defenses for them. Second, the homeless people facing ejection were permitted what was colloquially called a "fair hearing"—an administrative appeal before a state welfare agency official that was neither "fair" nor a genuine, impartial hearing, but that could offer some relief. City officials had wanted the people ejected to the streets *while* they waited for the hearing, which could take weeks. But we managed to ensure that homeless people would remain in shelter pending the results of a hearing decision. Finally—and this was probably the most important safeguard we won—the appellate court ordered that city officials share ejection paperwork with us at the same time it was given to the homeless people. This allowed us to seek out the individuals, explain the rules and their appeal options, and represent them at the hearing.

Partly due to these protections, the Bloomberg administration moved slowly in rolling out the shelter-ejection rules. By 2009, city officials had verbally threatened hundreds of homeless people with removal from shelter. But they had officially issued ejection paperwork to only around seventy homeless adults. Fortunately, my colleagues and I were able to track down nearly all those individuals and represent them in the "fair hearing" appeals process. What we found was alarming. I knew well, after years of dealing with the deeply flawed bureaucracy of city agencies serving poor New Yorkers, that errors in the implementation of the shelter-ejection rules were likely—including false accusations and the wrongful targeting of people with disabilities for removal from shelters. It turns out I was, as a colleague of mine put it, "insufficiently cynical." In fact, nearly all the homeless adults facing ejection to the streets were individuals living with serious mental illness and other severe health problems.

My colleagues and I personally represented dozens of homeless men and women in "fair hearings"—and, fortunately, we won many of those appeals. I represented a homeless man whose case was emblematic of many of the ejection cases. George was a US Army veteran who suffered from posttraumatic stress disorder, as well as injuries sustained from a parachuting accident. Both before and during his shelter stay, he had been treated for his mental illness by a psychiatrist at a local Veterans Administration hospital.

Although George had expressed an interest in supportive housing, the agency failed to initiate a housing application for nearly eighteen months. Only after issuing the shelter termination notice did the agency begin the application process—in fact, on the day before George's "fair hearing" began. George and his psychiatrist also presented evidence that he had been saving money and attending outpatient treatment, and also demonstrated that his savings and veterans' benefits alone—only a few hundred dollars per month—were insufficient to rent an apartment. George eventually won his appeal and moved to supportive housing.

Even more stunning—and hard to believe at the time, only a few years after 9/11—was the fact that the very first homeless person the Bloomberg administration targeted with expulsion from shelter was actually a survivor of the attacks. Thomas was a slight, quiet young man in his mid-twenties who had been homeless for two years. He worked for a brokerage company located in the South Tower of the World Trade Center, and he was on the thirty-sixth floor on the morning of September 11, 2001. He escaped with minor burns, but witnessed much of the devastation, including people falling from the towers. After the attacks, he stayed in his apartment for a week and reported feeling numb. Thomas lost his job with the company when it relocated to New Jersey. He later became homeless and entered the shelter system. He worked as a security guard, earning around seven dollars per hour—not nearly enough to secure his own apartment—and in the meantime began to suffer from depression.[26] The Coalition for the Homeless, with help from the Legal Aid Society, represented Thomas in his appeal. And luckily, before his hearing was completed, we were able to offer him an apartment in one of our supportive housing programs.

The Client Responsibility shelter-ejection policy was a window into aspects of the Bloomberg administration that remained shielded from most New Yorkers, in part because of a carefully cultivated image of Bloomberg and his top officials that was regularly transmitted by the media. First, the basic operations of municipal government, including its vast bureaucracy, were rife with systemic errors, along with inefficiencies and inept management. The seventy shelter-ejection cases, for example, had been administered, processed, and reviewed by multiple managers, supervisors, and lawyers—including, in many cases, agency commissioners and City Hall officials—yet nearly every one of them contained glaring errors. This flew in the face of Bloomberg's persona as a management expert who ran the municipal government like a sleek, efficient corporation.

Second, there was a mean-spiritedness to the handling of the ejection cases. When all was said and done, they concerned vulnerable people who had suffered in many ways, not least by living through homelessness. During the "fair hearings," I would regularly confront municipal attorneys and bureaucrats who exhibited nothing but contempt for the clients

I was representing. I had witnessed this phenomenon for many years in various parts of the shelter system, and among some city officials in both the Giuliani and Bloomberg administrations. But it was palpable to confront it in small, antiseptic hearing rooms, where people far more fortunate than the homeless clients argued ruthlessly, and often dishonestly, for the right to throw them out of shelters. This was far from the "kinder, gentler" regime that Gibbs had promised. It was also striking how many white lawyers and officials were fighting so furiously to throw Black and Latino people onto the streets.

Bloomberg also advanced his attack on the right to shelter for homeless families and children. In 2005, after the "pause" in litigation around the *McCain* case, the mediation panel that Justice Helen Freedman had appointed made some dangerous recommendations around ending the litigation and court oversight altogether, which was exactly what the Bloomberg administration had hoped for. But the Legal Aid Society strongly objected, and Justice Freedman also disagreed with the panel's risky proposal. In retaliation, the administration sought to dismiss the case altogether.

But in 2008, Bloomberg and Gibbs finally surrendered their yearslong attempt to eliminate court orders protecting homeless families and their right to shelter. They grudgingly agreed to a settlement in the *McCain* case, in large part because they were facing the blunt reality of testimony in open court from homeless parents and children who'd been grievously hurt by the administration's actions. The settlement ensured, like the *Callahan* decree did for individuals, that there was a legal right to shelter for homeless families and children.[27]

In his final years at City Hall, faced with defeat in court and failed policies, there was every sign that Bloomberg had fully disengaged from homeless policy. Far from reducing the size of the city's homeless population by two-thirds, during his tenure New York's nightly homeless population actually increased by 72 percent, and the number of homeless families had grown even more—by 83 percent. When Bloomberg left office, there were more than fifty thousand people sleeping each night in the homeless shelter system for the first time in modern history, and thousands more bedding down in other shelters or on the streets.

Bloomberg's luxury city had unquestionably come into being, but only in certain precincts of New York, and only for certain people. Homeless New Yorkers confronted a far meaner, far less glitzy version of the city, and a local government that instead of helping them made their lives immeasurably harder. They also encountered a far less affordable city whose neighborhoods, even those they'd once called home, had been transformed.

GENTRIFYING BEDFORD-STUYVESANT AND NEW YORK CITY

In the early 2000s, while visiting the Sumner Avenue armory, I began to notice the telltale signs of creeping gentrification in the western portions of Bed-Stuy: a wine shop, a café, an artisanal bakery, all with signifiers that their ideal customer base was white hipsters.

Census data from 1990 had shown that less than 1 percent of Bedford-Stuyvesant's population was white, with 82 percent Black and 13 percent Latino. Even in 2000, only 2 percent of the neighborhood's population was white.[28] But the upscale eateries and shops and, most of all, ornate brownstones and townhouses made the neighborhood catnip not only to white bohemians, but also to more conventionally affluent white professionals. The gentrification of Bedford-Stuyvesant continued into the 2010s, as property values rose and many Black residents were displaced. In 2020, 21 percent of the neighborhood's residents were white, and the Black share of the population had fallen to just over half—54 percent.[29] One of the most historically significant Black neighborhoods in New York was losing its identity.

As historian Michael Woodsworth described it in his history of community activism in Bedford-Stuyvesant:

> By 2015, the neighborhood formerly known as America's largest
> ghetto was awash in wealth. Though rates of concentrated poverty
> and incarceration in Bedford-Stuyvesant ranked among the
> highest in the city, brownstones were selling for $2 million and
> three-bedroom rentals in Stuyvesant Heights listed for $4,500
> a month. Longtime homeowners regularly got early-morning
> calls asking if they were ready to sell. Some cashed in, others
> defaulted on mortgages or were defrauded of their homes. Private
> investment firms scooped up properties by the bushel; thousands
> of low-income tenants were priced out or turfed out by their
> landlords eager to charge "market rates." Once upon a time
> speculators lined their pockets by making the ghetto; now they
> would reap windfalls from its destruction.[30]

The displacement of residents from Bed-Stuy, along with the neighborhood's transformation, mirrored Bloomberg's impact on New York City during his three terms at City Hall. His legacy ought to have been forever scarred by his racist policing tactics, record-high homelessness, flawed policymaking, and the brutality of his treatment of poor and homeless New Yorkers. But in elite circles, and among far too many middle-class city dwellers, most of them white, what they saw was a shiny, luxury city. What was lost was the other side of the Bed-Stuy image—the illegal boarding homes, lead-paint-infested apartments, crowded armory shelters, and Black and Latino families facing eviction and displacement from their homes and neighborhoods.

CHAPTER 6

THE EAU: SYSTEMIC RACISM AND HOMELESSNESS

It was in the empty house
That I came to dwell
And in the empty house
I found an empty hell.
Why is it that an empty house,
Untouched by human strife,
Can hold more woe
Than the wide world holds,
More pain than a cutting knife?

Langston Hughes
"The Empty House"

THE BODIES ON THE FLOOR

Nothing had prepared me for what I was about to witness on that steamy July night in the late 1990s. It was sometime around two o'clock in the morning in the South Bronx, on East 151st Street, a few blocks north of Mott Haven. My two colleagues and I entered the nondescript, low-slung brick building, whose functional design—really, its lack of any evident sense of design at all—practically screamed that it was a government office for poor people. We made our way past intake windows of thick, scratched, permanently clouded plexiglass, like those found at check-cashing stores and takeout joints in poor urban neighborhoods nationwide. After showing our IDs to security guards and a night-shift supervisor, who observed us with the same bored hostility I'd witnessed from so many other administrators in the homeless shelter system, we passed through battered metal detectors and entered the Emergency Assistance Unit.

And that's when we saw the bodies sprawled on the floor.

I had been told what to expect. Attorneys from the Legal Aid Society, who'd been fighting in the courts and elsewhere to protect homeless families, had visited the facility countless times over many years throughout the *McCain* class action litigation. But the sight of so many vulnerable children and families scattered on the floors of the bleak facility was still shocking.

The Emergency Assistance Unit was a warren of waiting rooms, narrow hallways, and small anterooms of concrete-block walls, which were covered with drywall and thickly painted a nauseating shade of taupe, all illuminated by glaring fluorescent lights. Covering nearly every inch of floor throughout the facility lay the bodies of homeless children and their parents—most sleeping, many struggling to rest, others sitting anxiously upright or staring into space. Some were sprawled uncomfortably on the beige, hard-plastic benches, but most were lying on the cracked, dirty linoleum floors, a few on flimsy foam mattresses. Some babies had been given portable cribs, but others were curled up with their mothers in a protective, desperate huddle I would recognize years later, when I cradled my own infant son in far more comfortable and fortunate circumstances.

Most of the adults, nearly all of whom were women, were huddled under thin white sheets or equally tattered blankets, clutching toddlers or their belongings—or both. The limbs of kids and adults spilled from the threadbare bedding, jutting beyond the thin, pale green plastic mattresses and onto the hard, filthy floors.

My colleagues and I walked slowly through the facility, surveying each room and being as careful as we could to avoid stepping on any of the sleeping bodies, which was a challenge. A few parents were awake, and we conducted quick interviews, writing down their names and the key facts about their cases; we gave them our phone numbers and urged them to visit our Lower Manhattan crisis-services office, where advocates could help them.

Then, well past three in the morning, we made one final sweep of the building. We found more than three hundred people on the floors and benches, mostly children, around half of them infants and toddlers. And that second time walking through the EAU, I noted something else—something that was so obvious that it should have been far more shocking than it was perceived to be: Nearly every one of the homeless children and parents was Black or Latino.

THE FRONT DOOR

The Emergency Assistance Unit, like the handful of other homeless in-take facilities that the city government had operated over more than four decades, was the front door to the vast municipal shelter system for home-less families and children. Every year, thousands of families journeyed up to the South Bronx to begin a grueling, wearying, hopelessly bureaucratic process of applying for a basic human need: shelter from the elements. They came to the EAU with their children, most of whom were very young; half of all homeless kids in New York City were under five years old. Often, families arrived carrying whatever they could. They came in various states of crisis—after being evicted, after fleeing a domestic abus-er, or after escaping apartments that were desperately overcrowded, un-safe, or both.

They came to the front door of the shelter system, but what they often found was a locked gate or a revolving door that hurled them back outside. For two decades, under a set of harsh policies crafted and implemented by the New York City mayors Rudy Giuliani and Michael Bloomberg and

New York State Governor George Pataki, government officials denied shelter to tens of thousands of vulnerable children and parents. These cruel policies forced desperate families to reapply for shelter over and over, and kept them in a state of purposeful bureaucratic limbo for weeks, even months at a time. They shuffled vulnerable families back and forth between temporary, often single-night shelter placements and the EAU. The harsh rules, born in the Giuliani years but honed to precision in the Bloomberg era, forced countless families to sleep on the floors of the bleak intake office, where sick children and adults became sicker and were denied even basic amenities like infant formula, diapers, and bedding. And in numerous cases, they sent desperate families back to hazardous dwellings, back to batterers, or to the streets.

But the EAU also served another deeply cynical purpose. It literally kept from view—in its bleak, windowless corridors and waiting rooms—the misery created by various mayors and their administrations. And it not only hid images of the hundreds of vulnerable kids and adults sleeping on hard floors from the public and media, but also obscured the racist inequalities of homelessness in New York City—the inescapable fact that the vast majority of those homeless children and families were Black and Latino.

NUMBERS

In New York City, the ongoing crisis of modern homelessness disproportionately, overwhelmingly affected Blacks and Latinos. Nearly 90 percent of homeless New Yorkers who sought shelter each year were Black or Latino—nearly double their representation in the city's total population, which was under 50 percent. By the end of the Bloomberg era, Black people made up more than 57 percent of all homeless households using the shelter system each year, while they accounted for only 22 percent of New York City residents. Latinos comprised nearly a third of homeless shelter residents, but only a quarter of the city's population. In contrast, white

New Yorkers constituted 32 percent of the city's population, but only 8 percent of homeless households using the shelter system.

When one looked only at homeless families with children—the people sprawled out on the floors of the EAU—the numbers were even more skewed and shocking. For one of the Coalition for the Homeless's annual reports on the state of New York City homelessness, I did a close analysis of the available data about homeless families and race during the Bloomberg era. In 2014, Black families made up 58 percent of all homeless families in the shelter system, but only 25 percent of all families citywide. Latino families constituted 36 percent of all homeless families, but only 29 percent of all families in the city. And white families comprised only 4 percent of homeless families—though they represented 33 percent of all city families.

Both the number and rate of total family homelessness rose sharply under Bloomberg, but homelessness among Blacks and Latinos rose at a higher rate. In the decade leading up to 2014—a time of rising family homelessness in New York—the total number of homeless families utilizing municipal shelters during the course of a year rose by 27 percent. But over the same decade, the number of Black families using homeless shelters increased by an alarming 41 percent, and the number of Latino families rose by 38 percent. In fact, compared to ten years earlier, 4,300 more Black families and 2,500 more Latino families used the shelter system each year—compared to just five hundred more white families.

One alarming finding in my analysis underlined the extremity of the racial inequality that defined the city's homelessness crisis. In 2014, one in every seventy-two households in New York City slept at least one night, often many more, in the homeless shelter system. But the disparities were stark—one in every twenty-eight Black households and one in every sixty-eight Latino households slept in the shelter system—compared to just one in 294 white households.

And that wasn't the most damning figure. During the same year, one in every forty-two New York City children had slept in a homeless shelter—already an alarming fact. But break the numbers down by race and ethnicity, and the picture was even bleaker—one in every seventeen Black children and one in every thirty-four Latino children experienced homelessness, compared to just one in 368 white children. And one in every seven Black children living in poverty slept in a shelter.[1] In the New Gilded Age, homelessness had become a routine, even expected, fact of life for Black and Latino kids.

CLOSING THE DOOR

The harsh mistreatment of homeless children and families at the EAU and other intake facilities dated back to the 1980s and early 1990s. Under the mayoral administrations of Ed Koch and David Dinkins, the problems at the EAU were mostly due to the mismanagement and neglect common to all municipal services for poor people. Legal Aid attorneys, led by Steve Banks, had successfully secured the legal right to shelter for homeless families with children in the 1980s in the *McCain* case, but they were still forced to file subsequent legal challenges to ensure basic, vital services—such as diapers and formula for infants at the intake centers, and timely transport from EAUs to shelters—when city officials failed repeatedly to provide them.

While conditions at the EAUs were bad, they grew much worse after the early 1990s economic recession forced thousands of New York families into homelessness. After months of the "overnighting" crisis, Legal Aid lawyers again mounted legal challenges, but city officials failed to comply with the resulting court orders. After Rudy Giuliani took office in 1994, his administration ordered the closing of all the EAUs except for the grim facility in the South Bronx.

Why did Giuliani choose to have only one entry point—a single "front door"—to a system that would eventually grow to more than two hundred family shelters? Well, with only one entrance, it was a lot easier to block homeless families from getting into the system in the first place. Giuliani's administration eventually began closing even that single front door.

Fitting with Giuliani's unsubtle political style, many of his administration's early attempts to deny shelter to homeless families were blunt and harsh. City officials for a time required all families seeking shelter to first phone a poorly staffed hotline; families who arrived directly at an intake center without having spoken with a hotline worker were turned away, and in that pre-mobile-phone era, there were few working payphones nearby. Many workers at the EAU were renamed "fraud investigators," with the single goal of rooting out, even inventing, reasons to deny a family's application for shelter.

In closing the "front door," Giuliani got help from his Republican counterpart in Albany, Governor George Pataki, who issued a series of dangerous, antihomeless regulations, often at the explicit request of City Hall. A particularly pernicious regulation from 1995 governed homeless people applying for shelter and how to determine their need for shelter. It shifted the burden of proof from the local government to applicants.[2] This simple but devious alteration in bureaucratic language led to years of misery and harm for countless homeless families and children.[3] Along with other state rules and directives, it effectively made homeless applicants "guilty until proven innocent," a blatantly racist construction, and created harshly restrictive "eligibility reviews" of all families seeking shelter. Under these rules, homeless families had to *prove* they were genuinely homeless, and more troubling, city bureaucrats were given wide latitude to deem a family "ineligible" for shelter—which would become a destructive loophole over the next decade. The Giuliani administration proceeded to deny families' applications for shelter on an unprecedented scale.

From 1995 to 1998 alone, the number of application denials for families seeking shelter rose at an absurd rate, from three hundred seventy to a staggering fourteen thousand.[4]

In the coming years, city bureaucrats denied shelter to tens of thousands of vulnerable homeless families for frivolous and shifting reasons. Many were deemed "ineligible" due to insufficient documentation, like birth certificates, which they often lacked access to, even when other city agencies already possessed them but refused to provide copies. Families were also barred if they had stayed with relatives or friends, even in horrifically overcrowded conditions; if they had relatives in other states, even other countries, that city bureaucrats claimed could house the families, even when those relatives adamantly refused; if they made simple mistakes on application forms; or if they failed to appear at intake interviews with children, even when the kids were in school or sick.

Over the years, we handled cases in which city bureaucrats claimed homeless families could sleep on the floors of their relatives' overcrowded apartments, or even in bathtubs—even when those same relatives repeatedly refused them entry. We also tackled cases involving domestic violence survivors who were told to return to their batterers, and cases in which teenagers and children were ordered to live in relatives' homes where they'd suffered abuse and neglect.

In the winter of 1996–97—in the middle of the Christmas and New Year's holidays—the Giuliani administration began implementing harsh rules that blocked homeless families who'd been denied shelter from reapplying within forty-eight hours. For the first time since the early period of modern homelessness, we documented cases of families and children sleeping outdoors, unsheltered, even as temperatures dropped. We swiftly organized efforts to assist the denied families and, working with some amazing clergy members, helped to create several sanctuary shelters in churches in the Bronx and Manhattan, where families could escape the cold while advocates and attorneys helped them prepare to reapply for shelter.[5]

At the sanctuary at West End Presbyterian Church, located on Manhattan's Upper West Side, I saw toddlers and other small children playing with Christmas toys that parishioners had given them and heard the stories of anxious, exhausted parents who were steeling themselves for a return trip to the EAU and another encounter with cold bureaucrats. The Episcopal priest leading the clergy effort, Archdeacon Michael Kendall, was quoted in a news report saying that the shelter-denial rule was "the cruelest thing I've seen yet" in homeless policy: "What faith do you know of that has as one of its tenets, 'Thou shalt drive thy brother and sister into the street'? All of our faiths talk about caring for orphans and widows, but we're doing the exact opposite."[6] That week, I accompanied him and a few families to City Hall, where Kendall spoke calmly but forcefully to the local media and members of the New York City Council about the cruelties of the policy.

Families were still forced to sleep overnight at the EAU, despite years of court battles. At one point, a professor of pediatrics with experience in animal research described the situation at the EAU as "worse than any animal housing I have ever witnessed."[7] The crisis continued well into Bloomberg's first term. In the spring of 2002, after the billionaire mayor took office, the novelist Jennifer Egan wrote a long, moving investigation for *The New York Times Magazine* about homeless families and the bureaucratic maze of deterrence rules. She even managed briefly to get inside the Bronx intake office:

Reporters aren't allowed inside the E.A.U. or even near its doors, but I did manage a brief visit inside the one-story brick building early this past winter. A series of windowless rooms, it has the bright, 24-hour feel of a casino. The place is crammed with children. . . . Every member of each family must be present in order for that family's case to move forward. There is a low din of crying and coughing, but I found the atmosphere weirdly hushed. Families sat or napped on long plastic putty-colored benches. Portable cribs were scattered around, many with older children folded inside them.[8]

Eventually, after months of intensifying crisis, high-profile news coverage (like Egan's article), and mounting court orders, Bloomberg finally ordered an end to the overnighting crisis. In 2011, city officials opened a new intake center, dubbed PATH (Prevention Assistance and Temporary Housing), on the East 151st Street site of the old EAU. But while reports of vulnerable families sleeping in that facility mercifully dwindled to almost nothing and conditions in the new building improved, the process of seeking shelter remained the same bureaucratic hell it had always been.

DENIAL

The main reason that Giuliani and Bloomberg intensified their deterrence strategy was, simply put, that it worked. For every family who persisted—enduring the nights sleeping on the floors of the EAU, the late-night shuttling between shelter units, the repeated notices of "ineligibility" slipped under a shelter door—many more would just give up and return to whatever intolerable, precarious living situation they'd left. Therefore, the heartless reasoning went, homeless families would be turned away and simply fade into the woodwork.

A year before Giuliani left office, his homeless services commissioner told *The New York Times*, "I can't screw the front door any tighter"—a frank admission that the main goal was to deny help to needy families, no matter what.[9] But the commissioner was wrong. The sad fact was that, under Bloomberg, the front door was sealed shut even more securely.

And access was barred when the need was greatest. In a 2014 report, the New York City Independent Budget Office analyzed applications for shelter during the previous decade (2002–12), the core years of Bloomberg's wholesale shelter denial and deterrence strategy. It found that the percentage of families deemed "ineligible" for shelter actually *went up* after the 2008 global economic crisis; indeed, 80 percent more families were denied shelter in 2012 compared to a decade earlier. This meant that, throughout the Great Recession and at a time of soaring unemployment and a spike in evictions citywide, Bloomberg's administration was turning away more homeless families seeking shelter than ever before.[10]

THE TWINS

For a good part of a year during the late 2000s, I spent several nights each week staffing an emergency hotline that the Coalition had set up for homeless families who had been denied overnight shelter at the Bronx intake center. The Bloomberg administration had recently implemented harsh restrictions for families reapplying for shelter after initial, often error-ridden denials, with the result that many families were turned away from the intake center and sent to the streets. For months, my colleagues and I got several calls each night from desperate families who had nowhere to sleep.

One chilly April night, I was contacted by Fernanda, a young Dominican-American mother. She explained that intake workers had denied shelter to her and her twin three-year-old sons, and they had nowhere to go for the night. I met them at Grand Central Terminal's main concourse, which provided some respite from the unseasonable cold. Fernanda was slight, soft-spoken, and timid; the boys were half asleep in a battered twin stroller, which was loaded with backpacks and plastic shopping bags containing the family's sparse belongings. We took a taxi to a small, modest tourist hotel in the Gramercy Park neighborhood, and I arranged a room for Fernanda and her kids for the night, making plans to meet at our office the next day to begin fighting for the family to get shelter.

Fernanda's twin sons were born prematurely, and both had developmental disabilities; one had been diagnosed with cerebral palsy. City officials claimed that Fernanda and her children could return to her father's two-bedroom Brooklyn apartment, which already had three adults and three children living there. Moreover, her father was recovering from major surgery, and a local agency that helped kids with developmental disabilities had said it couldn't serve Fernanda's sons in that overcrowded space.

It took six days to gather the necessary documentation regarding the family's medical problems and precarious housing situation, while Fernanda and her sons stayed at the hotel. My colleagues and I ultimately helped the family reenter the system—and this time, city officials reversed their earlier determination and deemed the family eligible for shelter. But I couldn't help but feel that this was only the beginning of a longer struggle—one small victory during an era when so many homeless families were turned away. The city government had expended so much time, effort, and money trying to keep Fernanda's family out of shelter, when the real battle was for Fernanda and her kids, and thousands more like them, to have their own homes.

RUNNING THE GAUNTLET

Back in the 1990s, during the heyday of Giuliani's harshest antihomeless policies, we used to describe the horrors of the EAU—the hundreds of bodies sleeping on the floor; the multiple nights families were effectively trapped in that bleak edifice; the bureaucratic indifference and red tape; the constant displacement of families, night to night or every few days, from one temporary shelter unit to another—as the gauntlet that homeless families had to run just to obtain even meager shelter. Legal Aid attorney Steve Banks used to call it an extreme example of "bureaucratic disentitlement," a concept in legal theory that describes how government agencies withhold benefits lawfully owed by erecting administrative barriers—like Medicaid "work requirements," drug testing of welfare recipients, or, in this case, by forcing desperate families to endure misery merely to secure shelter from the elements.

At the heart of the Giuliani and Bloomberg approach to homelessness and social welfare policies was a deeply racialized view of poor people seeking help. Black and Latino homeless families had to prove they were "eligible" for the most basic benefit—shelter from the elements—and the default assumption was that they were *not*. Even families seeking shelter immediately after an eviction were told they could live with some random relative or friend, even when those people were unwilling or unable to help. Indeed, even when families presented notarized letters from relatives declaring that a homeless family could not live with them, city lawyers routinely insisted that the relatives were "colluding" with the needy family—essentially asserting that countless Black and Latino families were engaged in a conspiracy to commit fraud.

The homeless families seeking shelter were de facto presumed guilty. But again, mimicking the systemic racism of the mass-incarceration system, there was almost no way to challenge the malicious assumption. In fact, under a Pataki-approved state rule—later discovered by Legal Aid attorneys to have been authored by Bloomberg officials and thus an example of *real* collusion—families who reapplied for shelter could only do so if they had "new evidence" to present. The artfully-written rule gave them no way to right a wrong committed in the first instance by government bureaucrats.

There were other ways the deterrence strategy relied on racist tropes about poor and homeless people. Giuliani introduced a rule that required poor people applying for federal food stamps, the most basic form of emergency food aid, to be fingerprinted. This punitive, counterproductive policy, which Bloomberg continued, treated poor families and individuals who needed food as potential criminals, scaring off many applicants—and denying New York City millions of dollars in federal funding. To make matters worse, Giuliani even tried to introduce fingerprinting into the homeless shelter system, until threats of legal challenges by advocates halted the plan.

The antihomeless and antiwelfare policies of the Giuliani and Bloomberg years, and the enormous, costly bureaucracies that grew up around them, were thus rooted in a series of fundamentally racist notions. First, with their marshaling of "fraud investigators," fingerprinting and redundant, pointless reviewing of ID and other documents, they assumed that poor and homeless people were trying to defraud the system en masse.

Second, and related to the "fraud" theme, city officials, along with their right-wing counterparts in the tabloid media, frequently claimed that poor people were trying to "game the system." As noted in chapter 5, the city claimed families were "pretending" to be homeless in order to get housing aid, even though Bloomberg had cut off nearly all such aid early in his mayoralty. One Bloomberg official defended its deterrence policy by claiming that shelter itself, as miserable as it was in the municipal system, was a costly benefit that people deceitfully tried to obtain: "Just because an advocacy group disagrees with our position that couples who are not eligible should not receive a scarce and costly benefit, does not mean the system is broken or that courts should run the shelters."[11]

Third, city officials, echoing hyperbolic and wildly distorted claims in the right-wing *New York Post* and other local outlets, occasionally claimed that large numbers of homeless people were arriving from outside the city to flood the shelter system. In 2013, Bloomberg himself gave the most extreme articulation of the long-standing, racist myth of New York City as a "welfare magnet." Discussing the soaring population of homeless families on his weekly radio show, Bloomberg said, "You can arrive in your private jet at Kennedy Airport, take a private limousine and go straight to the shelter system, and walk in the door and we've got to give you shelter"—revealing far more about the billionaire mayor's accustomed modes of luxury transportation than anything about the real lives of poor people.

Fourth, and threading through Giuliani and Bloomberg's policies as well as through decades of national debates on social welfare, was the racialized discourse about the "deserving and undeserving" poor—the notion that most homeless and low-income people refused to work, neglected "personal responsibility," and were, at the end of the day, culpable for their own homelessness and poverty. Despite the historic legacy of slavery, forced segregation, employment and housing discrimination, anti-immigrant xenophobia, and inequality, many politicians, and many Americans, blamed Black and Latino families for their poverty and housing crises. In this context, Giuliani crafted and Bloomberg perfected a regime of punitive policies—from workfare to fingerprinting, from eligibility reviews to fraud investigations—that were designed to trip up desperate families in crisis. This regime treated poor and homeless New Yorkers, most of them Black and Latino, not only as undeserving, but as if they'd been convicted of a crime before even being tried.

SHELTER AS JAIL

As recounted in chapter 4, in the summer of 2002, Bloomberg ordered the reopening of a shuttered municipal jail, the old Bronx House of Detention for Men, as a shelter for homeless families and children. After several weeks of legal challenges and the discovery of hazardous lead paint in the jail, it was shut down, although Bloomberg defended its use long afterward.

On the afternoon of August 5, 2002, a homeless sixteen-year-old named Jason-Eric Wilson returned to the temporary shelter unit he shared with his father and eleven-year-old sister. He and his family had spent the day fruitlessly seeking documents that EAU investigators had demanded before they would deemed the family "eligible" for shelter. Jason-Eric and his family had sought shelter that July after an eviction from their Brooklyn apartment, and they had already endured two weeks of the EAU version of hell—shuttled from the intake center to a temporary shelter unit, then back to the EAU, where they were forced to sleep on the floor and benches overnight, then to another temporary placement, and so on. City bureaucrats had declared the family "ineligible" for shelter despite Jason-Eric's history of mental illness—he had been hospitalized twice in the past year—and his father's battle with leukemia. With their latest temporary placement about to expire, they were awaiting yet another notice slipped under the shelter door telling them they'd have to go back to the EAU.

That day, Jason-Eric swallowed all the pills he could find in the shelter room, including some psychotropic medication. Soon afterward, his father found his unconscious body. He called 911, but an ambulance failed to arrive for half an hour. Jason-Eric died. His father knew immediately why his son had killed himself. As he told a *New York Times* reporter, "My son committed suicide because we were being threatened with being sent back there, to the EAU."[12]

Jason-Eric Wilson's death came during a summer of deepening crisis at the Bronx EAU, with hundreds of kids and adults sleeping on the floors, some for many nights in a row. Few could have predicted the heartless way that Bloomberg would respond to the worsening EAU crisis. On

August 11, six days after Jason-Eric Wilson's suicide, the mayor's deputies reopened the old city jail as a shelter for homeless families. And even though advocates and a state court eventually forced the site to be closed again, for those several weeks, more than eighty homeless families each night—in the largest, wealthiest city in the United States—slept in a jail. Small children and their parents, who had lost their homes due to evictions, domestic violence, or because their equally poor relatives could no longer house them in cramped quarters, bedded down each night in jail cells. Black and Latino kids and adults, whose likelihood of incarceration was already many times higher than those of white New Yorkers, were told that sleeping in the jail was preferable to sleeping on the floors of the EAU, as if those were the only two choices that a billionaire mayor and a vast municipal government could conceive.

CHAPTER 7

BELLEVUE: MENTAL ILLNESS AND HOMELESSNESS

With its ceaseless boom and bust cycles, capitalism is itself fundamentally and irreducibly bi-polar, periodically lurching between hyped-up mania (the irrational exuberance of "bubble thinking") and depressive come-down. (The term "economic depression" is no accident, of course.) To a degree unprecedented in any other social system, capitalism both feeds on and reproduces the moods of populations.

Mark Fisher
Capitalist Realism

THE WAITING ROOM

I nearly missed seeing Alejandro, huddled in a dark, dingy alcove of one of the shelter's overcrowded waiting rooms. But what caught my eye, even before I noticed his withered arm, skinny frame, and sad eyes, was his bright shoulder bag, emblazoned with an image of the classic 1980s X-Men, reimagined in phosphorescent green, Day-Glo purple, and pink. It was rare in those years to encounter a fellow comic book fan in most places, let alone one unabashedly displaying his devotion in such garish colors. But nowhere was it more unexpected than in the bleak chaos of the Bellevue men's shelter, the largest homeless facility on the island of Manhattan.

Alejandro was only one of hundreds of homeless men I saw crowded into the dismal, filthy, intersecting waiting rooms on the seventh floor of the Bellevue shelter during the winter of 2009–10, at the height of the Great Recession. I first saw him in December, when my colleagues and I received the initial reports of long waits for shelter beds and a worsening shortage of shelter capacity citywide, just as the winter cold was descending and more men were coming in off the streets to seek help. As court-appointed monitors of the shelter system with twenty-four-hour, unimpeded access to municipal shelters, we immediately began to investigate. I knew from long experience, and from previous legal battles with city officials, that the trouble spots were the intake shelters—the entry points to the vast, 7,700-bed system of shelter facilities for homeless adults. And this number didn't even include the more than thirty thousand homeless children and parents sleeping each night in family shelters that winter.

The Bellevue shelter, located on Manhattan's east side, a few blocks north of Bellevue Hospital's main building and adjacent to the city morgue, was the most troublesome of the trouble spots. For four decades it had been the intake point for homeless men—the front door to the municipal shelter system, just as the Bronx EAU was for homeless families. And as with the family intake center, city officials deliberately tried to make entry to shelter unbearable.

Back in the mid-1990s, we had successfully sued the Giuliani administration when it refused to add needed shelter beds one winter to address rising need. And the first evidence of that earlier capacity crunch and its deterrent effect had been found at the Bellevue shelter, where a coworker and I met desperate men who had given up waiting for beds and returned to the streets, even as temperatures fell below freezing.

So, beginning in December 2009, we began the painstaking work of gathering evidence for a legal challenge to the city's systemic mistreatment of homeless people. My colleagues and I spent dozens of late nights visiting the Bellevue shelter and other intake sites, from East New York and Crown Heights in Brooklyn, to Wards Island in the East River, to the Morrisania section of the Bronx. Every time we visited Bellevue, we found more than a hundred homeless men waiting for hours for shelter beds. Most were transported in battered old school buses to other municipal shelters in the Bronx or Brooklyn, usually arriving in the early morning hours; there, they'd be lucky enough to get a few hours of sleep before staff woke them before 6:00 a.m. for the return trip to the cramped Bellevue waiting rooms. Many would supposedly "refuse" a bed, though what it actually meant in those circumstances was difficult to determine. Some reasoned they'd get more sleep on a waiting room floor than by being shuttled from borough to borough. Others, including those with disabilities or limited English skills, never heard their names called in the noisy Bellevue corridors, but were listed by city bureaucrats as having "refused" shelter nonetheless.

Over more than two months, we collected evidence in the miserable waiting rooms and hallways of the Bellevue shelter, gathering homeless individuals' affidavits and our own firsthand observations. After weeks of litigation, a New York State Supreme Court judge ruled in our favor that Mayor Bloomberg and his administration had violated the *Callahan* consent decree, which required the city government to provide decent, suitable shelter to homeless men and women. The administration was forced to add more shelter beds and reform its shelter admission policies.

But for Alejandro, that legal victory, which improved access to shelter for so many vulnerable homeless New Yorkers in the following years, came too late. As I got to know him, I learned that he'd already spent a week being shuttled from shelter bed to shelter bed, and many more weeks of exhaustion camping on the floors. Later, he was assaulted by a rogue security guard at another shelter and gave up on the system altogether, seeking help at a so-called drop-in center, a facility with no beds where homeless men could wash up and store their belongings, and were grudgingly permitted to sleep upright in chairs each night.

Alejandro and I also bonded over comic books, comparing notes about favorite creators and characters. Over the following years, I ran into him at my local East Village comics shop and discussed some Justice League or Daredevil issues, Grant Morrison's weirdly operatic Batman comics, or the latest megacrossover event. At the same time, one of my coworkers did amazing work to help Alejandro finally get a studio apartment in a supportive housing building in the Bronx. One way that Alejandro qualified for the supportive housing residence, along with his disabled arm, was his diagnosis of bipolar disorder. He had struggled his entire adult life with sharp, chaotic mood swings, and during his years of homelessness, he also had difficulty securing treatment and maintaining his medication regimen.

When I met up with Alejandro after he moved into his home, he looked happier, healthier, and more grounded—so different from the frail shadow I first found crouched in a dimly lit waiting room at the Bellevue shelter, where he was one of countless homeless men struggling with mental illness that winter, waiting futilely for shelter. The waiting room, it turned out, was located in what was once Bellevue Hospital's infamous Psychiatric Building, where the "lunatics" of an older New York had once been confined.

CAUSES

Over the decades I've often heard mental illness cited as a "cause" of homelessness, but I never really understood this assertion. One of my aunts lived her entire adult life with schizophrenia, and for many years turned to alcohol to drown out the voices in her head. She had some very painful, even tormented years, but she never became homeless. Two other relatives were living with distinct but fairly serious psychiatric disabilities. They grew up in the same Cleveland suburb I did, and they were never homeless. I always knew that it was our middle-class status and government assistance—both of my cousins received Medicaid and Social Security disability benefits and one of them lived in a federally subsidized apartment building—that kept them from, well, losing a round of musical chairs.

What many people were getting at when they said mental illness "caused" homelessness was the easy stereotype: the guy on the street, wearing tattered clothes, who looked and acted crazy. And there was, of course, some truth in that stereotype. Unsheltered homeless people, although only a fraction of New York City's total homeless population, were by far the most visible part of the homeless community. According to research studies, roughly one-third to two-thirds of homeless people sleeping rough on the streets or in other public spaces lived with mental illness. And a smaller, but still significant, share of homeless single adults in shelters did as well. Yet given that most Americans living with mental illness were not homeless, how did so many wind up on the streets or in shelters—or, for that matter, in jails and prisons?

DEINSTITUTIONALIZATION

The first part of the answer was deinstitutionalization. Indeed, it had become a truism in both popular discourse and policy circles that deinstitutionalization was one of the primary causes of the modern homelessness crisis, though the true story was far more complicated and nuanced. In many respects, deinstitutionalization was the ultimate broken promise, an ambitious though protracted experiment, driven largely by all the right intentions—better, more humane treatment in the community for vulnerable people formerly confined in brutal conditions. But it was an experiment that ran headlong into cynical politicians and bureaucrats bent on slashing government budgets and strangling the remnants of the welfare state.

The origins of deinstitutionalization were rooted in the frankly barbaric way that the United States used to treat people living with mental illness. For well over a century, the "mad" and the "lunatics" were routinely interned in cavernous facilities, usually state-run hospitals, which were often little more than modern updates of Victorian-era asylums. During the first Gilded Age, Bellevue Hospital itself was an intake point for the notorious asylum dubbed the Octagon, located on Blackwell's Island (later renamed Roosevelt Island) in the East River. In 1887, the pioneering investigative journalist Nellie Bly wrote an exposé, titled "Ten Days in a Mad-House," for the muckraking *New York World*. She posed as a "madwoman" living in a boardinghouse, and a police court mandated her to the Insane Pavilion at Bellevue Hospital. There, her put-on "deranged" behavior convinced the "alienists" on staff to send her to the Octagon on Blackwell's Island, where she documented the brutal and sadistic treatment of patients.[1]

While Bly's articles and subsequent investigations forced reforms at Blackwell's Island and other large asylums, conditions remained appalling in many state hospitals well into the mid-twentieth century, and the treatment of patients still bordered on the barbaric. In the 1930s, the first prefrontal lobotomies were performed on people with mental illness or other brain disorders, with an estimated fifty thousand patients lobotomized in the United States by the end of the 1950s.[2] During the same decade, "convulsive therapy" was introduced in Europe, using insulin to induce seizures in psychiatric patients, before reaching Bellevue Hospital, where it remained a common treatment for years. In 1938, electroshock therapy was also developed in Europe and, within months, widely used at Bellevue and other American hospitals.[3]

By 1955, the population of individuals living with serious mental illness in public psychiatric hospitals in the United States peaked, with more than nine hundred thousand patients spending time in such hospitals over the course of a year—meaning that around one in every two hundred Americans resided in state hospitals at that time.[4]

The mid-1950s also marked a period of dramatic change in the treatment and care of people living with psychiatric disabilities. In 1954, the most important of a new generation of antipsychotic medications, chlorpromazine, was approved by the Food and Drug Administration. Marketed as Thorazine, this new treatment helped to stabilize many patients and minimize their most troubling behavioral symptoms. The use of such medications led to treatment philosophies that emphasized care in the community, rather than in institutional settings. And a growing reform movement, aligned with the civil rights movement, emerged to spark the process that came to be known as deinstitutionalization.

By 1980, the nightly state hospital population nationwide was only around one hundred thousand patients, a decline of more than 80 percent. Over the same period in New York, tens of thousands of resident patients were discharged from state hospitals, many of which were shuttered. From 1965 to 1979, the number of patients in state psychiatric hospitals in New York fell by 68 percent, from eighty thousand to twenty-seven thousand people nightly.[5] But in an era of austerity and neoliberal governance, state officials refused to reinvest the budget savings from downsized institutions into community care and, most crucially, into housing. Many of the discharged patients, particularly the poorest individuals, found themselves on the streets or in the vast shelter system.

THE PSYCHIATRIC BUILDING

Bellevue Hospital's reputation as the modern-day madhouse was likewise decades in the making. During the Gilded Age, Bellevue's Insane Pavilion, or psychiatric ward, was the waystation for the horrific Blackwell's

Island asylum. And by the 1930s, brutal treatments like electroshock therapy and induced seizures had become routine practice among Bellevue's psychiatric staff.

Many of these cruel yet supposedly scientific treatments were performed in the old Psychiatric Building, which later became the Bellevue shelter. The building was the prize project of Dr. Menas Gregory, an Armenian refugee who had begun his career as an "alienist" (the old term for psychiatrist) at the Insane Pavilion. He went on to become a Bellevue administrator and an adviser to Jimmy Walker, the flamboyant and corrupt Tammany Hall mayor of the 1920s. Gregory noticed that half of all Bellevue Hospital admissions consisted of individuals struggling with mental illness or addiction, while virtually none of the staff had psychiatric training. He therefore lobbied Walker's administration for funding to create a Psychiatric Building and, in 1926, won approval from City Hall.[6]

The building remains a bizarrely opulent architectural oddity. As one contemporary observer commented, it was hard to see why a mental hospital needed "cinquecento porticoes, Michelangeloesque stairways, carved pediments, and fluted cornices," adding tartly that the building "appears to have been based upon a misapprehension of the Villa Medici." The Psychiatric Building, which took seven years to complete, generated $3 million in cost overruns in its first year alone, a scandal that forced its corrupt lead contractor to flee to Europe with his generous advance.[7]

According to the historian David Oshinsky, when the Bellevue Psychiatric Building finally opened in 1933, it was "mired in controversy— the Italian Renaissance façade didn't quite match the somber mood of the Great Depression." At that time in New York City, one in three workers was unemployed, one in five schoolchildren was malnourished, and shantytowns were sprouting up citywide.[8] In subsequent decades, there were other scandals at the Psychiatric Building, including experimental treatment of children that included electroshock. Finally, in 1985, hospital administrators moved the psychiatric unit to the top floors of the main hospital complex a few blocks downtown. The Psychiatric Building was closed and converted into the largest homeless shelter in Manhattan.

GLOOMY ASPECT

In the era of modern mass homelessness, the divide between the Italianate, ornamental exterior of the Bellevue shelter and its new function—as a shabby refuge for New York's forgotten men—was as wide as during the Great Depression. As Oshinsky noted, the eight-story Bellevue Psychiatric Building always "looked more like a fine hotel than a mental hospital (if one ignored the high cement wall with wrought iron spikes on top)."[9]

By the twenty-first century, however, it more closely resembled a former luxury hotel that had gone to seed in some blighted, Rust Belt city. The Renaissance flourishes were dingy, the cornices chipped and weathered, the dark brick walls stained with years of runoff and crawling with tangled vines. The courtyard had become an unkempt jungle of overgrown shrubs and weeds, littered with the usual urban detritus of plastic bags and soda cans. The writer Ian Frazier succinctly described the place in a 2013 *New Yorker* article: "For gloominess of aspect, Bellevue is unique, with its high columns near the entryway surmounted by the words 'Psychiatric Hospital' (the building's original function)."[10]

The interior of the building was, if anything, bleaker and more decrepit than one might have expected. The floor plan was reminiscent of two tuning forks welded at their bases. The ground floor, devoted to an intake unit that funneled thousands of newly homeless men each month, was a web of waiting rooms, social service offices, and cubicles arrayed behind metal detectors and security officers. The remaining seven floors had rows of dormitories, with the largest holding more than twenty beds, situated at the vibrating ends of the tuning forks.

My primary sense memory of the Bellevue shelter was the omnipresent reek of ammonia cleanser, which lingered in my nostrils for hours after I'd left and that I occasionally encountered in subway stations and parking garages, triggering an olfactory flashback to the shelter. The building remained in constant disrepair, with pipes frequently cracking and erupting, water stains swelling on ceilings and walls, and flakes of plaster tumbling onto residents' beds.

Pursuant to the provisions of the *Callahan* consent decree, we used to conduct daylong, floor-to-ceiling "joint inspections" of the shelter, twice a year, alongside city officials. Not once, in the two decades I inspected Bellevue, did we not catalog pages of violations and hazards, even though administrators had weeks to prepare for the inspections. In showers and bathrooms, we'd routinely discover filth and creeping mold. I once found a broken window with a large, jagged shard of glass dangling over a resident's bed; a city bureaucrat positioned himself awkwardly in front of the window, hoping I wouldn't notice it. At the outset of one inspection, shelter administrators assured us that every resident's mattress was brand-new. After inspecting a few dorms, we discovered tears in every mattress, and sure enough, we soon found that nearly all the mattresses at the 850-bed facility had holes or wide gashes. Another time, we found excrement smeared on the walls of a room; this time, city bureaucrats staged an indignant, outraged protest about my inspection notes, apparently more upset that I'd scribbled the words "SHIT ON WALL" than by the presence of the feces itself.

The abysmal conditions of the Bellevue shelter would be nearly unbearable for almost anyone. But the residents of Bellevue had always been among the most vulnerable and frail in the entire shelter system. In order to placate local politicians and residents of the increasingly affluent Kips Bay neighborhood surrounding the facility, city officials had long reserved most of the beds for homeless men over fifty-five years of age; many were, in fact, far older, and some had resided at the shelter for years and years. I met many residents who were more than eighty years old, including one man who'd lived there for thirteen years.

But, as in most other shelters for homeless adults, enormous numbers of men at Bellevue were living with psychiatric disabilities. Two wings were devoted to specialized programs for men living with "serious and persistent mental illness," as the practitioners called it—primarily men diagnosed with schizophrenia or bipolar disorder. Many of the older men in the "general population" beds also struggled with mental health problems, mostly without medication or treatment of any kind. And Bellevue's intake unit for men new to the shelter system—encompassing the overcrowded waiting rooms and three floors of dormitories—saw thousands of men living with mental illness flow through every month.

When I recalled the hundreds of hours I spent at the Bellevue shelter over the years, I was always struck by how much of our work involved men with psychiatric disabilities—and how those men were always treated most harshly when crises emerged.

THE BLIZZARD

During the first winter I worked at the Coalition for the Homeless, in 1995–96, frigid weather and a rising homeless population pushed an increasing number of homeless men into the shelter system. But the Giuliani administration failed to add enough beds, triggering a full-fledged capacity crisis.

In December, my colleague Mike and I almost literally stumbled on the first evidence of its escalation. After midnight on a random week-night, we visited the Bellevue shelter, responding to vague reports that homeless men were being denied beds at the intake unit. We did a walk-through of most of the eight floors of the building, seeing nothing but the usual bleak surroundings. But in a ground-floor hallway, we noticed a security guard curiously positioned next to a closed metal door, and we forced our way past him. And there, in a disused section of the building, nearly a hundred homeless men slept on the dirty floors of three snaking hallways, covering nearly every inch of tiled linoleum.

In the following weeks, we saw the same conditions night after night, and shelter census records showed that the system had fewer vacant beds than there were men sleeping on the intake center's floors. The Coalition and its lawyers attempted to convince the Giuliani administration to add desperately needed shelter beds for the homeless men already on the floors, as well as the hundreds more who would seek shelter as the winter grew colder. City officials initially refused, then responded in sloppy and cynical fashion by reopening an armory in the Flushing neighborhood of Queens as a makeshift men's shelter—but only as an overnight facility. This meant that more than a hundred exhausted homeless men had to be shuttled by bus late each night to the Flushing armory, more than ten miles away, where they'd get a few hours of sleep, then be woken up before six o'clock for the return trip to Manhattan.

We eventually brought legal action to enforce the clear mandates of the *Callahan* decree, which required the city and state to provide lawful, adequate shelter. And a New York State Supreme Court judge eventually ordered Giuliani officials to open the Flushing shelter 24/7 and provide full services, such as meals, lockers, and social support. But over the many weeks it took to win the case, countless vulnerable men endured miserable treatment on the shelter floors, including many clearly living with mental illness.

The most vivid memory I have of that winter is from the historic blizzard that dumped nearly two feet of snow on New York City beginning on January 6, 1996. Worried about conditions at Bellevue, I walked through heavy snow from my East Village apartment, trudging up the middle of First Avenue—I saw a guy skiing on the thoroughfare, and no cars at all—until I neared the shelter. Just as I arrived, I met a tall homeless man in ragged clothes, approaching the shelter entrance from East 29th Street. And though I didn't notice at first, since the snow on the cross streets was still unplowed and quite deep, it turned out that the man had no shoes. He muttered a bit incoherently that he'd walked, in his bare feet, over from Union Square, nearly a mile and a half away, to get a bed. I helped him get inside the shelter, and the staff immediately found him some secondhand shoes and called an EMS team to examine him for frostbite and other possible injuries. And sure enough, the staff told me, he was far from the only homeless man to walk in off the streets, even during one of the worst winter storms in a half century.

SUSPENDED

One of the longest legal battles we fought with city officials about the rights of homeless people began under Giuliani and continued under Bloomberg, lasting for more than a decade. As recounted in chapters 4 and 5, both mayors sought the authority to expel homeless people from shelters for missed appointments or noncompliance with service plans or rules, targeting even those living with mental illness or disabilities. In the early days of the struggle, Giuliani's administration not only fought for the harsh new ejection policy, but also expanded existing rules that let shelter administrators temporarily suspend residents from shelter who'd engaged in dangerous behavior. But suddenly Giuliani officials interpreted "dangerous" to mean things like "smoking in a nonsmoking area"— and began evicting homeless men from shelters for up to a week.

We had always warned that the people most likely to be punished by the harsh ejection policy were those with psychiatric or cognitive disabilities, as they might have problems comprehending or following bureaucratic rules. And sure enough, at the Bellevue shelter I found Benny, one of the first victims of the new enforcement crackdown. Benny was one of the most gentle and easygoing people I'd ever met—a quiet sliver of a man barely five and a half feet tall, with a gentle smile and a distracted, slightly nervous manner. He had made the mistake of lighting up a cigarette one afternoon in a no-smoking TV room. Shelter staff and higher-level administrators ordered his suspension from the shelter for five days, but he didn't understand and stayed away for a week, sleeping on the streets near the Hunts Point Produce Market in the South Bronx. One reason he didn't understand was that Benny had an IQ of 55, a level once categorized under the defunct (and offensive) term "mental retardation."

We eventually worked with a helpful shelter caseworker and a sympathetic state official to find him a decent home in a Brooklyn residence for people living with developmental disabilities. Benny was so glad to escape the shelter at last. I visited him at his new home in Bay Ridge, sat with him in his clean, simple bedroom, and noticed that he'd shed some of the nervous energy he'd had in the shelter. But over the years, Benny was far from the only person with severe cognitive and developmental disabilities whom we found at Bellevue and other shelters.

THE ADULT FAMILIES

Another, smaller cohort of homeless New Yorkers was treated in an even more mean-spirited and harmful fashion during the Bloomberg era. City agencies had, for the purposes of providing shelter, typically divided the homeless shelter population into two major groups: families and single adults. But within the family population was a small group whom city bureaucrats called "adult families," which referred to families with no minor children—generally homeless couples, but occasionally a family whose offspring were aged eighteen years or older. In the Bloomberg years, the nightly population of adult families was around 1,500 families, comprising more than 3,000 people. The adult families had historically been treated far worse than families with children.

Their shelter facilities consisted of commercial "welfare hotels" whose owners were among the most infamous slumlords in New York City. In addition, adult families were denied even the dwindling housing resources that were targeted to homeless families with children, so they languished in shelters for long periods.

In December 2003, the Bloomberg administration moved the intake center for homeless adult families from the Bronx EAU to the ground floor of the Bellevue shelter. At the same time, and even though it was already winter, Bloomberg implemented a harsh new policy—the childless families who were denied shelter—or deemed "ineligible," in the legalistic jargon—were prohibited from reapplying for a week.[11]

We had been visiting the Bellevue shelter and the intake center newly established there, and we quickly learned of this brutal measure. Over the next three months, we did our best to assist families forced onto the streets, sometimes securing hotel rooms in addition to legal advocacy. Many of the people we helped had serious mental health problems and other disabilities, which was commonplace among the homeless childless couples we'd met. Some women were pregnant, but city officials sent them to sleep on the streets that winter anyway.

I remember helping a young couple, Rafael and Jasmine, who had been kicked out of a relative's overcrowded public housing apartment and spent time sleeping in hospital emergency rooms and subway cars before seeking help at the Bellevue intake center. Jasmine was around seven months pregnant, and Rafael had bipolar disorder, which made it hard for him to keep a regular job. Rafael talked a mile a minute while Jasmine sat quiet in our offices, enjoying the heat and a cup of hot chocolate. For three frigid nights, they'd slept outside near the intake center, occasionally slipping into the Bellevue Hospital ER to warm up. With the help of a Legal Aid attorney, we eventually overturned their shelter denial.

Finally, after three months and under pressure from clergy leaders and threats of legal action, the Bloomberg administration rescinded the denial policy—but still required "ineligible" couples and pregnant women to sleep on the floors of the Bellevue intake center.[12]

THE WHITE HOUSE

Every night, Bellevue's main first-floor intake unit was bedlam, with homeless men scattered in waiting rooms from the east side of the building to a grubby, chaotic space near the north entrance, where men boarded battered school buses until nearly three in the morning, when they were shuttled off to distant shelters.

My colleagues and I would make a circuit of the waiting rooms, counting bodies and interviewing the homeless men to track wait times, shelter history, and health issues. While searching for a restroom on the first floor, I discovered the White House—nothing more than a tiny, cramped, and—even by Bellevue's standards—exceptionally bleak room. Slumped in hard plastic chairs and sprawled on the floor under fluorescent lights were some of the most broken-down people one could find at Bellevue— men in tattered pants and thin coats, passed-out drunks, men talking to themselves, men with bruises and welts on their faces, and, for some reason I could never fully determine, a large concentration of Central American day laborers.

It turned out that the White House (I never learned the origin of the nickname) was the shelter staff's makeshift punishment room—the place they consigned the clients they disliked or chose not to deal with. Over the following months, we found some very troubled men with disabilities in that grim chamber and fought hard to get city officials to shut it down. But even a few years later, after we'd prevailed in court, it was possible to walk the now-less-chaotic hallways of Bellevue's intake unit and stumble upon a homeless man, usually pretty incoherent, who'd been condemned by some vindictive staffer to a long night on the floor of the White House.

RELICS

In some of the Bellevue shelter dormitories, particularly the one- and two-bed rooms, there were worn moldings high on the walls. One afternoon during an inspection, I asked a shelter administrator about them, and he confirmed what I'd already suspected. These were once the "padded rooms" dating to the shelter's time as a mental hospital, the old Psychiatric Building, when the staff hung padding over its aging moldings. The most brutal days of the madhouse era may have passed, but their remnants were visible in the sleeping rooms of homeless men at the shelter.

As a child of 1970s television, I remembered the refrain from the classic sitcom *Barney Miller*: "Ship 'em to Bellevue!" That popular-culture version of Bellevue—as the place that New York sent its "crazy" folks—rang down through the decades in movies and TV shows and the tabloids. In the decades since, various city and state administrations have tried to reform or even erase that image of Bellevue Hospital, along with the reputations of other public hospitals and state psychiatric centers.

The barrier between Bellevue the hospital and Bellevue the shelter was far from impermeable. In the 1980s, the hospital, like so many other public hospitals, became inundated with homeless patients as the modern crisis worsened. In 1989, four years after the former Psychiatric Building was converted into a men's shelter, administrators found that 43 percent of Bellevue Hospital's inpatient population was homeless—and, remarkably, almost three-quarters of its inpatient psychiatric patients were also homeless. Average stays in psychiatric unit beds had risen sharply, from ten days in the early 1970s to thirty-seven days by 1992.[13] Bellevue Hospital's acute-care psychiatric unit, created by closing and repurposing the Psychiatric Building, was transitioning into a longer-stay facility.

Since the 1980s, so many other hospitals have been overwhelmed by, and therefore drawn into, the ongoing homelessness crisis. The Bellevue shelter, for instance, was not the only municipal shelter situated in an old hospital building. Brooklyn's notorious Auburn shelter, adjacent to Fort Greene Park, was once part of Cumberland Hospital. Its vermin infestation and other hazardous conditions were detailed in an award-winning 2013 *New York Times* investigative series about a twelve-year-old homeless girl, Dasani Coates, and her family, and later in Andrea Elliott's book *Invisible Child*.[14] In the Greenpoint section of Brooklyn, two more old hospital buildings had long ago been converted to shelters. And on Wards Island, just down the road from the infamous Manhattan Psychiatric Center—almost the last of the dated state mental hospitals—one of the city's oldest shelters was located in the historic Keener Building, a former medical facility.

So many other hospitals have, like Bellevue Hospital in the late 1980s, functioned as de facto emergency shelters. In the late 1990s, I worked with fellow advocates to stop Lincoln Hospital in the Bronx from ejecting homeless people from its emergency room on subfreezing nights. But in general, most ER staff allowed homeless people to take refuge from the freezing cold, when sleeping on the streets was a matter of life and death.

New York hospitals' psychiatric units also provided essential care to homeless people, including short-term or outpatient treatment. Some of those patients got discharged to shelters (even though city officials tried to erect bureaucratic obstacles to these transfers); some were effectively dumped back on the streets, notwithstanding the laws and court orders blocking this practice; and some got sent to long-term state hospitals, even though such facilities were being downsized. Indeed, in 2015, even the once-scandal-plagued Creedmoor Psychiatric Center in Queens, long slated for closing, was briefly considered by Governor Andrew Cuomo as a potential shelter site, until overwhelming opposition by advocates and community leaders halted the plan.[15] Why, advocates asked, as they had so often in the past, should we spend millions to convert a residential care facility, even an imperfect one, into temporary shelter? Why should we continue allocating taxpayer dollars on a costly stopgap measure when what was missing was genuine housing?

Landmark research from the late 1990s helped show the need for supportive housing as an alternative to the shelter-only model. University of Pennsylvania researchers analyzed data on more than seventy-three thousand homeless individuals and identified three major groups of "shelter users": 80 percent of homeless people had brief, one-time shelter stays; 10 percent had longer, episodic shelter stays, coming and going over several years; and the final 10 percent had extended, continuous stays, sometimes spanning more than a decade.[16] The study found that the last two groups—the "episodic" and "long-term" shelter users—had high rates of mental illness, addiction disorders, and other health problems. The researchers conjectured that the "episodic" group most likely cycled between the shelter system and hospitals, jails, prisons, or other institutions.

The study confirmed what my colleagues and I had witnessed firsthand throughout the sprawling shelter system, and certainly what I'd seen in granular detail over hundreds of hours at the Bellevue shelter. There was a core group of older, often fragile men, many of them living with mental illness and other health problems. There was another cohort of somewhat younger men, whom I'd usually encounter in the intake unit, who also often dealt with psychiatric problems. Some of these men had just been released from prison or the Rikers Island jail complex, or they had recently been hospitalized. Many, when you asked them, couldn't provide a fixed address for years at a time; they were as rootless as they were homeless.

More than anything, the challenges they faced with mental illness were inextricably tied to their experience of homelessness. As a colleague of mine used to joke, with a bit of gallows humor and archaic lingo, "If you weren't crazy before you became homeless, you definitely were afterward." Homelessness often had a traumatic impact that lingered for years afterwards. The dismal conditions of the Bellevue shelter and other warehouse-style facilities, the daily grind to survive on the streets or in the subways, the brutal encounters with cops and demeaning treatment by municipal bureaucrats, the long, hopeless wait for a home, and, most of all, the lingering sense of instability and lack of control and fear—all of it was part of the wider, social context of mental illness and homelessness.

CHAPTER 8

CITY HALL: IDEOLOGY AND HOMELESSNESS

Neo-liberalism has been a huge success from the standpoint of the upper classes. . . . If the conditions of the lower classes deteriorated, this was because they failed, usually for personal and cultural reasons, to enhance their own human capital (through dedication to education, the acquisition of a protestant work ethic, submission to work discipline and flexibility, and the like). Particular problems arose, in short, because of a lack of competitive strength or because of personal, cultural, and political failings. In a Darwinian world, the argument went, only the fittest should and do survive. Systemic problems were masked under a blizzard of ideological pronouncements and under a plethora of localized crises.

David Harvey
"Neo-Liberalism and the Restoration of Class Power"

SCATTERED

My colleague Giselle and I knocked lightly on the shabby door, wary of alarming the family inside. A wiry young woman, guarded and with alert eyes, opened the apartment door just enough to see us, two white advocates making every effort to avoid unsettling the mostly Black and low-income residents of the rundown building. We explained that we were from the Coalition for the Homeless, investigating the conditions in units like hers, and that we'd received reports of serious problems in the building. With that, she let us into the dilapidated, seedy apartment for which the city government and taxpayers were inexplicably paying more than $3,000 each month—not even as housing, but as temporary shelter.

We'd managed to obtain the addresses of hundreds of apartment buildings in the Bronx that the Bloomberg administration was using, in a controversial and misguided way, as expensive shelter. At the program's peak, nearly three thousand homeless families—about one in four families in the system—were "sheltered" in apartments that could otherwise have been used as real housing for working-class and low-income families—all at staggering cost to taxpayers. And to make matters worse, the conditions in many of the scatter-site units were abysmal, and public dollars were enriching some of the worst slumlords in New York.

Ava, the young woman we met that day, took us on a brief tour of the cramped unit she shared with her two young children. When they arrived at the apartment, she told us, she found a dead rat in the oven, which was broken, as was the stovetop, so she had been relying on takeout and baby food. The unit was barely furnished, with only two army-style cots, and Ava said she slept together with her baby out of fear of vermin. The bathroom and kitchen were filthy when she arrived, and she'd only just begun to clean them.

Ava's story echoed those of countless other homeless families consigned to scatter-site shelter units. In 2013, I testified at a New York City Council hearing about the policy disaster of the program, describing the experiences of families we'd helped. One family, a father and his two teenage daughters, were sent to a decrepit apartment in the Bronx. On the first night the family slept there, they killed multiple water bugs and heard rats running around in the walls. On the second night, there was no water. The family had been there for almost a week before a caseworker finally reached out. When they complained about the terrible conditions, nothing was done. The family reported seeing rat droppings in the unit and a plantlike fungus growing in the bathroom. When the father attempted to knock it down, a black slime oozed out. The water bug infestation was so bad that they had to shake out their towels every morning before using them.[1] And their temporary, vermin-infested unit also cost taxpayers more than $3,000 each month.

A litany of problems plagued the scatter-site shelter program, including lease-holding tenants being forced out of buildings because unscrupulous landlords could make more money using their buildings as temporary shelter. The real scandal of the program was that it could have been ended quickly and with less expense had Bloomberg and his top officials avoided, or later reversed, their most damaging policies. As detailed in chapters 5 and 10, once Bloomberg cut off homeless families from federal housing aid, the number of families in the shelter system soared, eventually reaching record levels. Families like Ava's needn't have slept in slumlord-owned buildings, fearful of vermin biting their children. But the billionaire mayor and his technocratic aides had a plan, along with firm beliefs about poverty and the nature of homeless people. Though the plan and ideology were deeply unrealistic and resulted in failure, they refused to change course.

THE PEOPLE IN CHARGE

Rising inequality and deteriorating housing affordability during the New Gilded Age were the foundation of modern mass homelessness in New York City. But the crisis was also shaped by policy decisions rooted in neoliberal ideology and racial bias at City Hall. To a troubling extent, those actions were shaped by a handful of key public officials whose personal views, political philosophies, and implicit or explicit hostility to poor and homeless New Yorkers played an extraordinary role in defining municipal policy for decades, eventually influencing national strategies.

The template for New York City's failed response to the modern homelessness crisis was set in the first years of the crisis. The fundamental flaw was to treat homelessness as a *social services* problem, not as a *housing* problem. Thus, the city government's response to homelessness was centered within the Department of Social Services, as well as the Department of Homeless Services (which was created in the 1990s), both of which were overseen at City Hall by a deputy mayor who administered health and social services agencies. A different deputy mayor oversaw the housing agencies and infrastructure policy. By design, therefore, the municipal agencies tasked with responding to the problem of rising homelessness— by providing shelter, public benefits, and other emergency services—were forced to bargain with other parts of city government, as well as the federal and state governments, for the only real solution to the problem—affordable housing. And for the entirety of the New Gilded Age, City Hall failed to invest in sufficient housing resources.

The curtailment and, at times, elimination of housing aid for homeless New Yorkers became not merely a matter of municipal finances, but also an emblem of ideological entrenchment. Almost unique among American cities, many of which are dependent on federal spending for housing and services, New York has long had the fiscal resources necessary to solve the problem of mass homelessness on its own. By the 2020s, New York City's annual budget of over $100 billion exceeded those of all but four US *state* governments—one of which was New York State itself, with a budget surpassing $220 billion.[2] And this didn't even include the potential revenue New York could raise by taxing its wealthiest residents and corporations at more progressive and equitable rates.

The other key element of the template set during the 1980s was not only the abject failure of the neoliberal policy response to homelessness, but its exorbitant cost. Throughout the decade, it became increasingly clear that the failure to invest in housing-oriented solutions led to a larger homeless population, and hence the rising costs of a growing shelter system and other reactive, emergency-based responses. From 1981 to 1991, expenditures by the city's social services agency, which then administered the shelter system along with benefits and other services for poor and homeless New Yorkers, rose by an unprecedented 121 percent—outpacing the city's overall budget expansion by twenty-five percentage points. During the Giuliani and Bloomberg years, the increase was even higher. From 1994 to 2014, spending by the homeless services agency rose by 143 percent, to more than $1 billion per year. And this did not even account for other homelessness-related city expenditures, particularly the cost of policing, jails, and hospital care, which also soared during that period and afterward.

Thus, the conflation of neoliberal policies with fiscal conservatism was deeply misleading. As detailed in chapter 1, numerous studies have documented how government spending on supportive housing proved more cost-effective than leaving people homeless, given the significant expenses associated with shelters, hospital care, and jails. For homeless families, the public cost of shelter in New York City was also phenomenally high. During Bloomberg's mayoralty, average monthly spending to shelter a homeless family with children rose by 21 percent, to over $3,000 per month, and by the 2020s, it had nearly doubled, to $6,000 per month. Given the lack of affordable housing and city cutbacks in housing aid, homeless families also stayed in shelter for longer and longer periods. Under Bloomberg, average shelter stays for families with children rose from eleven to fourteen months, and then grew even longer by the 2020s, to seventeen months. By that point, the average total cost to shelter a homeless family was more than $100,000—far more than it would have cost to provide them with subsidized housing.

During my time as a homeless advocate, I had interactions—some brief and some quite extensive—with every New York City mayor from David Dinkins to Eric Adams. It was clear to me that each mayor's worldview and ideology—particularly those of Rudy Giuliani and Michael Bloomberg—had an outsize effect on millions of people. More revealing, though—and often alarming—was the time I spent with other officials. These unelected bureaucrats—whether commissioners of key agencies, middle managers, or heads of nonprofit organizations doing business with City Hall—made decisions that affected the lives of the most vulnerable New Yorkers. In fact, there was an eerie and unsettling distance between the homeless New Yorkers bedding down in far-flung districts of the Bronx, Brooklyn, and Queens and the stately, nineteenth-century edifice of City Hall, not to mention the antiseptic Lower Manhattan offices of municipal agencies. I came to realize that the lives of poor and homeless New Yorkers were largely dictated—and often damaged—by a handful of city officials, and that it was essential to understand both their mindset and their actions.

GIULIANI: RIGHT-WING IDEOLOGY AND HOSTILITY

For the volatile, bombastic Giuliani, there were countless moments over his two terms at City Hall that revealed his deep-seated hostility toward poor people and Black and Latino New Yorkers. Indeed, the Giuliani who embraced authoritarian, antidemocratic politics years later—by aiding Donald Trump's lawless attempt to overthrow the 2020 election—came as no surprise to those who had paid attention in 1990s New York City.

As documented in numerous biographies and profiles, Giuliani and his closest aides regularly threatened and attacked those they viewed as enemies—a long list that included former Dinkins administration officials, political rivals, civil rights leaders, and advocacy groups. In 1998, when the New York City Council passed a law limiting the size of shelters in order to make them safer, Giuliani threatened to open a shelter in the district of the legislation's lead sponsor. He targeted a building that housed a day care facility, mental health program, and senior center, threatening them with eviction until legal challenges and public opposition forced him to back down.[3] A year earlier, in retaliation for our advocacy, Giuliani's administration took away $3 million in federal homelessness assistance funds from the Coalition for the Homeless and Housing Works, a prominent activist group that also provided housing and services to people living with AIDS. After years of appeals to federal officials and a lawsuit, both groups saw their funding restored—and Giuliani lost control over the disbursement of federal homeless services grants.[4]

But by far the most extreme, and dangerous, act Giuliani committed against activists occurred in 1998, and it again involved Housing Works. The group had staged a peaceful, though boisterous, protest rally in City Hall Plaza, the site of countless similar gatherings over the years, to protest cuts to AIDS programs. In response, Giuliani ordered low-flying NYPD helicopters to buzz the crowd, which comprised around one hundred mostly Black and Latino people, some of them homeless and living with HIV. Additionally, Giuliani ordered police snipers stationed atop City Hall as an intimidating show of force against the protesters.[5]

Giuliani's hostility toward advocates for homeless New Yorkers, like his animosity toward Black and Latino civil rights activists, coalesced with his fervent embrace of right-wing, racist ideology about poverty, which was in vogue at the time. In the 1990s, conservative ideologues, Republican officials, and many so-called "moderate" Democrats embraced a philosophy that claimed that antipoverty programs and public benefits harmed poor Americans and actually *caused* poverty. Giuliani claimed that his brutal welfare program—which ultimately resulted in 775,000 poor New Yorkers losing public assistance over the course of his mayoralty—was "by far the best thing we're doing for the city."[6] His approach to welfare and homelessness was clearly guided far more by a right-wing, anti-government philosophy than by the impact on poor New Yorkers or the success of his allegedly work-oriented policies. Asked by a *New York Times* journalist which outcomes were more important, job placements or outright denial of benefits, Giuliani answered, "Decreasing the numbers of people dependent on the government."[7]

JASON TURNER: ANTIGOVERNMENT CRUSADER

The city official of the 1990s who most closely reflected Giuliani's own right-wing zealotry was Jason Turner, the architect of the mayor's brutal welfare policies. In interviews, he often told a story about how, as a twelve-year-old, he had read an article in the newsweekly *US News and World Report* called "How It Pays To Be Poor in America," which absurdly claimed that for millions of Americans, "idleness often turns out to provide almost as good a living as working at a low wage." A profile of Turner described his reaction: "'It just hadn't occurred to me that there were whole classes of people who didn't work, and who basically existed on government charity,' Turner would later recall. He immediately set to work scribbling designs for factories to put these dependents to work."[8]

Before coming to New York, Turner had been the architect of Wisconsin's draconian welfare reform program. The Wisconsin program became a template for the federal welfare reform legislation enacted in 1996 by President Bill Clinton and the Republican-controlled Congress. This radical reform essentially eliminated guaranteed cash assistance for poor Americans. The law replaced the Aid to Families with Dependent Children program, the safety net for poor families established in 1935 during the Great Depression, with a block grant to states, allowing them to craft an array of services that prioritized "welfare-to-work" programs. The 1996 federal welfare reform law gave Giuliani and Turner the flexibility needed to implement their cruel version of reform in New York City.

In a PBS interview in June 1998, Turner declared his intentions and philosophy in particularly revealing fashion, saying, "It's work that sets you free," the same slogan found on the gates of Auschwitz.[9] Turner had to make the obligatory apologies, but his Nazi quotation certainly reflected his deeply held views. In 1996, before arriving in New York, he had been interviewed by the right-wing Heritage Foundation and said, "What liberals have entirely failed to grasp is that social maladies, including poverty, are the result of learned behavior in which enforced idleness is a contributing factor."[10]

Turner got to work implementing his "work first" overhaul of New York's welfare system, importing the policy tools that had been workshopped in Wisconsin, but with a harder edge. These included "workfare," or newly created make-work programs for welfare recipients who could not find private-sector employment; "sanctions," or the partial or complete loss of benefits for allegedly failing to follow complex or impractical rules; "diversion," or bureaucratic barriers blocking people from securing benefits; "privatization," or contracting out government services to private entities; and systemic, spillover effects, in which loss of welfare benefits triggered the termination of other forms of assistance, such as housing, food aid, or health insurance.[11]

In New York City, Turner scaled up all these policies. The workfare scheme that emerged, the Work Experience Program, which was the largest of its kind in the country, typically involved menial labor such as collecting trash in public parks. Workfare also systematically contributed to the phenomenon of "churning"—that is, the rising number of welfare recipients with "sanctions" or suspended benefits who would then struggle to reinstate their benefits, only to be tossed off the rolls again. Many welfare recipients—especially parents of young children who lacked childcare, or people with chronic health problems—regularly missed or arrived late for workfare assignments, automatically triggering a loss of benefits. And the welfare system itself was rife with bureaucratic errors that resulted in people wrongfully losing aid, including misplaced notices, failed mail deliveries, and mandatory "face-to-face" meetings with welfare workers that were scheduled without notifying recipients.

The other weapon deployed by Turner was diversion and denial, in the form of a series of bureaucratic barriers that made it harder for poor New Yorkers to apply for and obtain benefits in the first place, or to reopen cases that had been closed or suspended. These "eligibility reviews" placed the burden of proof on poor people to gather hard-to-obtain government documents or provide a dizzying array of other extraneous information. The Giuliani administration also implemented a so-called fraud detection unit called Eligibility Verification Review, which imposed stringent eligibility barriers, leading to the denial of thousands of applications for welfare along with other legally entitled benefits, such as Medicaid and food assistance.[12] Taken together, the denial policies and tactics served their purpose—fewer and fewer New Yorkers sought or obtained government aid, even during economic downturns, and the welfare rolls plummeted.

Turner's impact on homelessness was twofold. First, almost by definition, nearly all homeless New Yorkers were eligible for welfare benefits and a range of other essential assistance, such as food stamps, Medicaid, disability benefits, and more. By shredding that safety net, tens of thousands of homeless people over the years had to struggle to obtain or keep the meager government aid they relied on to subsist. Moreover, the brutal design of a system that routinely closed or suspended benefits for a huge portion of recipients hampered homeless housing policy for years to come. Beginning under Bloomberg, the city government crafted rent subsidy programs that were intertwined with welfare benefits. This meant that when recipients lost their welfare benefits, they lost their rental assistance, and they ultimately lost their housing. Remarkably, one homeless services official who had worked under Turner in the welfare agency said that the fact that "only" one in four families with a welfare-linked rent subsidy had lost their aid was a "success."[13]

The second way Turner harmed homeless New Yorkers was by setting up the template for the "denial and sanction" approach to addressing homelessness, a tactic deployed at the EAU more than anywhere else (see chapter 6). This harsh philosophy—that reducing homelessness meant withholding or revoking access to shelters—shaped City Hall policy for years. Turner's extreme right-wing and antipoor outlook was perhaps best expressed, according to a *New York Times* report, when he was promoting Giuliani's "workfare for shelter" ejection plan: "At conferences and in meetings with shelter providers, Mr. Turner has expressed concern that some who were cut from the welfare rolls have been able to go to shelters and food pantries without restriction, sidestepping sanctions intended to push them to self-sufficiency. 'We need to create, if you will, a personal crisis in individuals' lives' that cannot be avoided by alternative programs," he said."[14]

GEORGE MCDONALD: RIGHT-WING IDEOLOGY AND CORRUPTION

Another key figure—this one from outside government, but entwined with City Hall politics—straddled the Giuliani and Bloomberg eras and illustrated the toxic amalgamation of right-wing ideology and the corrupting influence of money. George McDonald was a Republican former garment industry businessman who, in the 1980s, began volunteering to distribute meals near Grand Central Terminal. An intemperate and often loud-mouthed character, he became familiar to the local press corps for monologuing about homelessness on the steps of City Hall, claiming that he resided in an SRO building and had taken a vow of poverty.

Unlike advocates and experts on homelessness, however, McDonald did not believe homelessness stemmed from structural problems such as high housing costs and low wages, or from cutbacks to vital government programs. In the classic American blame-the-poor tradition, he believed homelessness could only be overcome through work and figuratively "pulling oneself up by one's bootstraps." He opened a shelter in Brooklyn built on his conservative philosophy—residents would be required to work *and* pay for their shelter, even though they were denied tenancy rights. McDonald grew this facility into an organization called the Doe Fund, named for a homeless woman nicknamed Mama Doe, who had died on the streets from exposure after police ejected her from Grand Central.[15] As noted in chapter 1, McDonald also parlayed his role as founder of the Doe Fund into a brief role at City Hall, where he helped Andrew Cuomo author the conservative "Way Home" report for an early 1990s homelessness commission.

Eventually McDonald found a lucrative avenue for his shelters and their residents in a program dubbed Ready, Willing, and Able. Beginning in the 1990s, he struck contracts with local business improvement districts throughout the city to have his clients perform street cleaning and other manual labor in well-to-do neighborhoods like the Upper East Side, midtown Manhattan, and the Wall Street area. The workers—who in many instances replaced unionized city government employees in a system similar to workfare—were supposedly paid the minimum wage. But the "cost" of shelter was deducted from their pay, meaning that the homeless workers earned only a few dollars per hour at best. The Doe Fund flouted labor laws by claiming to be a "training program" and labeling the workers "trainees," and therefore not subject to regulation.

In the mid-1990s, when Giuliani began "privatizing" the operations of dozens of municipal shelters, the Doe Fund got the contract to operate a large men's facility in Harlem. The Harlem shelter served working men, and the residents organized a strong "client advisory board," or residents' council, to address problems with administrators. When the Doe Fund took over operation of the shelter, the board was anxious about the change. As feared, despite promises to the contrary, all the residents of the Harlem shelter were required to enroll in the make-work program, and those with jobs were told to quit them. The shelter's resident leaders protested and held a boisterous protest meeting at the facility, but the Doe Fund would not budge. Most of the resident leaders were eventually forced to other shelters in the system.

McDonald also backed Giuliani and Bloomberg's attempts to undo the legal right to shelter. In late 1999, when Giuliani announced his plan to eject homeless people from shelters, McDonald submitted an affidavit supporting the rules—even though his organization had been named after a homeless woman who had died on the streets. McDonald defended his position by utilizing the typical right-wing talking points of the era: "Why would anyone want to protect someone's right to lie around a shelter doing nothing? . . . The advocates want to give the homeless an unconditional right to shelter and isolate them in government housing."[16] When Bloomberg launched similar attacks on the right to shelter, McDonald also supported those efforts.

McDonald's enterprise grew at an even faster rate. More BIDs contracted with the Ready, Willing and Able program for its workers to perform street cleaning, and Bloomberg's administration expanded the number of contracted Doe Fund shelters, providing the organization with a consistent labor force. A *New York Times* investigation found that McDonald's group had secured more than $260 million in contracts under Bloomberg.[17] But McDonald's relationship with the billionaire mayor was even more transactional and codependent than his relationship with Giuliani for one major reason: Bloomberg's money. As he had with dozens of other nonprofit homeless services organizations, Bloomberg leveraged his vast wealth to become a singularly generous donor to the Doe Fund, contributing millions of dollars to the organization through his personal foundation.

In one significant way, McDonald supported not only Bloomberg's policies but also his political ambitions, namely, the billionaire mayor's effort to overturn mayoral term limits and secure a third term. The Doe Fund's support for the legislation that changed the term-limits law was perhaps the most notable and controversial of any charitable group in the city. At a Columbus Day parade in early October 2008, weeks before the vote, a *New York Daily News* reporter spotted several Doe Fund workers in their blue uniforms, "holding huge professional-looking signs praising the mayor," along the parade route on the Upper East Side.[18] In the days before the vote in late October, *The New York Times* reported:

> The Doe Fund, a homeless-services organization, has received about $150,000 from Mr. Bloomberg since he took office. At the request of the mayor, the group's founder and president, George McDonald, testified for the mayor's proposal. . . .
>
> At least 11 Doe Fund employees, including several senior officials, testified in favor of the mayor's plan, but most of them did not identify their employer, describing themselves only as residents of their neighborhoods.[19]

But it turned out that the reporters initially missed the larger scale of McDonald's corrupt role. A follow-up *Times* investigation two years later found that Bloomberg had personally donated millions of dollars to the Doe Fund, including more than $10 million immediately after the repeal of term limits.

I was at City Hall the day of the hearing and saw firsthand that large numbers of Doe Fund personnel were present. It was a remarkable scene. The organization transported its homeless workers, clad in their usual blue jumpsuits and just off their street-cleaning shifts, in several vans. The workers were brought into the council's ornate main chambers, where the hearing took place, all of them wearing clothing emblazoned with the Doe Fund logo. The men looked confused and a bit shell-shocked, and they did not seem at all to be there willingly. I wondered at the time how many of them genuinely supported Bloomberg or the repeal of term limits. I doubted that these men, dependent on the Doe Fund for not only their jobs but also their shelter, had the autonomy to support or oppose the billionaire mayor.

While Bloomberg was clearly wielding his vast wealth to advance his own political aims, McDonald was a willing and able participant in that effort, as well as a recipient of the billionaire's donations. Over the years, reports emerged about McDonald and his family's lavish income from the Doe Fund. The *New York Post* reported that in 2007, McDonald was being paid a remarkable $403,000 per year, while his wife was paid $207,000 and his son, who had been appointed chief financial officer (an ethically dubious move), was paid $187,000. In addition, the Doe Fund itself was paying McDonald $147,000 in rent for use of his Upper East Side townhouse as headquarters for the organization—meaning that, in total, the McDonald family was taking in nearly $1 million each year from the nonprofit organization.[20] A year later, the *New York Daily News* reported that McDonald had quietly pocketed a $100,000 prize given to the charity by the right-wing Manhattan Institute to honor its efforts. It later emerged that the "prize" money came from a Bloomberg donation.[21]

In 2013, with Bloomberg's third and final term coming to an end, McDonald ran for mayor as a Republican, pledging to end the right to shelter for homeless New Yorkers.[22] McDonald's quixotic campaign was in keeping with his sense of grandiosity. But it was peculiar in that he was far from a charismatic figure, notoriously prone to tirades and explosions of anger. In 2019, the news outlet *Politico* reported that seven Doe Fund employees at the group's main office, all but one of them women, filed complaints about a hostile work environment. One employee described a "culture that has been created and allowed to continue by the Founder

[McDonald], which is one that promotes misogyny, allows bullying, is abusive and instills fear."[23]

For all of the melodrama and political wheeling and dealing that surrounded McDonald, underlying his wealth and influence was a putatively nonprofit organization. But it was a peculiar charity, uniquely suited to the era of neoliberalism, shaped by and dependent on the right-wing philosophy that had established it. Based on a fatally flawed premise—that homelessness was caused by broken, dependent people who didn't want to work, with employment as the sole solution—it could only participate in and fuel a process of exploitation of these new "homeless workers."

Well into the 2020s, the Doe Fund workers were still laboring in affluent neighborhoods—along Park Avenue, on the Upper West Side, next to Madison Square Park, and elsewhere. That work was once done by a unionized, decently paid municipal workforce that had benefits and labor rights. But beginning with the 1970s fiscal crisis, the city government eliminated those jobs and future neoliberal mayors never replaced them, resorting instead to a range of privatized schemes organized by the city's real estate and business elites. McDonald and his organization were an integral part of those schemes as suppliers of cheap labor, and they profited from that arrangement. All the while, the Doe Fund workers were paid a paltry sum and called "trainees" to skirt labor laws and wage requirements. They had as little control as any workers could—homeless men made into a surplus workforce doing grueling labor.

BLOOMBERG: TECHNOCRACY AND PHILANTHROPY AS POLITICAL PATRONAGE

Essential to understanding Michael Bloomberg's dozen years as mayor was recognizing his fundamental identity: a CEO, a billionaire, and a Wall Street and media tycoon. These were the keys to the public persona he crafted and to his exercise of power. And they helped to determine his views of homeless and poor New Yorkers, as well as the ultimately disastrous policies that he and his administration implemented to address homelessness.

As historian Julian Brash described him, Bloomberg was, in many ways, the epitome of the "charismatic CEO," a figure who arose in popular and political culture following the capitalist accumulation crises of the 1970s and amid rising distrust of corporations. Whether earlier figures like Lee Iacocca or Jack Welch, or later businessmen who also entered politics like Silvio Berlusconi or Donald Trump, Brash wrote that "the charismatic CEO . . . personifies the immense power of capital to restructure social, economic, and political relations. The charismatic CEO is seen as 'a particular kind of person'—a leader rather than merely a manager. Moreover, this leadership is typically proved in times of trouble."[24]

It was no mistake, then, that Bloomberg was elected at a time of crisis and turmoil in New York City, less than two months after 9/11. And it was doubtful he would have been elected if not for the attacks. Fully assuming the mantle of the wealthy, successful businessman who would wield his technocratic skills to steer the city out of crisis, Bloomberg went from virtually unknown beyond Wall Street to mayor of New York. And he sealed the deal by spending $73 million—nearly ninety-three dollars per vote—a historic sum for a New York City mayoral campaign at the time.[25] Bloomberg's lavish campaign spending presaged the ruthless and ultimately corrupt ways he would employ his wealth over the next twelve years.

As with the Doe Fund, Bloomberg strategically gave tens of millions of dollars to a wide array of charities and nonprofit organizations—civic groups, cultural organizations, schools, churches, and homeless service providers. The donations bought him the support of those groups and ensured their silence when they disagreed with his policies. As the political journalist Edward-Isaac Dovere wrote, "Bloomberg spent extensively as mayor of New York. He gave massive sums to nonprofit organizations and arts groups. He contributed enormous amounts in political donations out of his personal bank account. . . . He funded nonprofit organizations that boosted his policy agenda. When church groups or community organizations threatened to get noisy in opposition to him or his programs, he wrote checks that tended to quiet them down."[26]

The most glaring example of the weaponization of Bloomberg's wealth involved his campaign to overturn term limits. As *The New York Times* reported at the time, Bloomberg aides contacted many groups that held city contracts and had received donations from the billionaire mayor:

> An official at a social service group that receives tens of thousands of dollars from Mr. Bloomberg and has a contract with the city was startled to receive a call in the past few days from Linda I. Gibbs, the deputy mayor for health and human services. Ms. Gibbs asked whether the organization's leaders would be willing to call wavering council members to argue for Mr. Bloomberg's term limits legislation.
>
> "It's pretty hard to say no," the official said, speaking on condition of anonymity for fear of upsetting the mayor. "They can take away a lot of resources."[27]

Bloomberg's role as head of a media company also gave him enormous sway over New York's local media. Bloomberg News was expanding from its longtime focus on business to cover politics, public affairs, and national and international news. Thus the company was, for many local journalists, a potential employer, which made writing critically about Bloomberg the mayor a risky career move. But it was also true that Bloomberg's carefully crafted public image—successful CEO, technocrat, Manhattanite, and philanthropist—appealed to the rising class of journalists, who identified as upper-middle-class professionals and typically lived in affluent or gentrified neighborhoods.

By Bloomberg's third and final term as mayor, the technocratic, entrepreneurial, and philanthropic veneer that had masked his homeless policies—and generated positive press coverage despite the disastrous record—gave way to a clearer image of the true Bloomberg. As the homeless shelter population soared to record levels, the billionaire mayor responded testily to a series of public setbacks—and each revealed the antihomeless philosophy at the core of his worldview. For example, Bloomberg defended the unworkable design of his rent subsidy programs with an appeal to classic right-wing clichés, saying it was "not government's job to take away your responsibility for your own behavior or to be self-supporting."[28] Like his predecessor, Bloomberg was also prone to attacking advocates. Indeed, in a 2006 speech before the National Alliance to End Homelessness, he made cutting remarks to a room full of people who viewed themselves as advocates: "To rid our society of homelessness we must first liberate ourselves from the chains of conventional wisdom, from the fetters of political correctness, from the tyranny of the advocates and their unwillingness to admit that we're ever making progress."[29]

An even more revealing incident involved the yearslong struggle by tenants and advocates to end the poisoning of children by lead-based paint. During Bloomberg's second year in office, Cordell Cleare, a Harlem resident and tenant activist whose son had suffered lead poisoning, met with the billionaire mayor while serving as a staffer for a New York State senator. Years later, she told a journalist about the experience:

> As Cleare appealed to the first-term mayor about the lead paint
> dust causing an epidemic of brain damage among mostly Black
> and Latino children, Bloomberg interrupted her.
>
> "He said, 'Yeah, well, I just don't understand certain behaviors

in certain populations,'" Cleare recalled. . . . "Then he told me his foundation was trying to find out why people take drugs."

She understood the mayor's insinuation: Irresponsible minority parents, not landlords, were the ones to blame for lead-tainted paint dust coating the floors and surfaces of their poorly maintained apartments.

"I took it as an insult," Cleare said. "It was so mind-blowing to me that I honestly can't tell you how I came back. Everything just stopped right there, and I said, 'I'm talking about lead-poisoned kids.'"[30]

Bloomberg went on to veto lead paint abatement legislation passed by the New York City Council. And some time later (as detailed in chapter 5), his own administration sent homeless families to lead-paint-infested apartments where children were poisoned.

LINDA GIBBS: RIGHT-WING TECHNOCRACY

The key figure behind Bloomberg's approach to homelessness was unquestionably Linda Gibbs. She was commissioner of the Department of Homeless Services for four years before Bloomberg elevated her to Deputy Mayor for Health and Human Services, where she served for the remaining eight years of his mayoralty and oversaw the agencies serving homeless and poor New Yorkers. Her reputation was built on bureaucratic oversight and administrative leadership, not on policy or a vision for solving urban maladies. Nothing in Gibbs's professional background had prepared her for the complexity of the homelessness crisis—especially when it worsened just as she assumed her new job.

I had many encounters with Linda Gibbs, and I was often surprised how little she knew about the causes of homelessness, the vast system of shelters and services she oversaw, or the lives of homeless people. Even more alarming was her visceral resistance, evident even in the earliest encounters, to the idea that anyone other than the mayor and herself should have any input into homeless policy.

This controlling attitude surfaced in the wake of our first conversation with Gibbs, in January 2002, days after Bloomberg had appointed her as homeless services commissioner. As it had with the family shelter system, the outgoing Giuliani administration had failed to add capacity for homeless single adults as the wintertime cold drove more individuals to seek shelter. We were already preparing a legal challenge when Gibbs was appointed commissioner, so we hastily arranged a call with her in the hope that the new administration would respond appropriately. After some back-and-forth, Gibbs agreed to accelerate the opening of a new wintertime shelter to add beds for homeless men.

At the time, I believed the phone call to be a positive sign, and a welcome change from the adversarial relationship that had defined the Giuliani era. But later we learned that Gibbs took away something else entirely from that phone call. She resented the idea that the courts, advocates for homeless people, and attorneys representing homeless New Yorkers should have any involvement in the operation of the shelter system. In her view, only the CEO mayor and his appointees should have that power. Ultimately that phone call, and the events later that year involving the Bronx jail (see chapter 4), hardened Gibbs's opposition to any independent oversight of homeless services and sharpened her zeal to eliminate all court orders protecting homeless families and individuals. And it shaped her unremitting hostility to homeless advocates.[31]

More than that, Gibbs's later policy failures stemmed from a fundamental refusal to acknowledge that the homelessness crisis was rooted in worsening housing affordability—and that to address that root cause, the city government would have to create and allocate more housing resources specifically for homeless New Yorkers. In fact, for Gibbs and her boss, the ideological blindness was even more extreme—they believed the way to reduce the size of the homeless population was to *eliminate* housing aid for homeless people.

I had a firsthand experience of this during a conversation with Shaun Donovan. Prior to serving as head of the US Department of Housing and Urban Development under Barack Obama, Donovan had been Bloomberg's housing commissioner, and I met with him on several occasions as one of the leaders of a citywide affordable housing campaign. After one of those meetings, I buttonholed Donovan and asked for his help. Gibbs had just implemented her policy cutting off homeless people from federal housing programs. The homeless population was predictably growing, and homeless families in particular needed affordable housing resources—including apartments created and renovated by Donovan's agency. He sighed resignedly and said he could not help—he couldn't go up against Gibbs in City Hall, and she was determined to cut off homeless families from all subsidized housing resources, even those from his agency, no matter what.

After leaving city government in 2014, Gibbs, like many former Bloomberg administration officials, went to work for Bloomberg Associates, a consultancy that was part of the multibillionaire's larger foundation, Bloomberg Philanthropies. She even cowrote a book called *How Ten Global Cities Take on Homelessness: Innovations That Work*, which was a distillation of her outlook.[32] It was rife with corporate buzzwords like "strategic partnerships," "innovation," and "systems-level thinking." Most of all, it reflected the technocratic philosophy that homelessness, far from being the result of structural inequalities, was merely a problem to be managed.

In the book, Gibbs shared a telling anecdote. She mentioned the story of Jason-Eric Wilson, the teenager who killed himself in 2002 after his family had repeatedly been denied shelter on multiple occasions and had been forced to sleep overnight on the floors of the EAU (see chapter 6). Wilson's suicide was a tragedy that garnered enough public attention to lead to some reforms at the Bronx intake office. The circumstances of Wilson's death were plainly, inextricably linked to the brutal, punitive shelter-denial policies and practices inherited from the Giuliani era and later intensified by Bloomberg and Gibbs—policies that wrongfully denied shelter to tens of thousands of desperate families. Indeed, Wilson's father said that his son had killed himself out of fear of being sent back to the EAU.

In the face of all of this, Gibbs wrote that she "will always hold close the memory of Jason-Eric Wilson." Then, after a highly circumscribed and distorted account of the circumstances leading to his suicide—one that portrayed her agency's repeated denial of shelter to Wilson's family and their horrible mistreatment as merely a problem of missing paperwork and the family "shuttling around to government offices collecting the documentation"—she wrote the following: "That tragedy inspired me to put the system for integrated and shared case records across the finish line. HHS Connect now integrates select demographic detail, household data, service interactions, and case file documents from multiple city agencies. Rather than being sent to find these, families are now assisted by intake workers in composing their histories and telling their stories."[33]

What lay behind the tragic death of Jason-Eric Wilson, Gibbs seemed to suggest, was not a system that deliberately withheld shelter from vulnerable families, imposed arbitrary and excessive eligibility barriers on those in crisis, operated under a presumption of guilt for poor Black and Latino families, and maintained harsh, unwelcoming facilities. No, the problem was the lack of a database.

THE PRICE OF USING HOUSING AS SHELTER

The growing number of costly scatter-site shelter units—like the vermin-infested apartment where my colleague and I met Ava and her kids—was part of the catastrophic legacy of Bloomberg and Gibbs. In many ways, the program's flaws distilled the management and policy errors of the CEO mayor's administration.

The scatter-site shelter program also made the city's housing affordability crisis even worse. It effectively removed thousands of units of otherwise low-rent, rent-regulated housing from the city's housing stock. This created an incentive for the landlords to evict lease-holding tenants, something that we and other advocates increasingly encountered. An investigation by the local public radio station found a telling example of this dynamic: "Desperate for shelter space, New York City has been paying landlords in low income communities much more for their apartments than they could get in the private market. The result? Landlords are pushing out paying tenants to make room for the homeless. Melvina McMillan, a 40-year-old Flatbush woman, is one of those tenants now facing eviction. . . . 'We used to have like a lot of tenants. There's 83 apartments,' she said, describing her six-story building. 'Now roughly a dozen neighbors are hanging on.'"[34]

Most troubling of all, the scatter-site program served to enrich some of the worst slumlords in New York City, who owned many of the buildings used as costly temporary shelter. The most notorious of these slumlords were Jay and Stuart Podolsky, who benefited not only from the scatter-site program, but also from their ownership of several commercial "welfare hotels" also used as shelter. In 2013, *New York* magazine published a damning exposé of the Podolsky brothers by journalist Andrew Rice. Among other things, Rice's investigation uncovered their ties to a former Bloomberg official and their use of multiple shell companies and "front men" to obscure their ownership of at least forty properties used as shelter, which generated at least $90 million in revenue over two years. The article was succinctly headlined, "Why Run a Slum If You Can Make More Money Housing the Homeless?"[35]

By Bloomberg's last year at City Hall, just over half of all homeless families resided in for-profit shelter settings such as scatter-site units or welfare hotels.[36] Thus, beyond record homelessness and the incalculable misery inflicted on countless homeless children and families, there was another consequence of Bloomberg and Gibbs's ideological blindness and rigidity: Some of the most unsavory businessmen in New York made a fortune profiting from the crisis and their mishandling of it.

CHAPTER 9

ARMORIES: LABOR AND HOMELESSNESS

He is seeking to exorcise a history which is also a curse. He wants the old order, which came into existence through unchecked greed and wanton murder, to redeem itself without further bloodshed—without, that is, any further menacing itself—and without coercion. This, old orders never do, less because they would not than because they cannot. They cannot because they have always existed in relation to a force which they have had to subdue. This subjugation is the key to their identity and the triumph and justification of their history, and it is also on this continued subjugation that their material well-being depends.

James Baldwin
No Name in the Street

WORKING WOMEN

Glitter, mirrored glass, and pink-hued spotlights. Celebrities and fashion-industry groupies mingling amid the paparazzi and TV camera operators. Live performances by pop music stars like Marc Anthony, Destiny's Child, and Phil Collins. Statuesque models clad in nothing but tacky lingerie and stiletto heels, all unbelievably adorned with fluffy white wings. This was a Victoria's Secret runway show and PR stunt held in 2002 at an enormous, century-old building in Manhattan's Gramercy Park neighborhood. And in the same fortresslike edifice, built during the first Gilded Age, only a few dozen yards away through a battered metal door and up a flight of corroded stairs, was a shelter for homeless women.

Covering most of a Manhattan block and looming over Lexington Avenue, only four streets north of tony Gramercy Park, the 69th Regiment Armory had seldom seen a night like this. But in the years to come, it would host many more similarly gilded events. For the 165 homeless residents of the Lexington Avenue armory shelter—who heard the blasting music and felt the bass notes from the massive speakers through the hundred-year-old walls—the Victoria's Secret fashion show was a bizarre spectacle. I'd come to know 68 Lex, as the shelter was called, very well after dozens of inspections and troubleshooting visits throughout the mid-to-late 1990s. Because 68 Lex was what was known as a "working shelter," most of the homeless women were employed. They worked late-night shifts for meager wages at fast-food joints or cheap retail stores, and the shelter staff would often refuse them entry if their long work hours kept them out past the 10:00 p.m. curfew. So, on many nights, after my pager beeped, I'd hustle over to the shelter, often well after midnight, to stop the staff from denying shelter to residents. And sometimes I'd conduct an unannounced inspection of the facility, which, on its best days, was always cluttered, dingy, and rife with code violations and unsafe conditions.

But this Victoria's Secret extravaganza in November 2002, at the onset of the Bloomberg era in New York City—a fashion event whose plastic glamour, tabloid-hungry celebrity, and utter lack of irony seemed emblematic of the first decade of the new century—was something brazen and new. Here was the kind of shameless and frivolous glitz that didn't even pretend to notice the indigent women just a stone's throw away.

It became a cliché, and even a political slogan, to talk about the "tale of two cities" in New York—the billionaire elites contrasted with the legions of working poor, the fabulous wealth set against the harsh poverty. And there were indeed shelters located in affluent neighborhoods. In Brooklyn's well-to-do Park Slope neighborhood, the 14th Regiment Armory had a YMCA recreation facility frequented by Bill de Blasio before and during his tenure as mayor, and also contained a shelter for homeless women.[1] On Manhattan's Upper East Side—one of the wealthiest neighborhoods in the world—the 7th Regiment Armory stood on Park Avenue, only a dozen blocks away from the luxury townhouse of Mayor Michael Bloomberg. In the early decades of the twenty-first century, after renovations funded by affluent donors, the armory's vast halls would host a series of posh gallery shows, classical music recitals, and other arts spectacles for the city's elites—all while one hundred homeless women slept in a shelter on the armory's fourth floor.

But the large majority of shelters were found in low-income, Black and Latino communities—the same communities where New York City's increasingly impoverished working class resided. The geographical divide of wealth and poverty was growing wider as inequality worsened. So, as modern homelessness emerged in the New Gilded Age, city officials not only searched for out-of-the-way places to shelter the increasingly visible surplus population of homeless people. They also found literal fortresses in which to confine the poorest New Yorkers.

ARMORIES AS SHELTERS

Over the decades, New York City has used a dozen different armories as homeless shelters. In the 1980s, the four thousand shelter beds in armories made up around half of all municipal shelter beds for homeless single adults. Even in the early 2020s, after major downsizing, armories still provided one in ten shelter beds for homeless men and women.

Most of New York City's armories were constructed during the late nineteenth century's Gilded Age to train and temporarily quarter militias. While a few armories were, by the 1980s, still used for US National Guard units, many were effectively vacant. Because most were under government control—in this case, an obscure agency called the New York

State Department of Military and Naval Affairs—they could be converted into shelters virtually overnight.

For the tens of thousands of homeless New Yorkers who have slept in armory shelters over the decades, the fact that they were a hundred years old and never intended as residential buildings meant something else entirely: a litany of chronic, miserable, and often hazardous conditions, including unreliable utilities, warehouse-like dormitories, rodent infestations, gang-style showers, and the permanent stench of ammonia and other institutional cleansers. Getting a decent night's sleep in dormitories, sometimes with hundreds of residents crammed into cots three feet apart from one another, was a challenge. And tiny lockers and limited laundry access made it hard to keep work clothes clean.

The armories were immense, cavernous buildings that took up several city blocks and towered over their surrounding neighborhoods. They had huge drill floors, measuring forty thousand to sixty thousand square feet, under vaulted, usually arched ceilings fifty or more feet high. In the 1980s, the city government used the drill floors as sleeping space, with rows of hundreds of cots lined up under fluorescent lights. Some of the armories had well over five hundred residents—the Fort Washington armory in Washington Heights notoriously held twelve hundred beds, the Sumner Avenue armory six hundred, and the Franklin armory eight hundred—far exceeding the two-hundred-bed state limit. But in the early 1990s, as noted in chapter 2, advocates won class action lawsuits that forced nearly all the armories to be downsized to two hundred beds or fewer, effectively halting the use of drill floors as sleeping areas.[2]

The armories were designed to look like Gothic, medieval fortresses. They had turrets and arched doorways and tall, narrow windows with occasional iron grilles. Indeed, some armories even had cornices designed to allow for defensive measures such as pouring boiling oil onto attackers; all were designed so militiamen could fire upon crowds below. In many ways, as I came to discover over two decades of visiting armory shelters, the same things that made them seem impenetrable and impervious to assault also made them feel, for the homeless residents, like dungeons.

CASTLE GRAYSKULL: THE BEDFORD-ATLANTIC ARMORY, BROOKLYN

It was well after 2:00 a.m. on a simmering summer night in the mid-1990s. Talking to a homeless man on Atlantic Avenue, under the mammoth turret of the Bedford-Atlantic armory, I first heard the shelter's ominous, all-too-fitting nickname: Castle Grayskull.

I had earlier made a surprise, after-midnight visit to the armory after reports that the staff were denying beds to homeless men seeking shelter. Sure enough, I'd found a couple dozen men forced to sleep in grimy waiting rooms—some slumped over on benches, others passed out on the filthy linoleum floor—even though the 350-bed intake shelter had plenty of empty beds available. This was a sadly routine occurrence at many municipal shelters during the Giuliani years (see chapters 5 and 6), the result of the administration's deterrence policy that aimed to make the shelter system so horrendous and hard to access that many homeless men just gave up and remained on the streets.

After walking around the facility as discreetly as possible, I approached a shelter worker, alerted him that I was a court-sanctioned monitor, and explained how I'd found many violations of the long-standing *Callahan* consent decree. I proceeded to raise a ruckus, summoned a disaffected graveyard-shift supervisor, and managed to get the staff to provide beds to the exhausted homeless men.

Sometime later, I exited onto Bedford Avenue through the vast arched doorway, which still bears the vestiges of its functioning portcullis. The armory had been constructed in the 1890s, in the Romanesque revival style, to quarter the 23rd Regiment of the New York State Militia, and the edifice still had a martial aspect.[3] I stood on the corner of Atlantic Avenue, talking with one of the homeless guys who'd given up after being harassed; he knew the neighborhood and had decided to rough it on the streets until daylight. The guy offered to help get me home and flagged down a passing panel truck belonging to a neighborhood acquaintance, who agreed to take me to Manhattan for ten bucks. The driver later told me, as we crossed over the East River, that he had a couple of bales of marijuana with him in the back of his truck—which made that endless summer night even more surreal and ludicrous.

But before the contraband-laden drive to the bridge, the homeless man on the corner had been telling me about the terrible conditions in the Bedford-Atlantic armory, which he referred to several times as Castle Grayskull. When I later saw a picture from the 1980s-era *Masters of the Universe* cartoons, I instantly understood. The Bedford-Atlantic armory only needed the fearsome eyes above its mouthlike arched entryway, as well as the evil Skeletor and his minions, to become a real-life Castle Grayskull.

Over two decades, I began to appreciate the nickname even more. The Bedford-Atlantic armory had rightly earned its reputation as one of the worst-run shelters in New York City—a place marked by miserable conditions, sometimes brutal treatment by guards and staff, dark and cavernous barracks, and an inchoate feeling of menace. Despite all that, successive mayoral administrations have maintained Bedford-Atlantic as the largest entry-point shelter—meaning that around half of all homeless men entering the system have been forced to sleep inside Castle Grayskull.

THE SILK-STOCKING DISTRICT: THE PARK AVENUE ARMORY, MANHATTAN

According to historian Nancy Todd's encyclopedic history of New York's armories, the 7th Regiment Armory on Park Avenue was the "flagship" of the building type that would be replicated throughout the city in subsequent decades. Built between 1877 and 1881 in one of New York's fanciest neighborhoods, the armory reflected its affluent environs. Known as the Silk-Stocking Regiment before the Civil War, the 7th's civic reputation always augmented its military role.[4]

By the twenty-first century, the lavish wealth of the neighborhood was still on display, but never more so than at a singular birthday party one night in 2007. The billionaire head of the Blackstone Group, Stephen Schwarzman, held his extravagant, phenomenally expensive sixtieth birthday party at the Park Avenue armory with one hundred guests in attendance, including Donald Trump.[5] *The New Yorker* described the setting: "Part of the cavernous Park Avenue armory was transformed into a large-scale replica of the Schwarzmans' Manhattan apartment by Philip Baloun, the party planner who designed the Prince Charles gala at Lincoln Center. Replicas of Schwarzman's art collection were mounted on the walls, including, at the entrance, a full-length portrait of him by Andrew Festing, the president of the Royal Society of Portrait Painters. Dinner was served in a faux night-club setting, with orchids and palm trees. Guests dined on lobster, filet mignon, and baked Alaska, and were offered an array of expensive wines."

The lavish display of wealth was to become more commonplace in Bloomberg-era New York, with its billionaire oligarchy, and was characteristic of the luxury-obsessed hedge-fund titan Schwarzman, as *The New Yorker* reported:

> In 2006, he paid $34 million for a Federal-style house, on eight acres on Mecox Bay, in the Hamptons, that was previously owned by the Vanderbilt heir Carter Burden. Schwarzman also owns a coastal estate in Saint-Tropez and a beachfront property in Jamaica. He typically spends summer weekends and August in East Hampton; July in Saint-Tropez; and winter weekends

in Palm Beach. His children use the house in Jamaica; he rarely goes there. The five properties and their renovations appear to have cost Schwarzman at least a hundred and twenty-five million dollars. "I love houses," he told me recently. "I'm not sure why."

The women's shelter was located on an upper floor of the armory with a concealed side entrance, seemingly designed to keep it hidden from the genteel neighbors. When I first visited in the 1990s, it was still a city-run facility with, at-best, mediocre conditions. For some of the oldest residents, the Park Avenue armory was the last home they ever expected to have, and they made themselves as comfortable there as one could expect. But because the shelter was on an upper floor with no elevator, and thus had to be reached by a narrow stairwell, it became inaccessible for some aging women. There were terrible instances when residents who could no longer climb the stairs were involuntarily "transferred" to another, more accessible but usually less welcoming shelter or to a nursing home. Thus, these elderly women, who'd lost their homes and so much else, were displaced and uprooted yet again.

BOOGIE DOWN: THE FRANKLIN ARMORY, THE BRONX

Dubbed the Second Battery Armory when it was built between 1908 and 1911, the massive structure on Franklin Avenue and East 166th Street in the Bronx's Morrisania neighborhood won widespread praise from architectural critics. A 1910 issue of *Architecture* magazine described it as "probably the best in the city of New York. . . . The architecture is of a curious and fascinating style; powerful without being brutal, original without being bizarre. . . . The composition is exceedingly picturesque and has not been carried to a point which entails a sacrifice of the dignity so essential in a public building."[6] Decades later, the National Guard abandoned the building and the city government converted it to a shelter.

For most of its time as a shelter, the Franklin armory was temporary home to homeless men. Until the advocates' legal victories of the early 1990s (see chapter 2), some eight hundred men were sheltered there each night, most on the cavernous drill floor, until its court-ordered downsizing. Much later the city government closed a women's shelter in another Bronx armory, located on Kingsbridge Avenue, and the Franklin armory was converted to a two-hundred-bed women's shelter, with the same dismal conditions that thousands of homeless men had already endured for two decades.

But on one occasion I caught a firsthand glimpse of the miseries of the drill floor, repurposed as a temporary shelter. After New York City was battered by Hurricane Sandy in late October 2012 (see chapter 12), the Bloomberg administration shuttled poor families displaced from the Rockaways and other flooded areas to evacuation centers citywide, many of which were located in schools. But by November, the administration hastily closed the school-based evacuation centers and, with no advance notice to desperate families, moved them to drill floors like those at the Franklin armory, which were hastily reopened as emergency shelters. In sadly typical fashion, the planning was haphazard, and the conditions were dismal for the displaced families.

For me, the most shocking sight on the Franklin armory drill floor after Hurricane Sandy was the presence of infants and toddlers. City officials had bused dozens of evacuees to the building, which, like most armories, had never before been used to shelter children and families. Cots were either scattered or mashed together on the cold and unyielding floor beneath threadbare blankets. The families I interviewed, who all seemed dazed by unresolved shock and sleeplessness, complained of shortages of diapers and food, of being forced to share a single shower and crowded bathrooms, and especially about not knowing where they would be sleeping night to night.

One of those families was that of Tareste Etienne and his four children, who recounted their experiences to Nina Bernstein of *The New York Times*: "On Nov. 6 they were roused in the night, herded onto buses with hundreds of others and left at the Franklin Avenue Armory in the Bronx. 'It's like you were being processed to go to jail,' Mr. Etienne said, echoing many others who described waiting for hours in the cold to enter a vast sea of cots under constant fluorescent lights, with one shower for everybody and one toilet for men, where guards yelled into two-way radios all night."[7] The families were eventually relocated from the Franklin armory to temporary hotel placements, where they endured a long wait for housing aid.

The Franklin armory was also the one shelter that figured prominently in the history of hip-hop. In 1986, a young homeless Brooklynite named Kris Parker, who'd bounced around from sleeping on the streets to a youth shelter in the South Bronx and back to the streets, made his way to the armory on Franklin Avenue. There, he met a young caseworker named Scott Sterling, who also spent nights spinning records at local clubs. Together, Parker, who was already calling himself KRS-One, and Sterling, who came to be known as DJ Scott La Rock, joined with DJ Derrick "D-Nice" Jones, the cousin of a shelter security guard, to form the legendary hip-hop group Boogie Down Productions. Later, after the release of their classic album *Criminal Minded*, Scott La Rock was shot and killed in a fight in the Bronx. But KRS-One continued the group in honor of his friend and mentor.

Nearly a decade later, a longtime shelter supervisor and I sat in the drab, impersonal office used by the social work staff—the kind of gray, soul-deadening compartment that permeated the shelter system—and he pointed to the wall behind me. There, in the plaster, he told me, Scott La Rock had etched his name right around the time he ended his years of working in the shelter. The old-timer said that La Rock, with whom he'd briefly worked, had always treated the homeless men with respect. And he said there was a chance that La Rock had met KRS-One in the very office where we were sitting.

DO OR DIE: THE SUMNER AVENUE ARMORY, BROOKLYN

Over the years, I saw many depressing, deplorable things occur at the Sumner Avenue armory in Bedford-Stuyvesant: homeless men punished like misbehaving toddlers merely for complaining about poor conditions or food; shower rooms infested with black mold; shelter staff attempting to hide extra, prohibited beds behind improvised barriers on the frigid drill floor. But for some reason, the thing I remembered most about the Sumner Avenue armory was the bowling alley.

One day, a friendly and talkative maintenance supervisor offered to take me on a tour of the unseen parts of the 13th Regiment Armory, as it was officially known, which had been built between 1892 and 1894. It once had six hundred beds scattered across its drill floor, but after its court-ordered downsizing in the early 1990s, the two-hundred-bed men's shelter occupied only a fraction of the building. This was one reason a local nonprofit group contracted to operate the shelter, with the hope of creating a community center; the necessary repairs ultimately proved far too costly, and the group abandoned the contract.

The supervisor first took me up to see the upper stories, with uneven and creaky hardwood floors, peeling paint, and flaking plaster on the walls. We entered one of the gigantic turrets that looked out, from windows in curved walls, over the brownstones and rowhouses of Bed-Stuy. Finally, we descended to the armory's basement and walked through a dark, dank series of corridors. All at once, we happened upon the bowling alley. Everything was covered in a film of dust, and the skinny boards forming the lanes were crooked and curling up in places. The presence of this ancient alley was so incongruous—just a flight of stairs below a bleak homeless shelter—that I almost missed noticing the compartment behind the lanes where the "pin boy" of old once crouched to gather and reset the scattered bowling pins.

Another peculiar thing the maintenance supervisor told me was that there was an underground tunnel that connected the Sumner Avenue armory to the nearby Bedford-Atlantic armory and to others in Brooklyn. I never got a chance to explore those tunnels; in fact, I could never confirm that they really existed. But I welcomed the fanciful idea of a network of underground passages linking the century-old fortresses of New York. And I sometimes imagined they offered the homeless residents of the modern era a secret passageway or escape route from one armory to another, and maybe a way out of homelessness itself.

ARMORIES IN THE GILDED AGE

It was a striking and deeply troubling historical irony that these castles for New York's urban militias, which dated back to the first Gilded Age, had become makeshift, warehouse-like repositories for the poorest people of the New Gilded Age. In this way, the brutal history of the armories continued into modern times.

During the Civil War–era draft riots of 1863, workers rose up to oppose the conscription of poor New Yorkers into military service; the protests then morphed into violent attacks by Irish and other European immigrants on Black residents. In response to the draft riots and later worker uprisings, like the 1874 gathering in Tompkins Square (see chapter 2), the city's elites expanded the militias to put down future unrest. Hence began the great armory-building project of the Gilded Age.

The armories were never, as some have mistakenly believed, intended to protect New York City from invasion. Rather, they were designed to protect the elites from the workers. As historian Kim Phillips-Fein noted, the Park Avenue armory, for instance, was "a structure built in the late nineteenth century for a national guard regiment assigned to protect the mansions of upper Manhattan from the envious hordes it was feared might come marauding from tenements farther east."[8] As Todd noted in her history of the armories, the "primary role" of the National Guard was "as the keeper of domestic peace during the late nineteenth-century era of labor-capital conflict." She went on: "The antebellum disturbances and the Civil War Draft Riots paled in comparison to the labor-capital conflicts that plagued much of the nation during the Gilded Age, which spanned the last third of the nineteenth century. . . . Clever, ambitious and sometimes unscrupulous entrepreneurs and leaders of burgeoning new industries ascended to previously unimaginable heights of power; concurrently, many others descended into the depths of poverty and despair. America . . . was suddenly stratified, with an ever-widening gap between rich and poor."[9]

The brutal economic depression of the 1870s inspired further labor unrest, prompting New York City elites to mobilize a military response to worker movements. The first major effort by the militias to quell a labor rebellion was the Great Railroad Strike of 1877, when one hundred thousand workers nationwide protested wage cuts triggered by the monopolistic collusion of the Baltimore and Ohio Railroad and other rail companies. The strike spread to the Erie and Central lines in New York, with the governor declaring martial law in Albany. According to historians Edwin G. Burrows and Mike Wallace, however, it never reached New York City, largely because of "a phenomenal mobilization of military might directed at would-be strikers and supporters, and, in sharp contrast to other urban battlegrounds, a closure of ranks and hearts by the upper and middle classes against the urban working class and its depression-era hardships."[10] State militias and federal troops put down the strike, killing at least one hundred people, as New York City guardsmen were sent to Buffalo and other upstate towns.

The militias had also been sent earlier, in 1871, to quell worker protests and strikes near Rochester along the Erie Canal, and four years later to the cement works in Rosendale, in the Hudson Valley. In 1892, in one of the bloodiest and most violent reprisals, the National Guard put down the Buffalo Switchmen's Strike, during which workers rose up against several rail companies to protest poor pay and workplace conditions. The strike, which covered eight hundred miles of track, ultimately took seven thousand guardsmen to suppress.[11]

New York City was also the site of labor struggles subdued by the National Guard. In 1895, the militias used horrendous violence and massive force to put down the Brooklyn Trolley Strike. Labor groups representing conductors, motormen, and other workers called the strike in January to protest long working hours and low wages. The National Guard, with three thousand troops from Manhattan and four thousand from Brooklyn, violently suppressed the labor action, ending it two weeks later. As historian Don Mitchell described it, "The mobilization of military might worked. With the guns on their side and with scab recruits willing to brave the crowds for a paycheck, the trolley bosses were able to wait the strikers out. Striking workers, suffering the loss of pay, began to drift back to work (when the companies would have them), and the strike fizzled."[12]

In the late nineteenth century, in the midst of soaring inequality, the urban militias of the National Guard became essential to protecting the interests of capital and the gilded elites against increasingly restless workers. Ten armories were built in New York in the two decades after the Great Railroad Strike, and another dozen in the early decades of the twentieth century. As Todd wrote, "The sudden increase in armory construction during the 1880s and 1890s in New York State was the direct reflection of this meteoric rise in prestige and popularity of the National Guard during the Gilded Age."[13]

In 1874, budget cuts by the New York State Legislature halted construction of the Park Avenue armory. But the experience of the Great Railroad Strike of 1877—which paralyzed travel in much of the country for weeks—spurred wealthy magnates like John Jacob Astor and William H. Vanderbilt to contribute nearly $600,000 to finish construction. As the historians Burrows and Wallace noted, "When it opened in 1879 it was the finest armory in the world. Its huge hall, ample enough to accommodate regimental maneuvers, was stoutly defended by a bronze gate, a bronze portcullis, and a solid oak door half a foot thick. Loopholes for riflemen enfiladed all approaches, and two or three gatling guns could be quickly mounted in the tower to sweep Fourth [eventually Madison] Avenue."[14]

While the elites and their echo-chamber newspapers of the day praised the role of the militias in subduing labor unrest, there were critical voices. The labor-aligned *New York Sun* wrote that the creation of a virtual standing army threatened "a radical revolution of our whole republican system of government."[15] Another social-reform journal spoke out against the militarization of American cities in stark terms:

> [The country] is becoming a mighty armed camp, with enormous armories, not infrequently erected and furnished by individuals, for companies and regiments of troops who can be relied upon as being absolutely loyal to capital in any struggle between plutocracy or corporate greed and slaving industry. . . . And for this reason every true patriot and lover of the republic should discourage the war spirit and seek to check the spread of the military tendency which plutocracy is so energetically fostering at the present time. . . . [Armories are] bastiles of death which speak in such an unmistakable manner of the real materialism of the age.[16]

LABOR IN THE NEW GILDED AGE

The surviving armories of the twenty-first century still loomed over the low-slung neighborhoods of Brooklyn, Queens, and the Bronx, and even stood out in denser, high-rise Manhattan. But in the New Gilded Age, they presented a different kind of threat. It was not so much the imminence of militia attacks on the populace, given that only a handful quartered active National Guard units. In fact, when visiting armory shelters, I was always struck by the irony of how many military veterans resided in these fortresses: the homeless Vietnam-era veterans, many afflicted with posttraumatic stress disorder and other injuries, who made up such a huge part of the first wave of modern homelessness; the later cohort of Gulf War vets; and the subsequent, larger wave of Afghanistan and Iraq war veterans, many also with PTSD. By some measures, as many as a third of homeless men nationwide were veterans, and the number of homeless women who were also vets was increasing.[17]

But a larger, more indeterminate irony concerned the armories' historical role in managing, and ultimately suppressing, the labor unrest of the past—specifically, the armories' role in regulating, however violently, the discontent of the working class during an earlier Gilded Age and its aftermath. In the modern era of worsening inequality, the armories have assumed a more subtle role: bleak refuge and implicit threat.

In the New Gilded Age, the shelters concealed in New York City's armories were full of homeless workers struggling to survive. City data showed that at least a quarter of homeless adults in shelters and around a third of homeless families were employed. And others worked "off the books" in New York's vast underground economy.

Many were living vestiges of an older image of the working class—day laborers, handymen, welders, pipe fitters, carpenters, and other manual workers of all kinds. They had been discarded for one reason or another, whether due to layoffs, economic downturns, age, injury, or disability;

and sometimes those setbacks, followed by additional hardships, would lead to drinking, depression, or other struggles. I'd shake hands in greeting with homeless men whose rough, calloused hands bore the marks of longtime laborers. Many were clad in dusty, worn work boots, forced to stuff uniforms or canvas jackets into their too-small lockers. They were, in short, the working class of a vanishing era.

Then, too, there were the homeless workers who epitomized the urban working class of the twenty-first century. These were the countless homeless women I met who worked as home health aides, retail salesclerks, or house cleaners. There were other men and women I met who worked similarly low-wage jobs: bike messengers, warehouse workers, janitors, delivery people, even, in the upstate fields nearby the Camp LaGuardia shelter, farm laborers. I met innumerable security guards, working for low-wage rent-a-cop companies, who were homeless—including many who worked as guards in the shelter system itself.

During the Fight for Fifteen campaign launched late in the Bloomberg era—an ultimately successful struggle by community organizations and labor unions to get New York lawmakers to raise the state's minimum wage to fifteen dollars an hour—many of the fast-food workers on the front lines of rallies and protests were homeless. *The New York Times* profiled Terrence Wise, one of the leaders of the campaign, who worked sixteen-hour days at both Burger King and Pizza Hut and arrived home "around 11 p.m., after his daughters had gone to sleep. 'The kids started saying, "Daddy, we never get to see you,"' said Mr. Wise, 35. The situation worsened when Burger King cut back his hours and his fiancée was sidelined from work with a back injury. Despite his working two jobs, he and his family were evicted from their apartment, leaving them homeless for three months."[18]

And then, of course, there were the unemployed workers. As anthropologist Kim Hopper has noted, the disproportionately high unemployment rate of Black homeless men—and Black men generally—in the 1980s and afterward explained part of their overrepresentation in the homeless population; and this did not even account for the vast numbers of Black men incarcerated in prisons and jails, another factor contributing to discarded populations being made invisible.[19]

It was in this sense that the function of correctional facilities, armories, and shelters was not so dissimilar. They were brick-and-mortar reminders of where one might end up if the bottom dropped out. In the shifting late-capitalist economy of the New Gilded Age, so many low-wage workers had become literal surplus labor—what the British would call "surplus to requirements." They'd become the unneeded refuse of an age characterized by stagnant or falling incomes for the laboring class and fewer protections from dwindling unions or government, but persistently soaring housing costs. Where were they supposed to go if not on the streets? Where did the city place the broken, surplus laborers? New York's answer, in the newest age of inequality, was this: in the monuments and shrines to the last Gilded Age—within the armories.

CHAPTER 10

THREE-QUARTER HOUSES: "PERMANENT HOUSING" AND HOMELESSNESS

For this is the means and moment by which the city's very soil and bedrock, and the air above both, is turned into an urban commodity whose "use value," as the Marxists might say, is continually and ever more quickly outstripped by its price as a salable fiction—a number on a piece of paper or in the market's mind—to speculators. This is the signal moment in the defining activity of a city long animated by what Alexander Hamilton called its investors' "rage of getting rich in a day." Theirs is a particular faith, when it comes to real estate, long intrinsic to city life: that the price of its real estate will, day by day and year on year, charge ever upward like the "supertalls" that now line Central Park South and whose $100 million apartments in the sky aren't mainly places to live but to park and grow cash. And the truth that this faith has, year on year and decade by decade, by and large been borne out (with, of course, a few notable exceptions when everyone took a bath) is a fact vital to how the city has grown up, how it's grown out, and who runs its show.

Joshua Jelly-Schapiro
Names of New York

ALBERTA'S HOUSE

Over more than two decades working with homeless and poor New Yorkers, I witnessed some awful treatment of vulnerable people, including genuinely horrific conditions in shelters like Bellevue and intake offices like the EAU. But almost nothing was worse than what I saw one summer day in 2006 in a Brooklyn townhouse located in an ungentrified stretch between the Bedford-Stuyvesant and Bushwick neighborhoods. Shelters had been forcing homeless men to move to a place known as Alberta's House, calling it "permanent housing," and if they didn't go there, sight unseen in some cases, they'd be ejected from the shelter system. So, dozens of men had unwillingly been dumped there, and some told us horror stories about the site—overcrowded, infested with bed bugs, and run by a man who regularly threatened them and demanded they give him their food stamps and other meager benefits.

My colleague and I walked up to the door of the derelict, four-story brick building that afternoon and persuaded the man who answered the door to let us in, explaining half truthfully that we were looking for places to send our homeless clients. Of course, one glance at the squalid quarters and I knew I'd never wish anyone to stay even one night there. We visited a couple of filthy rooms crowded with austere steel bunk beds and thin mattresses. Spaces that would normally have housed one or two people at most had six or even eight beds.

Then we entered the ground-floor room at the front of the house. There, sprawled on the hard floor, were two passed-out older men, one so skinny he looked emaciated, lying on bare, shabby cloth mattresses soaked in urine. One of the men was spilling off his bedding onto the hard floor, and both were wearing ragged, dirty T-shirts and boxers. The sight of the broken-down men in that ragged room, smelling of piss and despair, was something I could never forget—far and away one of the most depressing places I'd ever seen homeless people forced to inhabit.

The guy who'd let us into the house said both men were sick and had just taken medication. We were tempted to call 911 but hesitated, thinking that involving the police might make their bad situation even worse.

But later we did report the house to state health officials. At that time, such officials rarely if ever took necessary steps to protect vulnerable people. But in this instance, they actually ordered the house shut down, as *The New York Times* reported: "Inspectors said that they found 67 men in bedrooms that were 'very overcrowded, dirty and having foul odor,' sleeping on mattresses infested with 'bedbugs the size of roaches,' and using bathrooms that were 'filthy without toilet paper, no soap, no towels and no washcloths.' The report . . . also noted that food, medical oversight and medical dispensation were inadequate."[1]

The operator of Alberta's House was a man named Daryl Evans, who ran at least two such illegal boardinghouses that had, over the years, come to be called "three-quarter houses." He was later charged by the state attorney general with illegally operating a care home and defrauding his tenants, but he couldn't see what he'd done wrong—in his view, he was just filling a gap in the housing system.

It wasn't hard to see how Evans came to that conclusion. For decades, New York City had relied on informal and illegal dwellings of various types to patch the holes in its inadequate stock of housing, whether they were cellars, illegal conversions, dormitories, or dangerous and unlawful boardinghouses like Alberta's House. But the problem had grown much worse in the early twenty-first century, fueled in part by a rising population of low-income people looking for any place they could afford.

As described in chapters 5 and 8, Mayor Bloomberg and Linda Gibbs spent nearly a decade running a vast, high-stakes social experiment on homeless New Yorkers—replacing federal housing aid with defective, short-term rent subsidies or with nothing at all. The outcome was devastating: unprecedented levels of homelessness and long-term harm to countless families and children. At the same time, they quietly subjected homeless single adults—many living with serious health issues—to similar dangers by funneling them into hazardous, unlawful dwellings.

New York City's leaders called these arrangements "permanent housing." But what the parallel experiments had in common was an unspoken assumption not only about the quality of housing these desperately poor and homeless people deserved—unsafe, exploitative, even life-threatening—but also something more alarming: a tacit admission in the form of official policy that, for poor New Yorkers, housing was never "permanent," and that much of New York's housing system was a revolving door back to homelessness.

ILLEGAL BOARDING HOUSES AND THE GREAT RECESSION

The first three-quarter houses I heard about were run by a quasireligious group that called itself the JUSTICE Organization and, in the mid-1990s, distributed flyers in homeless shelters looking for residents. The group had a few old houses in the Rockaways, which they loaded with bunk beds, and recruited addicts with promises of a Christian-influenced twelve-step treatment program, a cot, and strict house rules. In practice, they treated residents harshly, often kicking them out on the streets for no reason, in blatant violation of housing laws. I later worked with J. A. Lobbia, one of the best housing journalists I ever encountered, to include the JUSTICE Organization on the *Village Voice*'s annual list of the "Ten Worst Landlords in New York," and eventually the group closed down.

From then until the twenty-first century, the basic model of the three-quarter house remained the same. A fly-by-night organization, often no more than a single unscrupulous individual with creative paperwork, bought or leased a building, usually a single-family home or a townhouse. The group then recruited desperate people from homeless shelters, jails, hospitals, prisons, addiction treatment programs, even the streets. The group took a resident's welfare housing allowance as rent and demanded extra payments, including all of an individual's food stamp benefits. Many three-quarter houses posed as addiction treatment programs, sometimes calling themselves "recovery residences" or "sober homes." A few also pretended to offer services for people living with mental illness. But none of this was true. All of them offered little more than a cot, usually in a small room crowded with bunk beds. None of them treated their residents like genuine tenants with actual rights, meaning they would throw people out on a whim.

The three-quarter house name obviously evoked the old "halfway house" model, which dated back to at least the 1950s and was far more common outside New York. It referred to a supervised, restrictive boarding house for people discharged from prison or jail, often parolees. The idea was that it would be a stepping stone for "ex-cons" back to "society," hopefully leading to a job and their own home. The reality was always more complicated and fraught. As the Prison Policy Initiative, a progressive advocacy group, wrote in a 2021 report, "Contrary to the belief that halfway houses are supportive service providers, the majority of halfway houses are an extension of the carceral experience, complete with surveillance, onerous restrictions, and intense scrutiny."[2] And terrible conditions in the largely privatized halfway houses, including brutal treatment and exploitation, had been rampant nationwide—a model that was definitely reproduced in the three-quarter houses of early twenty-first-century New York City.[3]

Beginning around 2006, despite the fact that the dangerous and unlawful nature of three-quarter houses was well known, the Bloomberg administration made it official city policy to dump thousands of homeless adults into these illegal dwellings. One immediate result of the Bloomberg policy, which funneled more residents to the operators of these dangerous homes, was the proliferation of three-quarter houses throughout the city, effectively creating a dispersed skid row. Over more than two years we tracked the problem, and my colleague Lindsey Davis wrote a comprehensive report documenting our findings: hazardous, even life-threatening conditions in buildings; severe overcrowding; restrictive and punitive rules akin to the carceral model of many halfway houses; an absence of any support services, even in homes that claimed to be "rehabilitative"; routine exploitation, including demands for money that the indigent residents simply did not have; blatant denial of basic tenancy rights even though the residents were, under New York law, rent-paying tenants; and frequent threats and acts of violence against residents.[4]

We repeatedly informed Linda Gibbs and other top Bloomberg officials of these problems, yet they refused to halt placements into three-quarter houses, or even to take minimal steps, like requiring shelters to assess buildings for hazardous conditions before sending people there. But there was also a level of absurdity about the Bloomberg administration's actions. Just as the homeless services agency was placing vulnerable people in dangerous homes, other city agencies, like the Department of Buildings and the New York City Fire Department, were ordering the homes shut down. Indeed, by early 2008, we found at least ten illegal homes that had been "condemned" and vacated by city inspectors. I attended a hearing in the Bronx organized by a state legislator concerned about the proliferation of dangerous homes in his district. A uniformed Fire Department official testified about his agency's strong opposition to three-quarter houses. He highlighted the enormous risk of fire from overburdened electrical systems, and the fear that firefighters could die trying to rescue people from overcrowded dwellings. But under tense questioning by the legislator, he awkwardly refused to condemn the homeless services agency for creating and fueling the problem in the first place; it became clear that he had been instructed by City Hall not to call out another city agency for endangering firefighters.

Over time, we investigated and visited dozens of illegal boarding houses, meeting countless men and women who had even worse experiences there than when they'd technically been homeless. One of them was Pascual, who'd been dumped by a municipal shelter into an illegal home called Phil's Recovery Residence on Kingston Avenue in central Brooklyn. Pascual told us that he had multiple sclerosis and required regular injections, but the operator of the home would not allow a visiting nurse to enter the premises. He also got numerous bedbug bites while staying there. The operator of Pascual's residence was the same Daryl Evans who ran Alberta's House.[5]

The Fort Washington armory, at that time a shelter for homeless men diagnosed with mental illness, sent at least nine of its residents to a three-quarter house on Sumpter Street in central Brooklyn, a horrendously overcrowded dwelling with numerous documented code violations and no services whatsoever for the men. In July 2007, an exterior wall of the home collapsed, and the Department of Buildings ordered the house vacated. One of the men placed there was Mohammed, who told us that he had been approved for New York / New York supportive housing prior to being sent to the illegal boarding house. His approval documents recommended that he receive "ongoing psychiatric treatment" and other support services. Nevertheless, a shelter worker told Mohammed that, because Bloomberg had a plan to reduce the homeless population, the shelter "could not wait" for him to obtain supportive housing, and instead he would have to go to the illegal, collapsing house on Sumpter Street.[6]

My colleagues and I waged a frustrating, yearslong battle to get city and state government officials to protect the residents of three-quarter houses. We held multiple meetings with New York State Department of Health officials, and their pretzel-logic response was to assert that, because the homes didn't offer any real services, they couldn't regulate them as care facilities—even though countless people with disabilities were living in them.[7] Bloomberg administration officials were worse. It was clear that Bloomberg and Gibbs viewed three-quarter houses as an escape valve for the shelter system at a time when the homeless population was growing.

Another factor that fueled the growth of illegal boarding houses was the mid-2000s subprime mortgage crisis. Central Brooklyn, where the majority of three-quarter houses were located, was one of the areas of New York City hardest hit by the wave of mortgage foreclosures that triggered the Great Recession. Many of the Brooklyn foreclosures involved small multifamily buildings like townhouses. Over time, we came to discover that most of the shady operators of three-quarter houses didn't even own the buildings in which they crammed poor men and women. Instead, they leased the buildings from some entity that had acquired a foreclosed property. In this way, the homeless people dumped into three-quarter houses became more casualties of the worst housing-related financial crisis of the century.

NO STABILITY AND NO ADVANTAGE

After cutting off federal housing aid to homeless families in 2003, Bloomberg rolled out his first replacement subsidy program. It was called Housing Stability Plus, which reflected both PR spin and willful misdirection about its fatally flawed design. Unlike federal housing vouchers, which provided assistance as long as the poor household needed it, the HSP program was limited to five years, no matter the family's circumstances. Even worse, during those five years, the value of the rent subsidy, which began at levels close to that of federal vouchers, declined by 20 percent each year. This meant that a family of three or four people received a maximum monthly rent subsidy of $925 in the first year—barely enough at that time to rent a suitable apartment in a low-income neighborhood. The monthly subsidy declined to just $505 by the fifth year, and then fell to zero after that.[8]

Bloomberg administration officials defended the HSP subsidy's time limit and declining value by making the usual right-wing appeals to personal responsibility and the need to work.[9] But in the New York City labor market of that time, this was a deeply irrational expectation. In 2004, the minimum wage statewide was a skimpy $5.15 per hour, and the average wage for low-income workers was only $8.63 per hour.[10]

But there was another catch. Although Bloomberg officials tried to obscure this fact, it emerged that HSP recipients would have to maintain open, active welfare cases to receive the rent subsidy. Because welfare rules essentially barred paid employment, this meant that HSP recipients could not work. We heard from many people who wanted to work but were told they could not, or who were ordered to quit their jobs.[11] Their stories echoed that of Lisa Hendley, whose situation was described in a *New York Times* article:

> Ms. Hendley and her daughter, now 5, moved into a one-
> bedroom apartment in the Bronx in February 2005 after living
> in a shelter for victims of domestic violence. Ms. Hendley, a high
> school graduate, found an $8-an-hour job packaging groceries for
> Fresh Direct, the online grocery delivery service, in June 2005.
> But she said she quit the job after a Department of Homeless
> Services caseworker told her that she could not continue to work
> and receive the rental assistance. Ms. Hendley said that the
> apartment, which costs $820 a month, was infested with rats
> and roaches and often had no water. "I'm constantly running in
> circles, without end," said Ms. Hendley, who said she also lacked
> adequate child care.[12]

We also heard many stories about HSP families who lost their apartments because the city welfare agency had cut off or suspended their benefits—a continuation of the "churning" policy begun during the Giuliani years.[13] Only much later, more than two years after the launch of the program, did Bloomberg administration officials acknowledge, as the *Times* reported, "that many more families on Housing Stability Plus had faced such disruptions in their welfare than the city had predicted—65 percent instead of the anticipated 20 percent."[14] The scandalous 65 percent figure confirmed the existence of systematic errors in both the welfare system and the HSP program. But it was equally alarming, and revealing, that Bloomberg administration officials had moved forward with the program even while assuming that one in every five families would lose their rent subsidy and face eviction due to those mistakes.

By early 2007, three things had become inescapably clear. First, the early signs of the Great Recession were driving more and more New Yorkers into homelessness. Second, at the midpoint of Bloomberg's five-year plan to reduce homelessness, New York's homeless population was *rising*, and the number of homeless families approached record levels.[15] And third, the HSP program was not working, even by the administration's skimpy metrics. A Bloomberg official, in a moment of uncharacteristic candor, told the *Times* that, because landlords had grown frustrated with welfare and subsidy interruptions, the number of apartments in the HSP program had dropped by 14 percent since the previous year. He also acknowledged what previous officials had denied but was obvious: that the program's rules were a "work disincentive."[16]

With the collapse of the HSP program, Bloomberg and Gibbs announced another replacement rent subsidy: the Work Advantage program. Like its predecessor, the rent subsidy was time limited. But the Advantage program terminated rental assistance after only *two* years. To everyone familiar with the reality of housing in New York, it was obvious that the program was nothing more than a ticking time bomb for vulnerable families—when their subsidy was cut off after two years, most Advantage families would inevitably become homeless again.

By the end of 2009, according to an analysis by my Coalition colleague Giselle Routhier, around one thousand formerly homeless Advantage families had already returned to the shelter system, and thousands more were due to lose their rent subsidies the following year.[17] Four years later, we updated the analysis, and the findings were even more alarming. Nearly half of all Advantage families had returned to the shelter system. Some 8,500 formerly homeless families, with eighteen thousand children, had been forced back into homelessness by the program's deeply flawed design. And our analysis showed that the returning families had already cost the city government $287 million—an astounding figure that steadily increased over time as more families lost their subsidies and returned to the costly shelter system.[18]

The Bloomberg administration refused numerous calls to fix the Advantage program, and ultimately the flawed subsidy ended due to a budget skirmish with another stubborn, right-wing politician, Governor Andrew Cuomo. He objected to the state government covering roughly half the cost of the Advantage program, and his administration needed to make budget cuts amid the lingering economic downturn. The universal criticism of the Advantage program gave Cuomo an excuse to cut state funding for the program. But Bloomberg, too, chose not to pay for his own program going forward, and in 2011, he decided to shut it down.[19]

In the last year of Bloomberg's mayoralty, I attended a conference at New York University with Linda Gibbs as one of the featured speakers. She made her opening statement, praising Bloomberg and the administration. Then she was asked a question about Housing Stability Plus. She admitted that their internal data had shown early on that the program was a failure—that huge numbers of HSP families were losing their homes and returning to the shelter system because of the time-limited, five-year subsidies. So, she said, they decided to abandon the program and replace it with the Advantage program. But then she caught herself, and in a moment of what I could only think was accidental candor, she said something like, "So, why did we replace a five-year rent subsidy that wasn't working with a shorter, two-year subsidy? Well, the truth is, it was just too expensive to do more."

The cruel irony, of course, was that those "cheaper," time-limited subsidies ended up being *more* expensive for the city government and taxpayers—generating hundreds of millions in shelter costs as families were caught in a revolving door back to homelessness. But there was another cost to those flawed programs and the decade-long social experiment conducted by Bloomberg and Gibbs, which could not be measured in dollars.

There was overwhelming evidence that homelessness inflicted long-term, sometimes permanent damage on children. Research dating back to the 1990s found that, even compared to other poor but housed kids, homeless children were more likely to experience acute and chronic health problems, exhibit greater instances of developmental delays, and endure higher rates of clinical depression, anxiety, and behavior problems. Homeless kids were also found to miss more school days, perform worse on tests, and be more likely to repeat grades.

The Bloomberg and Gibbs social experiment, then, unnecessarily scarred and damaged the lives of tens of thousands of children. And the New York experiment had a nationwide impact. One in every six homeless families in the United States during those years resided in a New York City shelter. And other city and state governments began to experiment with time-limited rent subsidies. Indeed, in the early months of his second term, Donald Trump's administration talked about imposing time limits on federal housing programs. The revolving door back to homelessness became a template for the growth of family homelessness nationwide.

NEW YORK CITY'S HOUSING AFFORDABILITY CRISIS

This revolving door of neoliberal initiatives took place against the backdrop of New York City's worsening housing affordability crisis. A confluence of city, state, and federal policies, alongside structural shifts in the city's economy, decisively shaped the growing instability. And as with modern mass homelessness, the scale and severity became increasingly hard to comprehend.

By the 2020s, New York City's housing stock had grown to 3.7 million units. Of these, 2.3 million were rental apartments, and nearly half of those, around one million units, were rent-regulated. The rest were unregulated or "market rate" (1.1 million units) and public housing and other subsidized housing (two hundred thousand units). The vast majority of working-class and poor New Yorkers resided in rental apartments, and most of those renters lived in rent-regulated or government-assisted housing. In 2023, nearly one in four renter households earned less than $25,000 per year, and 40 percent overall earned less than $50,000.

The housing affordability gap—meaning the difference between rents and incomes—widened dramatically throughout the New Gilded Age. From 1975 to 2023, the median gross rent (i.e., rent plus utilities) for all New York City apartments nearly doubled in real, inflation-adjusted terms, from $830 per month to $1,650 per month (in 2023 dollars), an increase of 99 percent. In contrast, over the same period, median renter incomes had risen only 40 percent in real terms.

While much of that gap between rents and incomes grew in the 1980s and 1990s, it widened even more in the twenty-first century.[20] In 1999, the median share of income paid by tenants for rent and utilities was 33 percent, an already high rent-to-income burden. But by 2023, that figure was 54 percent—meaning that more than half of all renters in New York City met the federal definition of a "severe housing cost burden." The poorest renter households—those earning less than $25,000 per year—had an astounding rent burden rate of 86 percent. And Black and Latino tenants had much higher rates than white renters.

By any measure, the stock of housing in New York City that was affordable to working-class and low-income households was shrinking. In the proverbial game of musical chairs, it was as if more chairs were being removed each round, and each new game was starting at a faster clip. And this was exacerbated by the period's neoliberal housing policy regime.

New York City had a legacy of transformative housing movements and reforms, dating to the first Gilded Age and the decades afterward. As recounted in chapter 2, during that period, the city had enacted tenement reforms and rent regulation, built public housing, and launched state- and city-assisted housing initiatives. But political leaders during the neoliberal era largely abandoned government housing policies aimed at assisting working-class and poor New Yorkers. Instead, they fashioned housing policies to align with the interests of the real estate and finance industries that came to dominate the city's economy and politics.

From the 1990s through the 2020s, there were three major elements of City Hall housing policy. The first involved multiyear housing investment plans that were ostensibly modeled on Koch's landmark Housing New York plan but resulted in far less genuinely affordable housing. Bloomberg's New Housing Marketplace plan, for instance, allocated only 4 percent of its total housing units to homeless people, compared to 10 percent of the units under Koch's plan. Under Bloomberg's plan, only two-thirds of the housing units were targeted to families meeting the overly broad federal definition of "low income," which actually included many nonpoor families; in the 2010s, a "low-income" family could have had an annual income as high as $72,000, far exceeding the earnings of most renters. The remaining units went to households earning as much as $100,000 per year, far from the neediest families.[21]

The de Blasio housing initiative made some of the same mistakes, most of all concerning scale. The initial plan promised two hundred thousand housing units, but it was later modified to add an additional one hundred thousand units. The de Blasio housing plan improved on Bloomberg's by targeting nearly 80 percent of the apartments to low-income households. But due to the ambition to create a "bigger" plan, the subsidies were insufficient to aid the neediest families—and this at a time of record homelessness.[22]

A key problem with both the Bloomberg and de Blasio policies was that they prioritized the rezoning of neighborhoods to generate more housing. As housing policy analyst Samuel Stein has written, such rezonings granted enormous benefits to developers and property owners and asked for little in return. The city government gave them permission to build larger, usually taller structures with more floor space and additional housing units, thus generating greater profits. In exchange, the developers had to set aside a small number of units for households meeting the low-income threshold. However, as Stein noted, that federal standard was itself typically higher than incomes in surrounding neighborhoods, fueling gentrification beyond just the creation of additional market-rate developments.[23]

The housing plans and rezonings also worked hand in hand with the other real estate–friendly policy tool of the neoliberal era: property tax breaks for developers. The most damaging program, though lucrative for developers, was the 421-a exemption, named after its section of city tax law, which granted developers and owners a property tax abatement lasting at least twenty years if a portion of the units in new developments was designated as "affordable." Again, the prevailing rents in these "low-income" units, to say nothing of the market-rate rents, were often out of reach for tenants in surrounding neighborhoods. There were other major flaws in the program that helped accelerate gentrification, including a loophole that allowed some developers to build the "affordable" units off-site and rules that restricted affordable units to current neighborhood residents, which reinforced existing racial segregation.

Perhaps more than anything else, the most harmful housing policy shift that shaped New York City's affordability crisis was the weakening of rent regulation. The attack on the modern rent regulation system began in the 1990s through a series of legislative actions led by Republicans and conservative Democrats in Albany. The state legislation, backed by millions of dollars in campaign contributions from New York City real estate industry interests, allowed landlords to convert thousands of apartments to market rents once they reached a modest rent level, and permitted rents on regulated units to rise at much higher rates. The outcome was the deregulation of more than 150,000 formerly rent-stabilized apartments and higher rents on tens of thousands more.[24] And the weakening of rent regulation fueled gentrification of Black and Latino neighborhoods, making it easier for landlords to push out long-term tenants.

A persistent myth in New York housing political discourse underpinned all these policies: the idea that "more is better" and that simply building additional housing could resolve the affordability crisis. This offshoot of so-called trickle-down economics held sway through every mayoral administration from Ed Koch through Eric Adams, who made it a centerpiece of his housing platform in the 2020s. Long experience had shown that building more of the wrong kind of housing, particularly luxury housing, did little or nothing to ameliorate the city's housing affordability crisis—what was needed was more subsidized housing for the poorest households, as well as stronger rent regulation. But the "more is better" rhetoric served to obscure the systemic failure of City Hall and Albany to create genuinely affordable housing for the neediest New Yorkers.

FEDERAL HOUSING POLICY AND
THE REAGAN LEGACY

In New York City, the New Gilded Age was marked by a historical shift in housing policy—toward a system based largely on tax breaks and deference to the real estate and finance industries. This evolution was mirrored at the national level, beginning with the draconian cutbacks in housing aid under President Reagan and continuing for decades afterward.

As discussed in chapter 2, Reagan's dramatic cutbacks to the Department of Housing and Urban Development's budget marked the beginning of a sustained federal retreat from housing support, as austerity policies continued for decades, limiting new funding for an expanding population even while existing subsidies remained inadequate. As housing historian Alex Schwartz summarized the deteriorating trend: "Overall, accounting for inflation, budget authority decreased by 59 percent from 1977 to 2019. . . . If the federal government had continued to subsidize this number of additional low-income units every year since 1976 [i.e., 506,000 units included in that year's budget request], the nation would have had about 15 million low-income families living in federally assisted housing by 2004. . . . Instead, the federal government reversed direction and funded additional households at a much slower pace, so that little more than 5 million households received direct assistance by 2019."[25]

Moreover, there have been multiple years since the early 1990s during which the number of poor households assisted by federal housing programs actually *decreased*, usually during Republican presidencies. Indeed, the right-wing attack on key federal housing programs, from Ronald Reagan to George W. Bush to Donald Trump, played a central role in the federal withdrawal from efforts to address the housing affordability crisis.

The three largest federal housing programs have historically been public housing, the housing voucher program, and so-called project-based subsidized housing—and since the 1980s, all have stagnated or shrunk.

The number of public housing units in the United States peaked at over 1.4 million in 1994, but by the 2020s dropped to only 987,000 units. At the same time, the repair and modernization of the existing public housing stock has been deeply underfunded, leading to worsening conditions in the remaining apartments.[26] The housing voucher program increased marginally, assisting 1.8 million households in 2019, but still fell far below the rise in the population of needy households. And the number of project-based subsidized units has dropped sharply to 1.1 million units in 2020.[27] All in all, by the 2020s, fewer than one in five Americans who qualified for federal housing aid were able to obtain it.

There was, however, one federal housing initiative that thrived in the neoliberal era: the Mortgage Interest Tax Deduction. But this tax break primarily benefited affluent and middle-class homeowners. Nonetheless, in the twenty-first century the federal government spent well over twice as much on the mortgage tax break as it did on every other federal housing program combined.

THE TRUMP FAMILY AND THE DEVOLUTION OF GOVERNMENT HOUSING POLICY

There is perhaps no better illustration of the radical shift in government housing policy than the Trump family real estate empire. As Stein has written, Fred Trump built his massive real estate portfolio largely by exploiting the government housing programs of the postwar period, including Federal Housing Administration financing and project-based subsidies. The Trump Village complex in Coney Island, for instance, was financed by the FHA and the state's Mitchell–Lama program.

But the elder Trump also demonstrated how such government-assisted housing programs could be misused. In 1954, he was compelled to testify before the US Senate Banking Committee, and he admitted under oath that he'd wildly inflated building costs so that he could get a larger government-subsidized loan. In 1966, the New York State Legislature discovered that Fred Trump had used funding allocated for middle-income housing to build a shopping center.[28] But through it all, the elder Trump's connections with the local political machines—particularly in Queens and Brooklyn—insulated him from prosecution. Indeed, those same political alliances helped him to clear and displace residents from land he targeted for development. The site where Trump Village was built had been assigned to a union-based developer planning a residential cooperative for working-class tenants. Instead, Fred Trump secured control of forty acres, half of the initial site, and displaced hundreds of Black and immigrant families, under the false promise of homes in his new development.

In 1973, the US Department of Justice sued Fred Trump and his son Donald, who by that point was president of the family company, for widespread discrimination against Black tenants and applicants for apartments in the Trump Village complex. At the time, only seven of the development's 3,700 units had Black tenants, and the government's investigation found that Trump employees were instructed to mark applications by Black people with a large letter *C* for "colored." Both Trumps denied the charges and engaged in a legal battle to delay the case in the courts; the Justice Department ultimately settled the case with minimal penalties and the Trumps did not even have to admit any racist discrimination.[29]

By the 1980s, as Donald Trump took the reins of the company, he learned how to manipulate the emerging form of government housing assistance: tax breaks. To build Trump Tower, he became the first developer fully to exploit the 421-a program, which had been meant to incentivize residential construction. But it wasn't only the tax break that helped create the luxury tower. As Stein recounted, "Trump won many concessions to get his signature project built, including not just the tax break but a rezoning, a density bonus for a 'privately built public space' (the building's heavily guarded and commercialized atrium), and a shady agreement to use non-union undocumented immigrant labor—workers who, as Koch predicted, were never paid what they were owed."[30]

Every residential development Donald Trump built in New York City and elsewhere relied on some form of government financing. Indeed, a *Times* investigation from 2016 found that, up to that point, Trump had received at least $885 million in tax breaks in New York City alone.[31] And this enormous government subsidy occurred during an era when politicians and elites preached the need for austerity—yet did little or nothing to create affordable housing.

THE URBAN POLITICS OF THE NEOLIBERAL HOUSING REGIME

"Homelessness," historians David Madden and Peter Marcuse have written, "is not some quirk of urban life—it is a major segment of the housing system."[32] As such, it is impossible to understand the *why* and the *how* behind modern mass homelessness without understanding the shifting nature of housing in the urban economy during the neoliberal era.

Since at least the late nineteenth century, housing came to be regarded as a commodity. However, the emerging housing movements of that era and the early twentieth century contested the commodification of housing and the growing power of real estate capital in New York. As a result, government, which has always been a critical part of the development of urban space, for a time played a more progressive role. The outcome of these battles included, by the 1930s, health and safety protections in residential buildings, the regulation of apartment rents in privately owned housing, and the first-ever government-owned housing. But equally important, through agencies like the Federal Housing Administration and statutes like the Glass–Steagall Act, the production and, crucially, financing of *new* housing development was regulated by the government.

In the post–World War II era in particular, new residential construction was a joint effort by banks, local developers, and builders—and they relied on government action in a range of areas, from mortgage regulation to highway and infrastructure development promoting new growth.[33] Housing assumed what Madden and Marcuse called a "partially decommodified character." As they wrote, "The postwar expansion of housing in the United States did not take on the form of the partial or total nationalization of the housing system that it did in Europe. Instead it was built on massive government investment in infrastructure and equally massive government action around mortgage lending to finance private dwellings with debt."[34]

As sweeping as the housing reforms of the early twentieth century were, they did not entirely live up to the idealized reputation they later enjoyed. The political impetus for the construction of public housing, for instance, was far more about creating jobs for unemployed workers during the Great Depression than about building government-owned housing. And the housing policies and programs of the early twentieth century consistently discriminated against Black Americans. As Richard Rothstein wrote in *The Color of Law*, his landmark history of racist housing policies, "Actions of government cannot be neutral about segregation. They will either exacerbate it or reverse it"[35]—and the housing policies of the reform era exacerbated segregation in New York and urban America as a whole.

Nonetheless, the system that reigned during the postwar era, deeply flawed as it was, resulted in reduced class inequality, a moderate (though not nonexistent) housing affordability gap, and the absence of mass homelessness. But that system was upended beginning in the 1970s by two major forces. The first was the historic transformation in global capitalism that shifted the economic foundations of the wealthiest countries from industry to services. As a consequence, since the 1970s, real estate and finance played a larger role in the US economy and in capital accumulation, ultimately contributing to an accelerating cycle of economic crises. As the pioneering urban theorist Henri Lefebvre wrote in 1970, "It can even happen that real-estate speculation becomes the principal source for the formation of capital, that is, the realization of surplus value. As the percentage of overall surplus value formed and realized by industry begins to decline, the percentage created and realized by real-estate speculation and construction increases. The second circuit supplants the first, becoming essential. But as economists are accustomed to saying, this is an unhealthy situation."[36]

The other force involved the neoliberal political regime that emerged from the virtual laboratory experiment of New York City's 1970s fiscal crisis, which then spread nationwide during the Reagan era. The most sweeping policy shift of the era was the deregulation of housing finance, which reshaped the financial sector as a whole. It began in the 1980s under Reagan and built to the 1999 hollowing out of the Glass–Steagall Act, which had separated commercial banks and mortgage lending from investment banks to protect depositors from the risks of speculation—a major precursor for the 2008 financial crisis that triggered the Great Recession.[37] The consequence of these epochal changes was that housing came to be viewed more and more as a financial asset, housing lending and debt became much more risky, and new players entered real estate markets seeking purely to extract profits.

Beginning in the early 2000s, private-equity firms and hedge funds, which managed billions of dollars in investor wealth, began buying up enormous numbers of residential buildings in New York City. Between 2004 and 2008 alone, such outfits bought some ninety thousand rent-regulated apartments, representing nearly one in ten such units citywide.[38] In New York, the intensification of financial speculation in residential

real estate stemmed not only from hobbled banking rules; it also resulted from the weakening of rent regulation. Real estate speculators began
buying rent-stabilized buildings with the explicit aim of pushing out existing tenants, deregulating their apartments, raising rents dramatically, and bringing in more affluent households who did not have tenant
protections—another policy tool fueling the rampant gentrification and
displacement of the era. In the 2010s in my East Village neighborhood,
the second-largest property owner became the real estate firm controlled
by Jared Kushner, Trump's son-in-law, whose company helped displace
many longtime tenants.[39]

The result of the neoliberal policy retrenchment was what Madden and
Marcuse called the "hypercommodification" of housing, a phenomenon
in which a home's meaning and value were secondary to its utility as an
asset. Residential real estate was increasingly treated as a financial instru-
ment bought and sold for rapid profit. This trend unsurprisingly coincided
with the emergence of the so-called "FIRE" industries—finance, insurance, and real estate—as the largest employers in New York. By 2022, in
fact, the total value of all real estate in New York City was $1.3 trillion,
with $989 billion allocated to residential properties, and the total value
had risen by 17 percent since 2015 alone.[40] But little of that growing value
was captured by or shared with the general public, and even less with
working-class and poor New Yorkers, who made up the majority of the
city's two million renter households.

Contrary to the right-wing, antigovernment rhetoric of the era, the
neoliberal regime did not mean that government played a diminished role
in housing. Instead, government policies were aimed not at addressing the
affordability crisis, but at ensuring the accumulation of capital through
the ownership and development of housing. Far too often, the worsening
housing affordability gap in New York and elsewhere has been recounted

in neutral terms. The assumption was that the historical trends of rising rents and stagnant wages were long-term patterns or actions of "the market." But the neoliberal policies that reinforced and exacerbated them were far from accidental. They were the work of political actors, designed to achieve the goal of enhancing capital accumulation from the housing sector. They also reflected the ascendence of the new urban political coalition that had emerged in the neoliberal era, supplanting the former coalition of manufacturing and industrial labor with a new set of political elites from the finance and real estate sectors.

While the main architects of the neoliberal consensus were Republicans, the ideology became a bipartisan project. On the national level, Democrats like President Bill Clinton enacted some of the most sweeping laws deregulating the banking industry, as well as those weakening safety-net programs. Even President Barack Obama and congressional Democrats failed, in the wake of the 2008 crisis, to rein in the finance industry. In New York, the politicians who most zealously followed the neoliberal line included Republicans like Giuliani, Bloomberg, and Pataki, as well as Democrats like Andrew Cuomo and Eric Adams. Even self-identified progressive leaders like Dinkins and de Blasio governed largely as fiscal conservatives. With only a few exceptions, there was a bipartisan deference to the power of the real estate industry and to the hegemonic neoliberal ideology that shaped a housing landscape characterized by the impermanence of so-called permanent housing.

THE REVOLVING DOOR OF "PERMANENT HOUSING"

In 2013, Bloomberg's last year as mayor, I sat down to prepare the annual Coalition for the Homeless policy report about the state of homelessness in New York. The theme of that year's report was the record-high homeless population and how Bloomberg's policies had shaped that historic crisis. But as I pored through the data, the statistic that shocked me the most concerned the percentage of homeless families who had been homeless in the recent past. In the late 1990s and early 2000s, that figure was fairly steady, between 20 and 25 percent each year—an alarming but unsurprising rate. But after Bloomberg cut off homeless New Yorkers from federal housing aid and substituted his time-limited subsidies, the "return rate" shot up. By 2013, the city data showed, a remarkable 63 percent of homeless families—nearly two in three in the shelter system—had previously been homeless. For tens of thousands of poor New York families and children, the vast majority of them Black and Latino, the revolving door was not a metaphor, but a daily, lived reality.

This circuit, in which poor households were forced to return to homelessness—whether in shelters, on the streets, or in doubled-up, overcrowded dwellings—was hardly unique to New York. Across the country, a worsening affordability crisis and chronic shortfall in federal housing assistance left low-income families in unstable housing arrangements. As in New York, eviction was the primary cause of homelessness and undeniable evidence of housing precarity.

As Matthew Desmond documented in his landmark study *Evicted* and his subsequent research, the housing instability of low-income renters had reached epidemic levels: "If you study eviction court records in other cities, you arrive at similarly startling numbers. Jackson County, Missouri, which includes half of Kansas City, saw 19 formal evictions a day between 2009 and 2013. New York City courts saw almost 80 nonpayment evictions a day in 2012. That same year, 1 in 9 occupied rental households in Cleveland, and 1 in 14 in Chicago, were summoned to eviction court. Instability is not inherent to poverty. Poor families move so much because they are forced to."[41]

By the eve of the COVID-19 pandemic, 7.6 million renters nationwide were threatened with eviction each year, and 3.6 million cases were actually filed.[42] Systemic eviction, housing precarity, and homelessness grew more closely intertwined throughout the New Gilded Age. Politicians and policymakers talked about their efforts to create "permanent housing"; however, all the while, the revolving door kept turning, and the threat of displacement never vanished.

CHAPTER 11

WASHINGTON, DC, AND BEYOND: URBAN AMERICA AND HOMELESSNESS

As New York City has gone, so, in many ways, has the country as a whole. . . . As the American economy recovered from the blows of the 1970s, it was remade, as many noted, on completely different terms. The idea of using the state to remedy poverty and improve social conditions has given way to the sense that doing so is simply too expensive . . . Tax cuts have starved state and local governments, leaving them without the resources they need to provide education and other basic services. . . . Throughout the country, at every level of government, public budgets suffer as private fortunes grow. . . . The inequality that characterizes our society today seems to be accompanied by the constant sense that any hope for a better society, any notion of collective action, must be a pipe dream—irresponsible, impossible to afford.

Kim Phillips-Fein
Fear City

WASHINGTON, DC

Whenever I have visited Washington, DC—as I did dozens of times over some three decades, nearly always involving my work as a homeless advocate—I have traveled by train, arriving in the capital's majestic Union Station, a classical-style edifice built during the Gilded Age. It was marked by Romanesque pillars and allegorical statuary in keeping with the imposing, nineteenth-century architectural identity of Washington, and located only a short walk from the even more imposing US Capitol and other federal buildings. And every time, one of the first things I encountered was the overwhelming number of homeless people gathered there.

In Washington, DC, as in nearly every other city in the United States, most of its homeless population resided on the streets and in other public spaces, like Union Station and its environs. In the early twenty-first century, Union Station underwent a series of renovations meant to spruce it up and make it more inviting to urban professionals. I regularly saw business travelers, commuters, and tourists awaiting trains amid the typical array of overpriced coffee establishments, restaurants, and even some luxury boutiques. Then, in the same corridors and vaulted halls—or, more often, outside the station itself—I'd find dozens of homeless people, many of them in very rough shape, sleeping, panhandling, or searching trash containers for discarded food. It was a concentrated version of what has become an everyday reality in American cities: middle-class and affluent urbanites going about their routines while barely noticing the grim condition of other immiserated humans.

The municipal authorities in Washington, DC, alongside their federal counterparts, have long responded to the homelessness around Union Station according to the typical municipal playbook. They've resorted to brutal, police-driven initiatives, sweeping homeless people along with their blankets and tents and other belongings. When I attended Barack Obama's first presidential inauguration in January 2009, I couldn't help but notice that, amid the historically immense crowds gathering to welcome the nation's first Black president and the inescapable vibe of celebration and joy, the homeless people around Union Station and elsewhere were almost nowhere to be seen—systematically pushed away by the police and other authorities.

In 2023, the nation's capital had the fifteenth largest homeless population of any US city, according to federal estimates, which understated the true scale of the problem. Another federal report, which used a broader definition of homelessness, found 6,300 homeless kids in DC schools, representing 7 percent of all students.[1] The homeless population of Washington, DC, was overwhelmingly Black; federal estimates found that 84 percent of homeless Washingtonians were Black in 2023, compared with 41 percent of the city's total population.

Washington, DC, was as unlike New York City as any major East Coast city—low-slung and lacking skyscrapers, economically dependent on one major industry (the federal government), and largely southern in its attitudes and culture. It was also only a fraction of the size, with a total population in 2020 amounting to just 8 percent of New York's 8.8 million people. But Washington, DC, shared one feature with New York City that was decisive in creating and sustaining its homelessness crisis: remarkably high housing costs. By 2024, according to census data analyzed by the National Low Income Housing Coalition (NLIHC), a Washington, DC, household needed a "housing wage" of thirty-nine dollars per hour to rent a modest apartment, at a time when the local minimum wage was seventeen dollars per hour and the federal minimum wage was only $7.25 per hour.[2] That same year, there were only thirty-three housing units affordable for every hundred of the poorest households.[3]

Mass homelessness, which had first emerged in New York in the late 1970s and then spread nationwide in the 1980s, had become a defining feature of urban life in the United States. And New York City, given its outsize role in American society, influenced the approach to homelessness taken by so many other cities, for good and, mostly, for ill. For every positive reform born in New York—in particular the legal right to shelter, as well as supportive housing and the Housing First model—there were many more dangerous, damaging, and ultimately failed policies.

Throughout the New Gilded Age, American cities learned to address homelessness not by dealing with its root causes, but by relying on tools of urban control. This involved the punitive and racist criminalization of homelessness, the minimal provision of shelter and other emergency services, a reliance on charity and private organizations instead of genuine government action, and a rationing of dwindling housing aid. Meanwhile, this all occurred against the backdrop of a steadily worsening crisis and a persistent refusal to embrace the simple solutions that would end it.

CLEVELAND, OHIO, AND BOSTON, MASSACHUSETTS

I can still vividly recall the sense of shock and disbelief when I first witnessed people sleeping outdoors, exposed to the elements, on sidewalks and in plazas of the city where I had just moved. This was Boston, Massachusetts, in the autumn of 1983, when I had just arrived to attend college. It was the first time I'd lived anywhere other than suburban Cleveland, Ohio, and I was utterly unprepared for my first encounter with urban homelessness.

My reaction was much like that of most Americans in the early 1980s. While homelessness had begun to spread, a few years earlier, beyond the traditional skid row districts of New York City, it was the early 1980s recession and the Reagan cutbacks to housing programs that really forced mass homelessness into public view. Throughout my 1970s childhood, I had never seen people sleeping on the streets, even in my economically hollowed-out hometown of Cleveland. My high school's rundown neighborhood, known as the Near West Side and located near the central city, was marked by vacant storefronts and empty buildings. Traveling to and from there every day, I passed boarded-up warehouses and the abandoned factories and refineries lining the Cuyahoga River. After school, my friends and I often went downtown, which even on weekdays seemed strangely forsaken and depopulated. (In 1978, Cleveland had become the first city since the Great Depression to fall into default, a consequence of decades of deindustrialization, mismanagement, and pressure on the municipal government by banks and city elites.)[4] But even in the midst of Cleveland's 1970s economic crisis, I still never saw people bedding down on the streets.[5]

In the Boston area, it was a far different story. Dozens of homeless men and women slept each night in Cambridge's Harvard Square, literally next door to the wealthiest and most prestigious university in North America, as well as in nearby Porter and Central Squares. My freshman roommate and I got to know a homeless man named Daniel, who was probably around fifty years old and slept near the Harvard Square subway station. On particularly cold nights that winter of 1983–84, we occasionally invited him to sleep overnight in our dorm room. Daniel used to tell me about an overcrowded shelter in a church basement where he sometimes sought refuge, although on most winter nights there was a lottery to get a bed there. He eventually decided to try his luck down south—I've forgotten whether it was in North or South Carolina—in a town where he had family who might help him out.

In the early 1990s, I returned to live in Boston for a couple of years, completing my master's thesis while working odd jobs. One temp job regularly took me through the so-called Combat Zone, Boston's red-light district, where many homeless people congregated when they weren't sleeping in the Pine Street Inn or another shelter of that era. That period was a turning point for rental housing costs in metropolitan Boston. In 1994, rent control was abolished in Boston, Cambridge, and a few other communities. The repeal came from a Massachusetts statewide ballot initiative that had been pushed aggressively by Governor William Weld, a Republican, and the real estate industry, which financed a lavish and misleading anti-rent-control advertising campaign. In the wake of the repeal, apartment rents jumped dramatically in Boston and elsewhere, and many rental buildings were converted to condominiums, worsening an already acute affordability crisis.[6]

Three decades later, the greater Boston area developed one of the worst housing affordability problems in the United States. By 2024, according to the NLIHC, the wage needed to afford a two-bedroom apartment in metropolitan Boston was more than fifty-four dollars per hour, the seventh-highest rate in the country—two-thirds higher than the national average.[7] In 2019, Boston had the eleventh-highest homeless population nationwide, with a third of those affected being children.

SAN DIEGO, CALIFORNIA

Walking and driving around San Diego, which I've visited almost every year of the twenty-first century, I regularly witnessed the misery and wretchedness of unsheltered homelessness on full display. People lay passed out on sidewalks in ragged, dingy clothing. Older men begged for money on street corners or in front of the growing number of vacant storefronts that formed a buffer zone between the historic Gaslamp Quarter and the neighboring central business district, with its steel-and-glass office towers, as well as the more affluent residential districts lined with gleaming condos. Broken-down younger men self-medicated with alcohol or openly shot up with syringes. Camping tents and makeshift shelters, fashioned from blue plastic tarp, were lined up under bridges and along avenues in warehouse districts.

In San Diego, like many other California cities, the problem of homelessness has been shaped by the overwhelming effects of two forces: soaring housing costs amid stagnant incomes for working-class and poor residents, and the government's refusal to create anything like a sufficient supply of low-cost housing. According to federal estimates, by 2024, San Diego's homeless population was the sixth-largest of any US city, and it had grown by 17 percent over the previous decade. As in other American cities, Black people were disproportionately affected by homelessness;

only 7 percent of San Diego's total population was Black, compared with 22 percent of the estimated homeless population. Nearly two-thirds of homeless people were unsheltered, left to sleep in public spaces.

San Diego spent a pittance of its municipal resources on emergency homeless services and long-term housing. Instead, it relied on underfunded federal programs. During my years serving on the board of the National Coalition for the Homeless, I worked with colleagues from small cities or towns—in southern Mississippi, central Indiana, and elsewhere—which were forced to rely solely on federal homelessness grants due to the paucity of local revenues. In those communities, churches or charitable groups like the Salvation Army formed the bedrock of the limited homeless services.

But in San Diego, a large and prosperous city, the refusal by municipal leaders to spend local tax dollars on homeless services and housing was more ideological. San Diego, like a few other areas of California, had a long history of conservative political leadership, both Republicans and Democrats, and those officials often scapegoated their homeless residents instead of allocating necessary resources to help them get off the streets. In 2023, for instance, the city government enacted a ban on "rough sleeping" targeted at downtown San Diego, a harsh measure that was vehemently criticized by homeless advocates. But a former Republican mayor said that the ban didn't go far enough.[8] When I talked to homeless folks on the sidewalks of San Diego's Gaslamp Quarter, the lack of available shelter, to say nothing of affordable housing, was the main reason they gave for staying outdoors, even with the risks of getting swept up by the police.

AUSTIN, TEXAS

When I lived there in the early 1990s during my graduate studies, Austin still had the vibe of a countercultural community, a place where people who didn't fit into the conservative Texas macroculture could come to escape. While it was growing—Dell and other tech companies had just planted roots there—it still had the feeling of a large town, though one with classic urban problems like racial segregation, underfunded schools, and, of course, homelessness.

While attending school, I worked at a coffee shop near campus and got to know our regular clientele of homeless men and panhandlers. One older guy with a white beard and ponytail, to whom I used to give a coffee late in the shift when the manager was preoccupied, was almost an archetype of old-time Austin, somewhere between a hippie and a cowhand. He'd worked on ranches in his youth, had a mercifully brief stint in the army, and had struggled to make ends meet as a manual laborer until age caught up with him. As with so many older homeless men I've met over the years, I suspected there were deeper reasons that brought him to where he was, something you could see behind his pale blue eyes—a personal tragedy, perhaps a family drama, likely missteps and regrets—but he didn't share his full life story, and I didn't press. He told me about bedding down in some out-of-the-way spots near the university, if he managed to dodge the campus police, but how he preferred to sleep in parks downtown near the Texas State Capitol building.

In the Austin of the early 1990s, however, housing costs were still modest; the rent on my first apartment was only $175 per month, a fraction of what I'd paid in New York the previous year to share a one-bedroom place. But after I left in 1993, Austin grew at a rapid pace, driven by a torrent of tech money and, later, an influx of migrants from California and other states, as well as immigrants from Latin America. By 2020, Austin's population was 962,000, twice what it was when I'd lived there, making it the eleventh-largest city in the nation. Unsurprisingly, housing costs had soared. By 2024, according to the NLIHC, the wage needed to afford a two-bedroom apartment was thirty-seven dollars per hour—in a state where the minimum wage was the abysmally low federal rate of

$7.25 per hour.[9] That same year, Austin had only twenty-one affordable homes for every hundred extremely low-income households, the tenth-worst rate of any city in the United States.[10]

Homelessness predictably grew much worse. Between 2010 and 2022, Austin's homeless population grew by 52 percent, according to federal estimates. In May 2024, a local homeless coalition conducted its own one-night count of the homeless population and found 6,200 people, with five thousand of them sleeping unsheltered each night.[11] The demographics of the homeless population had also shifted to reflect that of other large, high-cost cities, with a rising number of families and children; by the 2020s, more than 2,300 homeless kids attended Austin's public schools.

Notwithstanding the work and struggle of homeless people, activists, and some of the remaining progressive elements of the community, the political leaders of Austin, like those of other American cities, often turned to the police as their first response to homelessness. In 1996, Austin enacted a "no camping" ordinance that resulted in the arrest and harassment of hundreds of homeless people. The law and subsequent police crackdown came after pressure by a local business alliance to "clean up" areas near the University of Texas campus, state government buildings, and gentrifying neighborhoods. The police campaign also generated vigorous protests by homeless people and their allies. Legendary Texas journalist Molly Ivins, whom I had the honor of meeting, camped overnight on Congress Avenue as part of one protest. Echoing a sentiment expressed by homeless people and advocates in similar battles nationwide, she wrote, "You cannot solve homelessness by getting people out of sight or by just sweeping them off the streets."[12]

CRIMINALIZATION OF HOMELESSNESS NATIONWIDE

Austin's various attempts to criminalize homelessness matched the chronically failed model pioneered in New York and then copied by virtually every other city in the United States. First, unsheltered homelessness was treated as a criminal matter, with the police leading enforcement efforts. Second, homelessness more broadly, including among families, was classified as a social services problem rather than a housing issue, ensuring that the crisis could only persist and worsen.

Many cities borrowed their antihomeless policing strategies from the Giuliani–Bloomberg model, which itself was informed by the discredited "broken windows" theory that criminal enforcement of "quality of life" problems—especially homeless people—reduced crime overall (see chapter 3). Beginning in the 1990s, New York Police Department commissioners like Bill Bratton, Ray Kelly, Howard Safir, and Bernard Kerik, along with lower-rank officials, spread their antihomeless policing strategies nationwide by advising other cities' police departments. After Bratton's first stint at the NYPD, he served in the early 2000s as commissioner of the Los Angeles Police Department, where he and his force targeted homeless people, particularly in the city's growing Skid Row district.[13] He was a frequently cited "expert" in the national news media throughout the twenty-first century, defending broken windows–style policing, long after it had been disproven, and occasionally making racist comments— most notoriously in a 2015 cable news interview about the routine police shootings of Black people, during which he referred to supposed problems "in Black society, in terms of . . . the disintegration of family, the disintegration of values."[14]

Antihomeless policing was accompanied by a proliferation of antihomeless lawmaking. Since the late 1980s, the National Homelessness Law Center (NHLC) has documented the spread of state and local statutes that criminalize homelessness, as well as the various enforcement tactics utilized by communities large and small. Many antihomeless laws were commonplace, involving the criminalization of using public space. In 2019, the NHLC analyzed the local laws of 187 communities and found that most of them included at least one statute that prohibited camping, sleeping outdoors, sitting or lying down, storing belongings in a public place, or, in a historical echo of mid-twentieth-century antivagrancy laws, loitering and "loafing." Also widespread were laws criminalizing behavior consistent with, though not exclusive to, homelessness, such as statutes outlawing begging, public urination, and scavenging (aka "dumpster diving").[15]

The criminalization of LA's enormous unsheltered homeless population, the largest in the country, was particularly brutal. A 2024 report by Human Rights Watch, based on three years of research and interviews, documented the extremity of the police crackdown on homelessness.[16] Los Angeles Police Department data showed that "38 percent of all LAPD arrests and citations combined were of unhoused people, including nearly 100 percent of all citations and over 42 percent of all misdemeanor arrests." Homeless people were given "99 percent of all citations and arrests for infractions like sitting or lying on the sidewalk, drinking in public, leaving behind personal property, violating park regulations, cannabis regulation, open containers, illegal possession of a shopping cart and minor alcohol and tobacco charges." In short, an enormous share of total police activity in Los Angeles was dedicated to the criminalization of homelessness.[17]

The nationwide rise of homeless encampments, especially in the years after the 2008 financial crisis, also triggered aggressive and frequent police crackdowns, particularly in California and other western states. In 2017, the NHLC documented both the rise in the number of reported encampments nationwide and the harsh response by local officials in affected communities.[18] Its study looked at nearly two hundred cities and discovered that half had statutes prohibiting camping in public spaces, a 48 percent increase from a decade earlier. It also found that half of the cities surveyed had either a formal or informal procedure for clearing encampments.[19] The report described the elaborate, and often costly, steps taken by localities to deter encampments:

> Other cities spend thousands of dollars on fences, bars, rocks, spikes, and other "hostile" or "aggressive" architecture, deliberately making certain areas of their community inaccessible to homeless persons without shelter. San Diego, CA, recently spent $57,000 to install jagged rocks set in concrete underneath an overpass in advance of the Major League Baseball All-Star game. Other cities, like Chicago, IL, simply fence off areas under bridges to prevent homeless persons from sheltering there. In either case, the money did not reduce the need for people to find shelter but potentially put people at greater vulnerability to exposure and hazards.[20]

As in New York City, the criminalization campaigns exacerbated the cycle of homelessness by perpetuating a revolving door between jails, prisons, shelters, and the streets, with homelessness increasing the likelihood of incarceration and vice versa. Targeting homelessness also undermined public safety by diverting criminal justice resources to address noncriminal, nonthreatening behavior, and it was extraordinarily costly. For instance, the NHLC found that a "study of Santa Clara County, California, estimated that homelessness cost Santa Clara County $520 million annually from 2007 to 2012 (not including spending on accommodation and direct services), and 34% of those costs were for criminal justice related expenditures, such as probation, custody mental health care, and jail/court costs."[21]

Police crackdowns on homelessness frequently served the interests of local capital—real estate developers and property owners seeking to gentrify neighborhoods, local and national merchants, and business associations aiming to "clean up" central business districts where unsheltered homeless people often congregated out of necessity. The wholesale criminalization of homelessness—along with the demonization and pathologization of homeless people—also became a political project of the national Republican Party, including Donald Trump. In 2024, the world's richest man and a far-right ally of Trump, Elon Musk, wrote on his social media platform, "In most cases, the word 'homeless' is a lie. It's usually a propaganda word for violent drug addicts with severe mental illness."

In Austin, the anticamping ban that homeless people and activists had managed to defeat in the 1990s was reinstated in 2021 via referendum. According to campaign finance disclosures, the ballot measure was promoted by a political group funded by wealthy residents and business leaders.[22] Among those Austin elites was Joe Lonsdale, a billionaire venture capitalist, cofounder of Palantir, a surveillance technology company, and fervent supporter of Trump. He was not shy about his views, at one point attacking "the Marxist idea that American capitalism causes homelessness, and that only far-left activism can fix it."[23] An investigation into his campaign found that "staff of Lonsdale's Cicero Institute have crisscrossed the country to sell state legislatures on the idea that Austin's ban is working, and that other states can best address rising homelessness by criminalizing it more thoroughly."[24] Lonsdale's think tank also supported the legal challenge to a long-standing ban on encampment sweeps in some states that, in 2024, was overturned by the right-wing majority on the US Supreme Court.[25]

THE SCALE OF MODERN HOMELESSNESS IN THE UNITED STATES

As in New York City, the criminalization campaigns in American cities served to mask a deeper, inescapable reality: the modern homelessness crisis was growing far worse throughout the New Gilded Age.

Modern homelessness has always been notoriously difficult to measure. Beginning in the early 2000s, the federal government required that states and the most populous localities produce an annual estimate of their homeless populations on a single winter night. From the start, there were significant problems with these "point in time" estimates—most of all, the problem of accurately "counting" the unsheltered homeless population, especially in large cities. Even reported tallies of the sheltered homeless population tended to leave out some people (like those residing in privately run or faith-based shelters). Finally, the point-in-time estimates by design ignored the "hidden homeless" population of people living in doubled-up, severely overcrowded housing or in other makeshift arrangements like motels. Nonetheless, the federal statistics offered a baseline of the size of the US homeless population.

By 2024, the federal government reported that there were an estimated 771,000 people who were homeless nationwide on a single January night of that year—the largest US homeless population ever recorded. Of these, some 274,000 people were estimated to be sleeping on the streets or other public spaces. Black Americans experienced homelessness at disproportionately high rates. The federal survey estimated that 31 percent of the US homeless population was Black, compared with 12 percent of the total population. Latinos were also overrepresented, with an estimated 31 percent of the homeless population, compared with 19 percent of the total US population. By contrast, white Americans comprised 36 percent of the homeless population, despite constituting 75 percent of the total US population.

The US homeless population had soared throughout the New Gilded Age. While the mandated "point in time" estimates only began in 2005, the US Census Bureau had attempted a similar single-night count during the 1990 decennial census, which reported 229,000 homeless Americans. While the two measures were both flawed and not entirely comparable, they suggested that the nation's homeless population in 2024 was three times larger than in 1990.

The one-night federal estimates, however, also failed to account for the number of Americans who *experienced* homelessness over the course of the year. By the first decades of the twenty-first century, databases of municipal shelter systems, like New York's, allowed researchers to calculate the "turnover rate" of shelter resources, meaning the number of different people who sought shelter over the course of a year. One study, which looked at nationwide data from 2007 and 2017, found a turnover rate of 7.3 people per bed in the earlier year and 4.9 people per bed in the later year.[26] These figures suggested that, during that decade, between 3.2 million and 4.7 million Americans each year used homeless shelters at some point.

Yet even these alarming statistics understated the problem because they only accounted for the "literally" homeless population—those people who slept in public spaces or in homeless shelters. The hidden homeless population of doubled-up households was significantly larger and revealed a deeper housing instability in the United States. Federal data on homeless students, for instance, used this broader definition of homelessness. For the 2021–22 school year, there were 1.2 million homeless public school students in the United States. Homeless kids made up one in every forty public school students nationwide, and the number of homeless students was growing at a rapid pace. Indeed, the 2021–22 figure was nearly twice the number of homeless students reported only fifteen years earlier.[27] Assuming an average family size of three people, these figures suggested that more than three million Americans with student-aged children were among the hidden homeless population of the early 2020s.

Using US Census Bureau microdata from 2019, a more comprehensive research study found that there were 3.7 million people living in doubled-up households nationwide, the majority of them renters.[28] As with the sheltered and unsheltered homeless populations, Black and Latino Americans were disproportionately affected, with Latinos experiencing a rate of hidden homelessness that was three times greater than white Americans. Doubled-up homelessness was also more common in the western and southern states than in the Northeast and Midwest, and somewhat more common in suburban areas than visible homelessness was.

All in all, the picture of US homelessness that emerged a quarter of the way through the twenty-first century was far more alarming than previous research had shown. More than three million Americans were, to use the narrowest definition of the term, *literally* homeless at some point during each year. Another 3.7 million Americans lived in doubled-up conditions. And while there was surely some overlap between the two groups, it was clear that, by the early years of the 2020s, at least two in every hundred Americans were experiencing homelessness each year.

But mass homelessness has never been spread evenly across the United States. It has afflicted Black and Latino Americans, poor families and individuals, and people struggling with disabilities at much higher rates than others. But most of all, it has affected city dwellers. Federal data from the early 2020s found that less than one-fifth of the nation's homeless population lived in rural areas. More than 80 percent of the US homeless population resided in predominantly urban or suburban districts, and the large majority in what the report termed "major cities."

THE HOUSING AFFORDABILITY CRISIS IN AMERICAN CITIES

According to the federal 2024 point-in-time estimates, the twenty-five metro areas with the largest homeless populations accounted for just over half the nation's total homeless population—some 389,000 people out of a total estimate of 771,000. After New York City and Los Angeles—which, combined, accounted for a remarkable 27 percent of the total US homeless population—the list included areas likewise characterized by severe housing affordability problems, including Seattle, San Diego, Denver, San José, Oakland, Phoenix, Sacramento, San Francisco, Las Vegas, Portland (Oregon), Chicago, Orange County (California), Boston, and Washington, DC.

Nearly all ranked among the highest on the list of cities with high housing wages. In 2024, the NLIHC found, for instance, that San Francisco, San José, New York, San Diego, and Boston all recorded housing wages of more than fifty dollars per hour, the amount required to afford a modest two-bedroom apartment. Even some suburban communities, like California's Orange County (nearly fifty-four dollars) and New York's Long Island (forty-eight dollars), had remarkably steep housing wages.[29] The state of California had the highest housing wage, just ahead of Massachusetts and New York.[30] And in terms of the cities that had the most severe shortages of rental housing affordable to extremely low-income households, the 2024 analysis found many of the same locations: Las Vegas, San Diego, San Bernardino, Dallas, Los Angeles, and Phoenix.[31]

By the 2020s, the nation's housing crisis had reached critical levels. An all-time record twenty-two million renter households paid more than 30 percent of their income in rent, the federal definition of rent burden, and of those, twelve million paid more than half their income in rent, exceeding the threshold for severe cost burden. In the twenty-first century alone, the number of very low-income households nationwide grew by more than four million, but only around one in five such households received housing assistance.[32] During the 2010s, the number of low-cost rental housing units fell by nearly four million.[33] And the greatest losses of affordable housing were occurring in the wealthiest cities.

URBAN AMERICA IN THE NEW GILDED AGE

One sign of the epochal transformation of urban America was the growth of income and wealth inequality. By every measure, the United States has become vastly more unequal since the end of the 1970s. Even a cursory look at statistics on household wealth and earnings confirmed this trend. From 1980 to 2019, the median real income (in 2019 dollars) of the bottom fifth of American households increased only slightly, from under $13,000 to $15,000 annually. By contrast, the top fifth of households nearly doubled their real median income, reaching $255,000 annually. And the income gains were even greater among the top 5 percent of American households; over that time, their median real income rose to more than $400,000, an increase of 94 percent.[34]

The gap in wealth between the poorest and richest Americans was even greater. From 1983 to 2016, the real median family wealth (in 2016 dollars) of the top third of American households more than doubled, from $344,000 to $858,000. Meanwhile, the bottom third's median wealth shrank from $12,000 to $11,000. Even more alarming, by 2016, the richest third of American households held 79 percent of all wealth nationwide, while the share for both the bottom and middle third had fallen sharply.[35] Racial income and wealth inequality also worsened dramatically in the New Gilded Age. In 2016, the median wealth of a Black family was $17,600 and that of a Latino family was $20,700, while a white family's median wealth was $171,000.[36]

By 2021, the top 1 percent of American households controlled an absurd 31 percent of all US wealth—nearly a third of the nation's total.[37] This level of concentration surpassed even that of the nineteenth-century Gilded Age, creating what amounted to a new oligarchy.

Throughout the neoliberal era, as discussed in chapter 10, the primary mechanism for capital to accumulate surpluses and profit shifted from industry to finance and real estate, primarily housing. As urban theorist

David Harvey has noted, "Urbanization . . . has been a key means for the absorption of capital and labor surpluses throughout capitalism's history."[38] Investment in the urban environment—whether in bridges, tunnels, or other infrastructural projects, but above all housing—has always been a means for capital to address crises of overaccumulation. And this always required the intertwined cooperation of the state and the banking sector, as such investments were necessarily debt-financed and speculative. They were also inherently prone to trigger crises. In the "golden age" between World War II and the 1970s, such risks had been moderated by a stronger state regulatory regime. But the neoliberal shift to deregulate banking and finance, accompanied by austerity policies that sought to extract more value from urban environments, instigated a period of crisis after crisis that has defined the New Gilded Age.

As Harvey wrote in the wake of the Great Recession, "There have been hundreds of financial crises since 1973 (compared to very few prior to that), and quite a few of them have been property- or urban development-led."[39] The worst global economic downturn since the Great Depression was fueled by the mid-2000s foreclosure crisis. Financial chicanery and fraud by Wall Street banks and other players in the finance and real estate sectors—such as the creation and exchange of complex financial instruments backed by securitized mortgages, a legacy of the banking deregulation of the 1980s and 1990s—played a key role. More than six million people lost their homes to foreclosure, and the national unemployment rate soared to double digits. By 2012, homeowners had lost $7 trillion in equity, with the harshest impact on nonwhite households—the median wealth of Black households fell by 53 percent and that of Latino households by 66 percent, compared with 16 percent for white households.[40]

But all in all, the intensified frequency and severity of accumulation crises in the neoliberal era resulted from the larger and riskier role of housing in capital accumulation. As urban theorist Brett Christophers has written, so-called late-stage capitalism increasingly came to rely on rentier arrangements, meaning surpluses and profits derived from assets.[41] Housing was one of those key assets, a hypercommodity financed primarily through debt and thus subject to speculative risk. These finance-driven crises, including the 2008 global crash and others abroad, came at a faster and faster clip.

The prevalence of crisis and instability in an increasingly commodified housing sector helped to widen the affordability gap. The consequence was a worsening shortage of housing accessible to the poorest American households. By 2023, that shortfall had reached an astounding 7.3 million housing units, forming the foundation for the worsening crises of mass homelessness and displacement.[42]

SOLUTIONS

Having lived through the emergence of modern homelessness, I was among the millions of Americans who were left wondering, as the crisis deepened, "Why hasn't the country solved this problem, or even attempted to solve it?" I wasn't blind to the politics of the era—the Reagan presidency had reversed many New Deal–era policies, and the white backlash to the civil rights era was in full force. Nor was I especially naive about the enormous structural and social changes occurring nationwide. But it was hard not to think that, in a sensible and compassionate society witnessing so much visible, preventable misery, the public might have pushed the nation's leaders to enact solutions.

Simply put, the solutions to the problem of homelessness have never been mysterious or terribly complicated. At its core, homelessness has always been a housing affordability problem, and the principal remedy is therefore obvious: create and maintain sufficient affordable housing for poor and working-class Americans. It is equally obvious that the private market would never provide an adequate supply of affordable housing for the poorest Americans, so government would have to play the central role. Moreover, there were examples of other wealthy, developed nations that had largely accomplished that goal and had remarkably low rates of homelessness, like Japan, Canada, and most of western Europe.

In considering solutions, one does not even need to think in utopian terms about eliminating all homelessness or poverty, but merely ending *mass* homelessness. These are social-democratic, eminently achievable solutions that rely on proven models, and as such, they don't even depend on a more comprehensive rethinking of American cities, a transformation that would ensure far more social and economic justice. In summary, ending mass homelessness involves a combination of the following policies and principles.

1. GUARANTEED OR UNIVERSAL HOUSING AID

Dating from the progressive victories of the New Deal and the Great Society eras, many large-scale public benefits in the United States have been entitlements. That is to say, when one qualified or met the "need standard" for those programs, one automatically received those benefits, and their funding levels were adjusted to account for rising and falling need. This has never been true of housing aid. Federal housing programs have historically been subject to annual budget appropriations, which meant that there has always been less federal housing aid available than the number of people who need the assistance—which is the primary reason why, by the 2020s, four out of five low-income Americans who qualified for federal housing programs could not get help.

Making housing assistance an entitlement—a right—for low-income Americans could be accomplished in several ways. The most successful approach in other countries has been social housing—that is, government-owned housing with guaranteed levels of affordability, or alternatively nonprofit-owned housing with the same guarantee ensured by the government. This would include supportive housing for people living with disabilities and other special needs, with an emphasis on the Housing First approach. Compared to other advanced capitalist countries, far too few housing units have been owned and administered by the US federal government. Of the nation's roughly 145 million total units in the early 2020s, fewer than one million were public housing apartments; in comparison, Canada had nearly 900,000 units of social housing despite having a population only one-eighth the size of the US population.[43] This has left the private market as the last resort for housing for poor households.

The other way to provide guaranteed housing aid would be with housing vouchers, which pay the difference between what a needy household could afford and rents in private-market housing. This approach has been widely used throughout Europe, at a much larger scale than in the United States, where the federal program reaches only five million people, a fraction of poor households that need housing aid. In 2004, Great Britain, a country with one-fifth the population of the United States, provided a voucher-like housing benefit to 3.8 million people. Likewise, the Netherlands, with a population of only seventeen million people, provided housing vouchers to nearly one million people, roughly 30 percent of all renters.[44]

2. PREVENTION AND RENT REGULATION

The other key policy tool to end mass homelessness and to prevent the cycle of housing instability would involve comprehensive, universal prevention programs. Key to these would be right-to-counsel laws for housing courts, guaranteeing legal assistance for poor tenants facing eviction. More important would be nationwide rent regulation and tenant protections in privately owned housing, akin to the rent-regulation laws that have existed in New York and some other communities. One of the over-looked features of rent regulation in New York City is its guarantee that tenants can renew leases and remain in their residences, as well as limiting rent increases and providing other safeguards.

3. ANTIDISCRIMINATION PROTECTION AND ENFORCEMENT

The degree of racial and ethnic segregation in American housing and neighborhoods, already extreme throughout the New Gilded Age, worsened during the twenty-first century. This exacerbated the legacy of racist policies and programs—including urban renewal, federal housing programs, redlining, blockbusting, exclusionary zoning, and tenant discrimination—that shaped American cities and suburbs in the postwar era and effectively contributed to the creation of majority-white enclaves and Black and Latino ghettos. While there have been federal, state, and local statutes outlawing housing discrimination based on race or ethnicity for decades, they need to be strengthened and comprehensively enforced.

4. ENSURE A RIGHT TO SHELTER

As homeless people and advocates have long argued, the easiest way to eliminate problems like the criminalization of homelessness would be to solve the problem itself—to get homeless people off the streets and into homes. Until that occurs, one necessary and interim measure would be to extend the right to shelter to homeless people nationwide—essentially to guarantee that people without homes need not turn to the streets and public spaces. Indeed, coupling this safeguard with universal Housing First assistance would radically reduce the unsheltered homeless population. And some cities have had success in replacing the police as the so-called first responders when dealing with homeless people, instead deploying teams of public health workers who can assess health needs and provide access to Housing First units.

More than anything, the right-to-shelter protections that were won by advocates in the early years of the modern crisis have saved countless lives. In 2005, I led an effort to pass a law requiring New York City to report the number of deaths of homeless people. Since then, each year, the city government has documented between one hundred and two hundred deaths of unsheltered homeless New Yorkers.[45] While these numbers represent far too many deaths, the comparison with cities without a right to shelter was striking. In 2023, in Los Angeles, where three-quarters of homeless people lacked shelter (compared to 5 percent in New York), there were some nine hundred deaths of homeless people. The large majority died on the streets or other public spaces. And there were more than two thousand homeless deaths in the surrounding county, with public officials admitting that these figures were an undercount.[46] In San Francisco, whose total homeless population was one-twelfth the size of New York's, there were 278 reported homeless deaths in 2020.[47] The National Health Care for the Homeless Council conducted a review of cities in 2018 and found sixty-eight communities that tracked homeless deaths, with 5,720 such deaths reported. Extrapolating from that data, it estimated that annually there were as many as forty-seven thousand homeless deaths in American cities, the vast majority among people without shelter.[48]

WHY HAVEN'T WE SOLVED
THE PROBLEM OF HOMELESSNESS?

Why has the mass homelessness crisis been permitted to worsen? The question never stopped troubling me because, while ambitious, the solutions to the modern crisis were far from impossible to achieve. Other advanced capitalist countries had enacted them in one form or fashion, and as a result had remarkably small homeless populations. And such measures were well within the capacity and resources of the United States and the federal government. How did the United States in the modern era fail to embrace and enact proven solutions, and instead make the problem of homelessness even worse?

Some of the explanations were obvious. The structural economic changes that emerged from the 1970s were accompanied and exacerbated by a neoliberal and right-wing transformation in American politics. Those political movements—stretching from the Ronald Reagan era, through the rightward shift of the Democratic Party under Bill Clinton, to the George W. Bush era and the reactionary, oligarchical ethnonationalism of Donald Trump—were themselves rooted in American cultural history. The United States has long been divided around the themes of the "deserving" and "undeserving" poor, a historical fissure seeded in the nation's Protestant Christian colonial past and the systemic racism of the slavery and Jim Crow eras. Charity was long considered the only and best response to poverty. Even then, the American capitalist identity was shaped by the notion—often unforgivingly judgmental—that individuals bore personal responsibility for their economic well-being. Poor people, it was typically said, needed to "pull themselves up by their bootstraps."[49]

This trope in American history was especially prevalent during the first Gilded Age. Horatio Alger, one of the literary progenitors of the American narrative of escape from poverty and improvement through hard work and religious faith, was inspired by his experiences working with homeless and poor children in New York City during the economic crisis of the 1870s. According to Richard White's history of the period, this was the backdrop for Alger's best-selling book *Ragged Dick*, which told the story of the rise of a homeless street urchin: "In Alger's version of America, a homeless, illiterate child, living in a box in an alley, needs only good advice if he is made of the right stuff. . . . What follows is a course of self-improvement and progress. Dick starts saving money, stops drinking and hanging out with the guys, and learns to read and write. He learns the 'satisfaction of self-denial' and the pleasures of property."[50] Of course, the other side of this cliché was, according to White, the "undeserving" poor character: "To indicate that not all children were made of the right stuff, Alger introduces an Irish villain—Mickey McGuire—whose name conveys his shortcomings."[51]

It goes without saying that for most of American history, Black people were most often cast in the role of the "undeserving poor," both in fiction and reality. Along with the modern homelessness crisis, the 1970s ushered in one of the historical periods of "white backlash" in the United States, a reaction by white Americans and conservative political forces to the victories of the civil rights era. While the nation has always had an enormous gap between the wealth of white and Black people, dating to the slavery era, in the aftermath of the civil rights movement, that gap gradually narrowed, from eight to one in 1960 to five to one in 1980. However, after 1980, the gap began to widen again, reaching six to one in 2020, coinciding with another period of white backlash following the election of Barack Obama as president.[52] Racist policies on the national and local levels, the steady loss of manufacturing jobs in cities with large Black communities, and the growing concentration of wealth among the richest fraction of the nation's population led to growing disparities and high rates of Black poverty.

More pernicious, though, was the legacy of anti-Black racism that politicians of the New Gilded Age mined to attack poor and homeless Americans. From Reagan's attacks on "welfare queens" to Bill Clinton's rhetorical divide between "working people" (white) and those supposedly stuck in a "cycle of dependency" (Black), from Giuliani's multiple attacks on Black New Yorkers to Trump's endless barrage of racist and xenophobic invective, a distinctly American racist ideology underpinned the politics and policies of the era. Given the weight and legacy of systemic racism, it was enough to say that solutions to the homelessness crisis were never enacted solely due to deeply entrenched racial disparities and underlying racist ideology. I used to think, as I walked through the EAU or various shelters, where nearly every homeless person was Black or Latino, that if the math were reversed—if 90 percent of homeless New Yorkers were white—would things have been different? The question basically answered itself.

The received cultural notions of personal responsibility and charity, so thick in the American collective memory, also shaped a suspicion of, and often an antipathy to, government aid for the needy. The right-wing political shift in the United States intensified such antigovernment messages. In his first inaugural address as president, Reagan famously condensed the rising conservative political sentiment with the memorable phrase, "Government is not the solution to our problem, government is the problem." This sentiment has been repeated by political leaders of both major political parties for decades.

In the end, what remained one of the fundamental barriers to solving the dual homelessness and housing crises was that far too few Americans viewed government as the solution to these escalating challenges. The weighted legacy of the myths of "personal responsibility" and the alleged virtues of free markets undermined genuine progressive action on housing policy, much as it has in other contested issues like health care and safety-net programs. One consequence was that private charity and nonprofit organizations were compelled into the breach.

CHARITY, PRIVATIZATION, AND THE COMPROMISED ROLE OF NONPROFIT ORGANIZATIONS

Charity has long stood at the forefront of efforts to address modern mass homelessness. In the early years of the crisis, churches and their congregations mobilized soup kitchens for the new "derelicts" and "vagrants" appearing on city streets. The same groups, along with faith-based charities like the Salvation Army, also opened food pantries and emergency shelters. Even in pre-1980s New York City, where the municipal government had long played a role, however incomplete, in providing emergency shelter, religious groups like the Bowery Mission and dozens of churches and synagogues were among the first "service providers" to respond to the growing homeless population of the modern era.

The central role of private organizations in providing services for needy people was a singularly American phenomenon. In other advanced capitalist countries emerging from the Great Depression, the various forms of welfare state assistance—pensions, national health care, housing programs, care for people living with disabilities, child care, and, critically, income supports and food aid for unemployed and poor people—were primarily carried out by the government. In the United States, the welfare state that emerged from the New Deal was far more limited in scope and liberality. There was no national health care, for instance, and other forms of assistance, particularly housing aid, depended on year-to-year budget allocations rather than demonstrated need.

The role of private organizations in providing social welfare assistance expanded in the 1980s under Reagan and then exploded in the 1990s. The 1996 federal welfare reform law not only eliminated the entitlement to cash assistance for the poorest families in the United States, but also replaced the former benefit with "block grants" to state governments— huge allotments of federal funds that gave local officials wide latitude to craft new policies, as detailed in chapter 8. Many state and municipal governments directed that funding to private organizations, essentially making these entities a proxy for government and its services. This created numerous complicated and morally dubious relationships between nonprofit organizations and governments. Some groups were ordered to enact policies that they opposed but nonetheless carried out. Others saw a rise in demand for assistance without a corresponding increase in funding, leading to a decline in service quality and burnout among frontline workers. Many became dependent on government funding and tempered their participation in policy debates.

Many homeless advocacy groups, established in the first years of the modern crisis, continued to work as service providers. They eventually grew into nonprofit organizations, which expanded programs and secured government funding. This symbiotic relationship with government created obvious conflicts. As discussed in chapter 8, government officials in New York regularly threatened the leaders of contracted service providers whenever they opposed a dangerous policy or challenged the actions of City Hall, and the same thing happened routinely in other cities. Some advocacy groups, like Housing Works and the Coalition for the Homeless, had diverse funding bases and were more insulated from political pressure, while others, like the National Coalition for the Homeless, largely chose to forgo government funds altogether. But such arrangements and resolute independence were rare.

Even more problematic were the inherent limitations of being a nonprofit organization. Under the US tax code, such groups were exempt from paying the same taxes as for-profit corporations. But there were strings attached, the most restrictive being a prohibition on political activity or messaging. Thus, during the entirety of the neoliberal period, while the Republican Party was engaging in a project to dismantle the welfare state and eliminate or radically weaken government housing programs, advocacy groups like ours could not speak frankly about these policies. In addition, when politicians who shared this antihomeless ideology were campaigning for office, we could do nothing about it—nor could we support the handful of politicians who championed progressive policies aimed at ending homelessness.

Advocates in New York and elsewhere successfully fended off some truly dangerous policies during the neoliberal era, genuinely saving lives. And we managed to force government leaders to create housing and other vital services for thousands of homeless people. But much of the time I felt frustrated, especially by having to engage in a defensive, rearguard action for so long, and I had some regrets. Perhaps the biggest regret—and I came to blame myself for this as much as anyone—was that our strategy and tactics relied too much on conventional advocacy, persuasion, and argument, and too little on grassroots organizing and activism. With remarkably few exceptions, most of the advocacy work since modern mass homelessness emerged has involved attempts to convince government officials to implement sound policies or reverse bad ones—using an array of traditional tactics, from policy reports to press conferences to meetings with officials, and even the occasional march or rally. These efforts have generally been led by people trained in public policy (like myself), social work, or a related field, often by white people (also like myself) who've never been homeless.

I came to realize, without taking anything away from the achievements of advocacy groups, that more effective strategies are needed to win major changes in federal and local policy. This involves organizing homeless, formerly homeless, and precariously housed people into a genuine movement. This also involves forcefully engaging with the politics surrounding the housing and homelessness crises. The right-wing forces that fiercely oppose progressive efforts to end mass homelessness and the housing crisis are powerful. Overcoming them requires equally determined and creative political movements.

In the twenty-first century, several such movements have secured significant victories. In New York, housing and tenant movements in 2019 won major progressive reforms of the rent-regulation laws—changes that revised the weakened rent laws of the 1990s and were designed to preserve tens of thousands of affordable apartments and protect millions of tenants.[53] In the 2020s, housing movements emerged in places as diverse as Minnesota, Massachusetts, Utah, and California,[54] and while most of those movements were focused more on removing barriers to new housing construction than on robust government support for affordable housing, they were welcome signs of a rising grassroots response to the housing crisis.

PATHS NOT TAKEN

Understanding why modern mass homelessness has endured is essential to ending it. Likewise, obscuring those causes has been a vital weapon of the right-wing project. The same dynamic exists with other critical issues and debates of the New Gilded Age. Corporate health insurers fund opposition to government health care; fossil fuel companies lobby against renewable-energy policies, even bankrolling fraudulent "research" denying climate change; and corporate and business groups resist regulations and attack labor unions.

But like so many others, I often wonder what this era might have looked like if, say, different leaders had been elected, different policies adopted, and different public reactions emerged to the ongoing misery in urban America. Before his death, the British cultural theorist Mark Fisher wrote eloquently about "lost futures," identifying the period of the 1970s and 1980s as a fulcrum—a time when hope for better, even utopian futures had been abandoned. It was no longer possible to imagine better days ahead as Reagan and his conservative doppelgangers took power, and as globalization and the dismantling of the welfare state marched forward.[55]

Fisher was mostly focused on cultural production, but his larger theme—feeling haunted by futures that one sensed innately would never come to pass—resonated with me. Over decades working as an advocate, investigating the homelessness and housing crises, battling the brutal and harsh treatment of vulnerable people, and, most of all, watching desperate people survive in public spaces every day, it's impossible not to feel haunted.

CHAPTER 12

NEIGHBORHOODS AND HOMELANDS: MASS DISPLACEMENT AND HOMELESSNESS

With planetary urbanization, a planet-full of people can no
longer find steady work or steady homes, and a huge unwieldy
inertia persists.

Andy Merrifield
The Politics of the Encounter

CROSSING THE GAP

It was in the grimy hours before dawn, in October 2022, when the first
day's bus from Texas pulled into Manhattan's Port Authority Bus Terminal. Around fifty passengers disembarked, all exhausted, bedraggled, and
carrying few personal belongings. They were immigrant asylum seekers
from various parts of Central and South America, who had been sent by
bus to New York City under orders from the governor of Texas. I interviewed several individuals and families, jotting down their names and
basic information about their asylum cases and upcoming hearing dates,
and, most of all, their need for clothing and food. The mutual aid group
with which I was volunteering had been formed to provide emergency
help for recent immigrants to New York, collecting donations of appropriate cold-weather apparel, as well as basic items like socks, underwear,
diapers, and toiletries.

One woman, Estela, was from the outskirts of Otavalo, a large town in

Ecuador, which lay north of Quito, where I had briefly lived and worked as a teacher in the late 1980s. This lovely town, which I had visited several times, was where many Ecuadorian immigrants originally lived before moving to New York. It was not uncommon to see musicians from Otavalo playing in subway stations with traditional instruments like the *zampoña*, or pan flute, and wearing Andean indigenous garments. Estela, who was in her late twenties, arrived with her husband, who barely spoke, and their two children, aged seven and four. She said they left Ecuador due to threats of gang violence in her community. After making their way to northwestern Colombia, the entire family traveled on foot through the Darién Gap, the roadless isthmus of dense jungle that separates Colombia and Panama, and which had become notorious as a corrupt, lawless transit corridor for countless migrants fleeing South America for the north.

In New York and other cities, there were millions of people who'd undergone similarly grueling treks to North America, expelled or displaced from their homelands by repression or economic dislocation. Likewise, there were countless internal migrants in those cities, discarded from vanishing industries and gentrifying neighborhoods. The waves of displacement of the New Gilded Age, whether from deindustrialization, gentrification, the climate crisis, or mass migration have long been treated as discrete crises. But there was a thread connecting these phenomena. To borrow a term that came into vogue in the early 2020s, they formed a polycrisis—the intersection of various kinds of displacement and removal. These mass displacements have occurred on a wider scale and with more frequency since the 1970s. Deindustrialization and the financialization of the capitalist economy ran through the advanced capitalist nations and spread to much of the Global South. Gentrification took hold in cities worldwide. And the climate crisis caused bigger and more frequent disasters, displacing millions while contributing to waves of migration across regions and even continents.

Like mass homelessness, these crises have their roots in the epochal shifts in global capitalism, particularly in cities, and the same strain of neoliberal policies that emerged in New York during the 1970s fiscal crisis, all against the background of systemic racism and rising xenophobia. Mass displacement in its many forms has become the new normal—a defining feature of the New Gilded Age.

DEINDUSTRIALIZATION: ECONOMIC DISPLACEMENT

The economic and fiscal crises of the 1970s, following structural trends set in motion in the preceding decades, radically altered New York City. What had been a vibrant, bustling, industrial, and commercial metropolis, firmly established as a world capital, became a far different place—characterized by growing inequality, the dominance of finance and real estate, and precarious service-sector employment for the working class. In these ways, New York signaled the coming transformation of the rest of urban America.

In the years after World War II, New York City's economy was relatively balanced across various employment sectors, with manufacturing at its core. In 1950, nearly a million New Yorkers worked in factories and workshops, making up 29 percent of total employment—a share similar to that of manufacturing employment nationwide.[1] But even though total employment in the city rose, before the eve of the 1970s, to 3.8 million workers, manufacturing's share of the total decreased to 22 percent—and then fell off a cliff. Between 1969 and 1977, New York City lost 639,000 jobs—one in six jobs citywide. Nearly half of that loss (291,000 jobs) came from manufacturing employment. By 1977, only 16 percent of jobs in New York City were in that sector, a rate that would continue to deteriorate into the twenty-first century; by 2024, only one in every hundred city jobs was in manufacturing.[2]

New York was ahead of the national trend of deindustrialization. Corporations had already moved many manufacturing jobs from New York to southern states, drawn by their laws blocking labor unions coupled with the white supremacist regime suppressing Black workers. Ultimately, however, industrial capital found even cheaper wages and more opportunities for labor control in the countries of the Global South, and it therefore moved most manufacturing employment entirely out of the United States. The number of manufacturing jobs nationwide peaked in 1979 at nearly twenty million—around one in every four US jobs—but declined steadily over the following two decades, with even sharper declines in the early twenty-first century. By 2024, there were only thirteen million manufacturing jobs nationwide—despite a much larger workforce. This constituted only 8 percent of all US employment.

Deindustrialization hit cities particularly hard. Of the more than five million manufacturing jobs lost since 2000, more than one million alone were in just ten metropolitan areas—and this included cities with the worst housing affordability problems and largest homeless populations, like Los Angeles, Boston, San José, Houston, San Francisco, and New York.[3] The impact of manufacturing losses hit urban Black communities disproportionately hard. Many Black Americans had fled to northern and western cities from the South to seek employment in the growing industrial sector, only to see that sector hollowed out by white industrial flight—one of the major factors behind unequal rates of poverty and homelessness among Black people across the country.[4]

Amid the process of deindustrialization, it was a common mistake to imagine that the working class was vanishing—that the loss of manufacturing jobs had somehow erased actual labor. Nothing could have been further from the truth. As urban theorist Andy Merrifield has written, "Simply put, technological expansion under capitalism *actively produces* an unproductive service class. As the mode of production develops, what looks like the disappearance of the 'traditional' working class is, in actuality, a reconstitution of this traditional working class. The growth of a service class reflects a *deepening* of capital-labor relations, not its supersession."[5]

The new jobs that defined the lowest rungs of labor in New York not only paid less than manufacturing jobs had, but they also were almost entirely nonunion positions. Indeed, in New York City, the rate of unionized nongovernment workers fell steadily in the twenty-first century—to only 13 percent by 2024—which was still higher than the national rate of 6 percent.[6]

Above all, the defining feature of the new jobs was their precarity— workers had few protections, especially during economic downturns, and could easily be fired or replaced, leaving them in a cycle of uncertainty.

GENTRIFICATION: URBAN DISPLACEMENT

The neoliberal era was also marked by the spatial and demographic reorganization of New York and other cities. A key process in this urban transformation was gentrification—the conversion of working-class and poor neighborhoods, most of them majority Black and Latino, into middle-class and affluent white districts. The term gentrification, which obviously derived from "gentry," signifying the elite classes, was coined by British sociologist Ruth Glass in the 1960s to describe the changes in London neighborhoods like Islington. As Glass wrote at that time, "One by one, many of the working class neighbourhoods of London have been invaded by the middle-classes—upper and lower. . . . Once this process of 'gentrification' starts in a district it goes on rapidly, until all or most of the original working-class occupiers are displaced and the whole social character of the district is changed."[7]

Gentrification has often been romanticized as simply the improvement of blighted neighborhoods, or as a matter of cultural or aesthetic changes to such areas—with the unfortunate, though often overlooked, by-product being the departure of some older residents. However, it was actually a broader, more comprehensive process of urban change—the culmination of a three-part historical process of how capital shaped the urban environment in the neoliberal age. As housing analyst Samuel Stein has explained, "First comes *investment* in a built environment; second, neighborhood *disinvestment* and property abandonment; and third, *reinvestment* in that same space for greater profits."[8] As Stein went on to explain, widespread gentrification was deeply rooted in the historic shift in urban capitalism: "As the complex process of deindustrialization unfolded, capital became both more mobile and, ironically, more grounded. . . . Investments in land and buildings filled the literal and figurative space left by urban industrial flight. Real estate went from being a secondary to a primary source of urban capital accumulation. This switch is the genesis of gentrification in the United States."[9]

In New York City, capital and government had invested in a city that was largely shaped, from the first Gilded Age through the post–World War II period, by manufacturing and industry. Road networks and mass transit were designed to bring workers and goods to and from factories and work sites. Even neighborhoods that, by the twenty-first century, were almost entirely residential or dotted with retail spaces and office buildings—like Chelsea, Long Island City, Chinatown, Red Hook, the Lower East Side, and many parts of central Brooklyn—had been centers of manufacturing decades earlier. Other neighborhoods were shaped by their role in housing the industrial working class.

These neighborhoods were also molded by racist government housing and development policies, like redlining and urban renewal, that segregated Black and Latino New Yorkers in lower-income enclaves. Indeed, the racialized urban policies of the postwar period helped to shape the terrain for eventual gentrification by displacing Black and Latino tenants from many urban spaces, followed by "improvements" and investment in public amenities, such as parks and roads. This was the reason many of the most contested sites of gentrification in New York City in the twenty-first century have involved historically Black and Latino neighborhoods like Bedford-Stuyvesant, Bushwick, Crown Heights, and Fort Greene in Brooklyn; Harlem and parts of the Lower East Side in Manhattan; and even sections of the South Bronx.

Gentrification always required the removal and displacement of those Black and Latino communities. The two largest Black communities in New York City have historically been in central Brooklyn and Harlem. In Bedford-Stuyvesant, the heart of the former, between 1990 and 2020, the Black share of the neighborhood's population fell from 82 percent to 54 percent, while the white share rose from under 1 percent to 21 percent (see chapter 5). In Central Harlem over those three decades, the Black share of the population fell from 89 to 51 percent, and the white share grew from 1 to 16 percent. Indeed, the Black share of New York City's total population fell from 26 to 20 percent over that same period, reflecting the outmigration of Black people to other cities in the South and West.[10]

On the Lower East Side, Puerto Rican and other Latino residents were pushed out of the neighborhood as early as the 1970s, especially from the area called Loisaida, which covered much of Alphabet City along the neighborhood's eastern stretches. The housing abandonment of that decade had already led to a 9 percent decline in the area's Latino population by 1980, and those who remained were increasingly concentrated in the public housing complexes lining the East River.[11] As urban theorist Neil Smith has noted, housing disinvestment and abandonment had long been a tool of gentrification for an unscrupulous segment of the real estate industry. Cutbacks in maintenance and basic upkeep, sometimes coupled with nonpayment of utilities and property taxes, were, in the long term, logical within a profit-making calculus. This was particularly true on the Lower East Side of the 1980s, where land and property values were poised to rise faster than the income generated by long-standing, low-income tenants.[12]

Gentrification served a useful purpose for urban capital in the earliest phase of the New Gilded Age. In the wake of the 1970s austerity regime imposed on New York and other cities, civic leaders turned to private capital to make investments in "distressed communities," and to generate profits through the "revitalization" of those neighborhoods. Over time, the "real estate state," to borrow Samuel Stein's apt term, marshaled a range of policies friendly to banks and developers to incentivize investment and development in the newly affluent districts. This included tax breaks, rezonings, the weakening of rent regulation, targeted investments in urban amenities like local schools, and the privatization of public services and spaces, as with the "business improvement districts" and the "conservancies" administering valued parks. Finally, civic leaders and the local press could be counted on to praise the outcome: the newer, shinier, sleeker environs with luxe dining and shopping experiences for the affluent residents.

Less remarked on were the people who'd been displaced and replaced. The longtime residents, old neighbors, and anchors for communities were overlooked, even though they had been the very people who began to revive poor neighborhoods in the first place, via sweat equity, community mobilization, and grassroots organizing for better schools and urban services. And, of course, among the first to be displaced—in this case, using the state-sanctioned violence of the police—were homeless people.

THE CLIMATE CRISIS: GLOBAL DISPLACEMENT

I met Natalia one November when she was staying at a nondescript hotel in midtown Manhattan. It was the kind of generic establishment that catered to middle-class tourists, those visiting New York for the first time to take in a Broadway show, gawk at the skyscrapers, and typically complain about paying $200 per night, at that time, for a room in a modest chain hotel, where the nightly rate would have been half that amount anywhere else.

But Natalia's room cost $300 each night, and far from being a tourist on holiday, she was there involuntarily. She'd been made homeless by Hurricane Sandy, whose massive storm surge struck New York City on October 29, 2012, causing billions of dollars in damage and displacing tens of thousands of New Yorkers. Most of those who became homeless, like Natalia, lived in the coastal areas like Far Rockaway in Queens, Brighton Beach in Brooklyn, and Midland Beach in Staten Island—communities with working class and poor residents. A Russian immigrant who worked as a housecleaner, Natalia had lived in a basement apartment in Coney Island, a few blocks from the beach, but the swell of water—which, at its worst, rose to nearly ten feet above normal tide levels—flooded her home. Natalia had arrived at the midtown hotel after several grueling nights in a makeshift "evacuation center" and then a congregate shelter, and she had not begun to work through the shock of losing her home and nearly everything she owned. When I met her, I was volunteering with some Legal Aid Society colleagues to help her complete FEMA applications for short-term cash assistance and temporary housing, which was made more difficult by the fact that her basement apartment was not entirely legal. This was a common problem for the people displaced from the poorer neighborhoods devastated by Hurricane Sandy.

The city government's response was haphazard at best, kneecapped by the fact that, at the time Sandy struck, the municipal shelter population was at a record high of nearly fifty thousand people, with virtually no vacant beds—hence the exorbitant rates demanded by the commercial hotels. Making matters worse, many municipal shelters were themselves evacuated because they lay in the storm's flood zones. The 850 residents of the Bellevue shelter were temporarily relocated. So were hundreds more from shelters in Brooklyn and Queens, as well as homeless people who'd slept in the Staten Island Ferry Terminal.[13] Moreover, Sandy's storm surge had pushed up the East River and overflowed the Manhattan waterfront as far north as 14th Street, ultimately flooding a Con Edison power plant in my East Village neighborhood and knocking out electricity for the southern third of the island. During the weeks without power, and amid an unseasonable cold snap in the city, thousands of people slept in homeless shelters that had no heat and lighting.

The Bloomberg administration had clearly not planned for the onset of worsening storms related to climate change. In the days immediately after Sandy, it opened emergency "evacuation centers" in schools and other government buildings for the thousands, like Natalia, who'd escaped their flooded homes. Over the following three weeks, and with no advance notice, city officials closed the centers and hastily—often in the middle of the night—shuttled evacuees to hotels or substandard accommodations. One notorious example was the Franklin armory in the Bronx. As noted in chapter 9, the site was already a shelter for homeless women, with two hundred beds in barracks-style rooms. But city bureaucrats hastily added dozens of cots to the armory drill floor, marking the building's first use as a shelter for families and children. Evacuees were eventually relocated to commercial hotels, like the one where I met Natalia.

But thousands of displaced families and individuals languished for months due to a lack of affordable housing and the government's failure to provide assistance. Natalia had been paying around $800 per month in rent for her basement room, but she would never find an apartment at a comparable price. In March of the following year, a Bloomberg administration official wrote to evacuees to tell them that regardless of whether they had been lucky enough to find permanent housing, the city's Hotel and Interim Placement Program would be ending on April 30, only six months after Sandy devastated New York.[14] Given that homeless families often had to wait in shelters for more than a year for housing aid, six months was a wildly unrealistic time frame. While advocates mounted legal challenges to the hasty end of the program, many desperate families had to turn to the traditional shelter system, where they encountered even longer, often fruitless waits for housing assistance. Or they sought refuge in the overcrowded, invisible quarters of New York City's "hidden homeless" population.

A "hundred-year storm" that occurred far sooner than anticipated, inflicting more damage than predicted, Hurricane Sandy was a harbinger of stronger storms to come. A study published in *Nature* estimated that, of the approximately $60 billion in damages caused by Sandy, as much as $14 billion was clearly attributable to anthropogenic climate change.[15]

Numerous scientific studies have concluded that the effects of the climate crisis—in particular, warming oceans and higher sea levels—have increased the force and destructiveness of hurricanes.[16] Moreover, research has shown an even stronger link between climate change and other extreme weather events, including heat waves, droughts, wildfires, and floods. The California wildfires of January 2025, for instance, destroyed more than ten thousand homes in Los Angeles and caused billions in damage.

So-called natural disasters have occurred with far more frequency, and a far higher price tag, during the New Gilded Age. According to the National Oceanic and Atmospheric Administration, the number of billion-dollar weather and climate events in the United States has risen every decade, from an average of three per year in the 1980s to twenty-eight in 2023. By the 2020s, more than sixty million American homes were in areas determined to be of "moderate risk" or worse from flooding and other environmental disasters.[17]

If anything, the climate crisis has caused far more severe homelessness and displacement outside the United States. Huge swaths of central and southwest Asia, South America, Africa, and Central America suffered historic heat waves, floods, and drought, exacerbated by climate change, during the first decades of the twenty-first century. And those climate disasters, along with economic and political forces, helped push millions of people to migrate.

MASS MIGRATION: HOMELAND DISPLACEMENT

New York has long been a destination city for immigrants from poorer countries. By the end of the first Gilded Age in 1910, the foreign-born share of New York City's population had peaked at 41 percent, part of the explosion in mostly southern and eastern European migration to North America of that era. By the 1970s and 1980s, however, only around one in five New Yorkers had been born outside the United States. But the renewed waves of in-migration that began in the 1990s—spurred in part by changes in federal immigration law, but mostly by widening economic disparities between the United States and countries of the Global South—again increased the number and percentage of foreign-born New Yorkers. Likewise, the legacy of US imperial interference in Latin America, including the funding and support of dictators, paramilitary groups, and death squads, continued to destabilize much of the region. By 2018, New York City's immigrant population had grown to 3.1 million people, the largest in its history, and foreign-born New Yorkers made up 38 percent of the total population and 45 percent of the workforce.[18]

But two years into the COVID-19 crisis, New York City experienced an even greater increase in immigration that, unlike earlier influxes and due to its politicized origins, significantly expanded the city's homeless population. While the broader trend of migration from Latin America, Asia, and Africa to the United States had been years in the making, the arrival of thousands of asylum seekers in New York was the consequence of bad-faith political gamesmanship by Republican politicians in border states.

In the spring of 2022, Texas Governor Greg Abbott began trans-
porting recently arrived immigrants by bus to New York, Los Angeles,
Denver, Philadelphia, Washington, DC, and other cities with Democratic mayors. By early 2024, Abbott claimed he had bused more than one
hundred thousand immigrants to so-called "blue" cities outside Texas, at
a cost of $148 million.[19] However, while Abbott's cynical actions estab-
lished the pattern of migration, they were responsible for only a portion
of the movement from the border to other communities; according to one
analysis, Abbott's policy may have accounted for only around one in every
five busloads of immigrants arriving in northern cities. By the summer of
2024, just over two years after the Abbott-initiated buses had first begun
their journey north, an estimated 210,000 immigrants—the vast majority of them with pending asylum cases—had arrived in New York City,
with the state of Texas having transported around forty-five thousand of
them.[20] The arrival of buses carrying immigrants initially overwhelmed
city officials and charitable organizations, although many of the latter,
like the mutual aid project where I volunteered, rallied to provide emergency aid and legal assistance for the asylum seekers.

But the response by the newly installed mayoral administration—Eric
Adams had taken office in January 2022, a few months before the Abbott
buses arrived—and the conservative Democratic governor, Kathy Hochul, was nothing short of disastrous. City officials were slow to add shelter capacity, for both immigrant families and individuals, and many of
the new shelters were deeply inadequate. State officials initially provided
little to no assistance, and other necessary emergency services, like food,
clothing, and legal assistance, were slow to arrive.

In the months before the first Abbott bus arrived in April 2022, New
York City's total shelter census hovered around sixty-six thousand people
per night.[21] Over the next two years, the total nightly shelter population
in New York doubled—to an astounding 132,000 people, by far the high-

est level in the city's history.[22] That increase reflected a nearly 20 percent rise in the nonimmigrant homeless shelter population, but the large majority of the new homeless population was made up of immigrants.

During the first two years of the wave of new immigrant arrivals, city officials placed thousands of asylum seekers in vast tent shelters located in inaccessible parts of the city, such as Floyd Bennett Field—a former airport in Brooklyn abutting Jamaica Bay that had been converted to federal parkland—and Randall's Island in the East River. During my visits to Floyd Bennett Field in 2024, I saw dozens of Latino immigrants trudging in the rain from the tents, which were located on Runway 19—an abandoned airstrip—to an athletic complex housed in an old airplane hangar a quarter mile away. There, they could purchase snacks or fast food, but that was all. In deference to complaints from the white community that used the complex, there were newly posted signs bluntly declaring, "No Public Restrooms"—I had never seen them before the immigrant had arrived. The tents on Randall's Island sheltered some 2,200 immigrants, and like those at Floyd Bennett Field, the residents faced growing hostility from neighboring communities that used the island for recreation and youth sports leagues.[23] In other neighborhoods, the anti-immigrant-shelter opposition grew violent, with mob-style protests and even bomb threats.

But for homeless immigrants, the most serious problems concerned the deplorable conditions in the massive new shelters haphazardly created over two years. Heavy rainfall caused flooding at the Randall's Island tent complex.[24] In the giant tents, families with small children were often sheltered in congregate settings alongside individuals. The living conditions and food were miserable, and security guards and staff mistreated the residents. All these complaints resounded like a deafening, historical echo of those heard routinely over decades from homeless New Yorkers sheltered in the vast municipal shelter system.

One other historical echo was even louder. Faced with the growing number of homeless immigrants, Adams took a page from the Giuliani and Bloomberg playbook and mounted a vocal attack on the right to shelter. He eventually turned to the courts to overturn the *Callahan* consent decree. After months of litigation and negotiation, and anxious about the consequences for future homeless populations as courts were growing more ideologically conservative, the Coalition for the Homeless and the Legal Aid Society reached a settlement with the Adams administration in March 2024. The limited agreement set two-month time limits on shelter stays for young adult immigrants, although they could extend their stays if needed. Most important, it maintained the existing right-to-shelter protections for homeless families and children, who made up nearly 80 percent of homeless immigrants. But the compromise was clearly a setback provoked by the anti-immigrant xenophobia and Trumpian politics of the period.[25]

Mass displacement and migration from country to country, even continent to continent, grew on a global scale in the twenty-first century. Millions of refugees and other displaced people fled their homelands, often seeking refuge in Europe and North America, although the majority settled in the countries of the Global South.[26] As larger parts of the planet were affected by the climate crisis, many fled territories beset by drought and famine, while many millions more escaped violence or economic deprivation for better opportunities in the advanced capitalist countries.[27]

In 2024, the Adams administration opened a "processing center" for immigrant adults in my East Village neighborhood, using a boarded-up Catholic school located across the street from Tompkins Square Park. I'd regularly see long lines of Latin American and African young men outside the center or resting on benches in the park. Many gathered outside a nearby mosque, whose sidewalks were packed with bicycles and e-bikes used by the deliverymen who worked in the area. Many of the asylum applicants, although forbidden from working legally, nonetheless found jobs as *deliveristas*, restaurant dishwashers, construction workers, or in some other part of New York's underground economy. One day in Tompkins Square Park, I talked with a young man from Caracas, Venezuela, a city I'd visited in the late 1980s, long before the US embargo and the economic collapse. He told me how much his country had changed (he hadn't even been born when I visited), describing his time in Colombia before braving the Darién Gap and traveling north through Central America. Above all else, he wanted my help finding a job so he could leave the processing center and tent shelters behind and find a real home.

THE SURPLUS POPULATION AND HOMELESSNESS

All these forms of displacement had something in common—people were discarded from employment, neighborhoods, whole regions, and even nations. The New Gilded Age stage of capitalism not only created mass displacement; it also produced enormous groups of redundant, superfluous workers, forming a vast surplus population. In the nineteenth century, Karl Marx had described how the system of capitalism itself, even in its earliest industrial stage, inevitably created a surplus population of workers—what he referred to as the "industrial reserve army."[28] As the value of labor rose, the rate of profit and capital accumulation declined, and, as a result, capital laid off workers. As theorist Søren Mau has explained:

> Marx distinguishes between three forms of this relative surplus
> population, which he considers to be a necessary condition of
> capitalist production: the *floating* surplus population, that is,
> workers belonging permanent to the labour force but temporarily
> under- or unemployed; the *latent* surplus population, in other
> words, proletarians who are not regularly a part of the workforce
> but can be drawn into wage labour when capital needs them
> (Marx cited the example of rural populations, but we could also

mention domestic workers of proletarians on public benefits);
and finally the *stagnant* surplus population, which is the lowest
strata of the working class: those who have "extremely irregular
employment" but, unlike the latent surplus population, generally
do not have access to means of subsistence outside of the wage
relation. Taken together, these different subgroups within
the relative surplus population make up what Marx calls the
industrial reserve army.[29]

This phenomenon has been inescapable for well over a century. The
most glaring signs have been widening inequality, along with the rise of
mass unemployment, the decline of relative wages, and the impoverish-
ment of the working class. The other factor that created and sustained this
relative surplus population was the rising productivity of capital—in brief,
advances in technology and efficiency that reduced, or even eliminated,
the need for labor. And it was this process, in combination with the first,
that tended toward a larger surplus population over time.

As Mau and others have observed, for much of the twentieth century,
especially the "golden age" between World War II and the 1970s, there
was widespread belief that this dynamic, the expansion of a growing surplus population, did not play a significant role in the developed capitalist
countries. The rise and fall of unemployment and poverty were viewed as
cyclical. These trends were described in the news media as almost natural
events, referred to as the "business cycle," or the ebb and flow of economic
prosperity. To a large degree, this owed to the fact that, in the decades
after the Great Depression, Keynesian and welfare-state policies (e.g., the
New Deal programs in the United States, and similar programs elsewhere)
were prevalent throughout most of the advanced capitalist countries and
cushioned some of the worst effects of the periodic accumulation crises.
At the same time, imperial control of much of Latin America, Asia, and

Africa extracted value from colonized territories for "first world" capital.

Indeed, one reason the emergence of modern mass homelessness was greeted with such shock was that it was a visceral, in-your-face indictment of this collective myth: the generalized sense that things improved and returned to "normal" as the economy recovered from a downturn. And it undermined the wholly American faith in progress and the notion that "things are always getting better."

Entering the twenty-first century, it became clear that the postwar era of economic growth, reduced inequality, and relative stability was, in fact, an exceptional period. Instead, the decades after the 1970s have seen continuous growth in the surplus population, and, most troubling of all, a growth in what Marx called the "stagnant" population: the poorest workers with the most tenuous connection to the labor force. Internationally, the steady growth of surplus people was evident even before the 1970s in the metastasizing cities of the Global South, where mass waves of rural-to-urban migration led to the explosion of shanty communities and slums, many with vast underground or "informal" economies.[30]

In the United States, evidence of the growing surplus population was most glaringly obvious in two places. The first revolved around prisons and jails, and, indeed, the wider carceral system. In 1970, the nation's total prison population was 199,000 people, but by the mid-1990s—amid the police crackdowns seen in New York and elsewhere, and a national political panic about crime rates— it surpassed one million, eventually exceeding 1.5 million by the 2010s.[31] By the twenty-first century, the United States had the world's largest prison population and ranked just behind Rwanda in incarceration rates. But even these inconceivable statistics understate the scale of the nation's multifaceted carceral system. In 2021, there were an astounding 5.6 million Americans under the control of the criminal justice system, including 1.8 million in prisons or jails and 3.8 million on probation or parole. In comparison, in 1980, that total number was just over 1.8 million. In more than four decades of the New Gilded Age, the number of Americans under carceral control grew by 368 percent, and the prison population alone increased by 305 percent.[32]

The second repository for the growing surplus population was, of course, mass homelessness. Over time, homelessness evolved into something more than mere urban misery, the most extreme version of American poverty, as bad as all of that might be. Mass homelessness, the most visible and, in some ways, the earliest sign of the mass displacement of the era, morphed into the ever-looming threat facing the discarded, surplus populations of the New Gilded Age.

CONCLUSION: PLACELESS

We think of the past as finished and the present as open-ended,
but this is not [Walter] Benjamin's opinion. In his "Theses on
the Philosophy of History" it is the past that is incomplete,
and the present that has a chance to bring it to fruition. What
happens, happens, and does so irretrievably; but the meaning
of such events is in the custodianship of the living. . . . We can
also ensure that those in the past who were defeated in their
fight for justice and friendship did not die in vain. . . . The dead
cannot literally be compensated for their suffering, but that
suffering can be invested with new significance by our actions
in the present.

Terry Eagleton
"The Marxist and the Messiah"

HOMELESSNESS AND URBAN SPACE

The change was so gradual that at first it escaped notice—but over time it
became the "new normal," a regular part of urban life. Beginning in the
1980s, public spaces in New York and other American cities began to be
altered in response to the rising number of unsheltered homeless people.
And the goal was to keep them away and keep them out of sight, to make
them invisible.

Benches in parks, at bus stops, and inside transit terminals were rede-
signed to prohibit anyone from lying down on them. Gates and barriers
were erected around parks and plazas to prevent entry, especially at night.
Public restrooms were shuttered and abandoned, and coffee shops and

restaurants installed locks or passcodes on their bathroom doors to keep out unwanted visitors. Store owners installed sprinkler systems, switched on at night and in the early morning hours, to prevent people from sleeping under awnings or in doorways. Metal spikes were installed on railings, low concrete walls, and anywhere else someone might want to sit down and rest for a spell.

Such features of "hostile architecture," as it came to be called, made life progressively harder for homeless people, delimiting the urban space in which they moved about, sought respite, and struggled each day to survive. And it made life harder for the nonhomeless public as well. In New York and other cities, many public plazas and spaces were privately owned—often created as part of some development tax break that required them to be open to the general public. But under the pretext of barring homeless people, such "public" spaces came to be closed or gated, thereby blocking out the broader populace as well. As much as anything, the spikes, gates, and confinement of public space served as a signifier that common, shared urban space was not only shrinking—it was intended for some people and not for those labeled "undesirables." In this fashion, the privatization of public space morphed into a form of urban control.

Hostile architecture was merely the most visible mechanism of control affecting homeless and displaced people throughout the New Gilded Age. Over decades, urban elites responded to mass homelessness not only by altering physical space, but also by intensifying social control over the lives of homeless and poor people. The criminalization of homelessness—or, better put, the use of state violence, via the police, and the power of detention and incarceration—was the other palpable, unremitting means of controlling homeless city-dwellers, in particular Black and Latino people. The police further circumscribed the use of public space—indeed, the very presence of homelessness—determining who could or could not be in a park, on a subway platform, or on a sidewalk.

The removal of homeless people from urban space also advanced the goal of gentrifying areas to benefit affluent white residents, as well as the interests of real estate and finance capital. Gentrification represented wider-scale displacement—in this instance, of whole neighborhoods and districts—aimed at destabilizing communities. The grassroots, collective efforts of Black and Latino activists to improve parks, schools, and local services were turned against those very communities, as investment capital and white gentrifiers moved in and pushed out longtime residents.

Such displacement helped to fuel the housing precarity that formed the substructure of modern mass homelessness—the ever-looming threat of eviction. Losing a home was the proverbial tip of the iceberg, the discernible feature of a much larger, churning process of displacement. In this sense, homelessness served as an ever-present threat, and thus a species of control over poor and working-class urbanites in an age of inequality.

HOMELESSNESS AS THREAT

During the first Gilded Age, workers in New York and other cities contended with many of the same challenges as those in the neoliberal era: structural economic change (in the form of industrialization) and worsening inequality. Waves of immigration, alongside manufacturing development, led to the enormous growth of cities—but also generated an anti-immigrant backlash. Far more brutal was the white supremacist counterattack to Reconstruction and the end of slavery, which led to Jim Crow and helped to oppress and displace millions of Black people. American workers also confronted an oligarchical leadership, with a small number of wealthy individuals controlling immense wealth and vast sectors of the economy, and a corrupt political system allied with those elites. Indeed, the very name bestowed on the era borrowed from Mark Twain's novel, which tellingly was not called *The Golden Age*, but instead *The Gilded Age*, emphasizing a polished surface concealing deep-rooted flaws. As historian Richard White has written, "The pithy title covered a convoluted plot whose moral was the danger of speculation over honest labor. The 'Gilded Age' exposed the rot beneath the gilded surface. . . . The Gilded Age was corrupt, and corruption in government and business mattered. Corruption suffused government and the economy."[1]

Working-class and poor Americans of that era suffered tremendously, perhaps nowhere more than in the overcrowded "slums" of New York and other burgeoning cities. But they also fought back, whether it was the Great Railroad Strike of 1877 and other labor uprisings, or the tenant rent strikes at the turn of the century. Unions and socialist political movements flourished, setting the stage for subsequent labor victories and welfare-state reforms to come. But those movements generated a fierce, often violent backlash from elites. In the same vein as the Tompkins Square police riot of 1874, the suppression of transit worker strikes and furious construction of armories revealed government leaders—pushed by their elite patrons—utilizing police departments and militias to stamp out worker dissent. The threat of state and elite reprisals was clear, as unmistakable as imprisonment or a truncheon blow to the head.

The threat to poor workers in the New Gilded Age is far more subtle, if no less brutal. Down deep, every working-class and poor urbanite knows that homelessness is a looming threat. Indeed, when one in every fifteen poor New Yorkers – including one of every seven Black children living in poverty – slept in a homeless shelter over the course of a year, it was impossible to view homelessness as an unusual or rare experience.[2] The dismantling of the social safety net, particularly the welfare-state programs that cushioned the blows of unemployment and periodic capitalist crises, has augmented those fears and anxieties.

And that was one of the principal aims of the neoliberal project. From the draconian cutbacks to government services and the municipal workforce in 1970s New York, to Reagan's housing cutbacks, to Clinton's attack on entitlement programs such as welfare, the goal was to weaken and dismantle government assistance and protections for working-class Americans. Low-wage workers, already fearful of job loss and eviction, are far less likely to organize for higher pay and better working conditions if they know there is no safety net to rescue them from losing it all—from becoming homeless.

It was in this sense that historian Kim Phillips-Fein, urban theorist David Harvey, and others described the New York City of the 1970s fiscal crisis as a testing ground for the neoliberal state—a model of governance that has since been replicated internationally from the 1980s through to the early decades of the twenty-first century. By the 2010s, however, there was growing evidence that the right-wing, neoliberal political regime that dominated American politics—from Reagan to Clinton to Bush on the national level, and from Koch to Giuliani to Bloomberg to Andrew Cuomo in New York—had been supplanted by an even harsher brand of politics. Trump and his far-right allies trafficked in a discourse that was explicitly racist, xenophobic, misogynistic, and nationalistic, and their political project was allied with the growing billionaire oligarchy of the age. But many elements of the neoliberal model—from lavish tax cuts for the wealthy and corporations, to sharp cutbacks in housing, health care, and food assistance—remained core features of the ascendant far-right political movement.

While the neoliberal template involved the shrinking of certain state functions—especially welfare-state programs and the regulation of banks and corporations—it also required a larger role for government in the management and control of the lives of poor people and the growing surplus population, via the carceral state and, of course, homelessness. What's more, so-called "private sector" mechanisms of control began to flourish. As Matthew Desmond and others have written, being poor and precariously housed in American cities entails various forms of exploitation: by slumlords, including the wealthy investment firms that increasingly own large portions of housing in poor and working-class communities; through the predatory financial arrangements prevalent in poor urban neighborhoods, like payday loans, layaway purchase plans, and check-cashing storefronts that charge exorbitant fees and interest; and even in local groceries and bodegas, where food costs more than in suburban supermarkets. As James Baldwin wrote in the early 1960s, "Anyone who has ever struggled with poverty knows how extremely expensive it is to be poor; and if one is a member of a captive population, economically speaking, one's feet have simply been placed on the treadmill forever."[3]

In New York City, I saw this exploitation of homeless people firsthand. "Three-quarter house" operators routinely demanded food stamps, benefits, and cash payments from residents, or they'd throw them out onto the streets. Unscrupulous landlords demanded "side payments" from homeless families hoping to use rent subsidies to lease an apartment. Business improvement districts and predatory nonprofit groups paid homeless workers shamefully low wages, far below the legally mandated minimum wage, to perform the work once done by a unionized municipal workforce. Slumlords like the Podolsky brothers even exploited government programs, making hundreds of millions of dollars over the years by operating the most decrepit shelters and welfare hotels.

The system of municipal services for homeless people routinely exercised significant control over their lives. Obtaining and keeping basic benefits—for food, cash assistance, and health insurance—required an enormous, exhausting amount of time and effort, not to mention the grueling ordeal involved in entering the shelter system. And homeless services based on the "continuum of care" model frequently involved repeated intrusions into the lives of shelter residents, all premised on the false notion that they were broken people who needed to be repaired, and who had to accomplish certain arbitrary goals before they could get housing—assuming the inadequate, rationed supply of housing aid was even available.

But in a larger sense, the loss of control represented both by homelessness and by the wider displacement of the New Gilded Age went far deeper. To be homeless meant losing one's place in the world—not only one's home, but one's standing in the city's civic, political, and economic life. Indeed, a study that analyzed tens of millions of eviction and voter records from the 2016 election found that areas with high eviction rates had significantly lower voter turnout, concluding that "the impact of eviction reverberates far beyond housing loss, affecting democratic participation." These findings built on earlier research documenting how high rates of poverty, foreclosure, and incarceration also led to lower voting rates, showing that "political quiescence may emerge, even for individuals with prior histories of political participation, as a product of living in a community where exposure to trauma and disadvantage is common."[4] The instability of housing precarity and losing one's home, to say nothing of homelessness itself, thus whittled away at poor people's already diminished control of their neighborhoods.

Homelessness and displacement were a way of making urban communities perpetually unsettled and less powerful—more precarious, less communal, and crucially, less engaged in the wider society. The sense of being secure in one's home, keeping the same job for years, or feeling rooted in one's neighborhood or homeland—those sentiments came to seem like relics of a lost world, appeals to ancient memory and nostalgia, even though they existed within one's lifetime.

The displacement marked by homelessness echoed strongly the displacement underpinning the neoliberal era, such as the way Black and Latino tenants have been pushed out by waves of gentrification and segregated by racist government policies; the way workers have been displaced by structural shifts in the late capitalist economy; the way communities have been disrupted by neoliberal housing policies; and the way whole populations have been displaced by the climate crisis and other wider forces, forced to relocate to other places.

In the end, to be homeless was merely the most extreme iteration of the new state of urban life, which is to be placeless.

HOMELESSNESS AND FORGETTING

Nearly everyone misunderstood the modern homelessness crisis at first. It wasn't clear, in the initial years, how deeply rooted it was in the structural changes of the period, and no one predicted how persistent and widespread the problem would become. Nor did anyone foresee how many people would be lost to homelessness.

News accounts from the early 1980s treated the first signs of modern homelessness as a novel urban phenomenon, and homeless people as almost a new species of city dweller. A *New York* magazine cover story from 1981 blared, "The Homeless: Shame of the City," and featured vivid tales of broken-down New Yorkers struggling on the streets. A 1984 cover of *Newsweek*, headlined, "Homeless in America," featured a stark black-and-white portrait of a grim-faced mother and her kids, evoking the Walker Evans photos from the Great Depression. But even those accounts, often in the mode of amateur ethnography, treated the problem with sympathy and shock. The expanding homeless population in New York City in the late 1970s and early 1980s was initially considered a short-term crisis, something the city government would overcome and then return to "normal"—never suspecting what the new normal would become.

Flashing forward to the twenty-first century, what is striking is how undeniably, disconcertingly normal homelessness has become. The sight of desperate, impoverished, often deeply unwell people laying in miserable circumstances on sidewalks has evolved into a commonplace, expected, even accepted part of urban life. When well over a quarter million

Americans sleep unsheltered each night, the vast majority of them in cities, it is not possible anymore to greet the sight of homeless people with shock or surprise. Indeed, a quarter of the way through the century, more than two-thirds of Americans have lived their entire lives in the era of modern mass homelessness. They simply can't recall a time when people sleeping on the streets was not the backdrop of American society.

As an advocate and policy analyst, I often calculated the enormous cost, in public dollars and resources, of homelessness. And researchers have analyzed the cost to homeless people in terms of mental and physical health and educational setbacks for children. But what about the unmeasurable cost to a society that has allowed homelessness to become normalized? What happens to a culture when preventable suffering is an everyday sight? What is the psychic, even spiritual toll taken on the American public by persistent, visible homelessness? Over the decades, I saw some of the consequences of that normalization of the crisis. "Compassion fatigue" and some mixture of pessimism and cynicism helped fuel the backlash era and its aftermath. These sentiments were weaponized by right-wing politicians, who demonized and pathologized homeless people and blamed them for their plight. At the same time, hostile architecture and criminalization campaigns sought to hide or elide the problem of homelessness—to make it invisible. But when a growing majority of Americans have known only a time of mass homelessness, what I saw most often was a loss of hope.

LOSING PLACE

Homelessness has always fundamentally been about loss, absence, something that had been taken and displaced. It's right there in the word itself, which originated during the first Gilded Age, and in its more modern derivations, such as home*less* and *un*housed. Homelessness signals a lack of something vital—something that is missing and must be reclaimed.

But even if it is recovered, the scars of that loss remain, as does the awareness that even as one escapes homelessness, even temporarily, the threat of it has not vanished.

Homelessness also means a loss of control—and not only control over one's personal, everyday life, although that is an essential element. It narrows one's field of vision and possibility to the confines of a daily struggle for survival. Homelessness involves a loss of social control. Losing one's home to displacement, or the omnipresent fear of it, fractures one's ties to community and makes collective struggles—for affordable housing, labor rights, and social justice, to say nothing of engaging in a democratic society—so much harder.

To be homeless is not to have agency, not to have a choice where to sleep at night, nor where to return the next night, nor how to spend the day, nor how to move about in public space. It means losing that control to another power, usually government authorities or their agents. Being homeless means being told what to do or what not to do, and where you can and cannot go, and what is required to obtain basic necessities like shelter, food, and clothing. During the New Gilded Age, being homeless means being subject to a wide array of mechanisms of control and even punishment.

Most accounts of homelessness—at least those that weren't advancing a typical right-wing, blame-homelessness-on-homeless-people agenda—have dwelled on a personal tale of loss. There was the origin story, as it were: a fall from grace, or perhaps at least from the trappings of a so-called normal life. Then there was an account of the period of suffering, featuring the grim details of life on the streets or bouncing from shelter to shelter. Finally, because most of these have been American stories, the narrative resolved into one of redemption, of rising above adversity, of overcoming homelessness.

What the stories rarely told were the next chapters or, crucially, the tale of the next person or persons who took the formerly homeless protagonist's place. That is, to return to the children's game metaphor, we never heard about the next round of musical chairs that took place after the first one, then the one after that, and on and on. Some players managed to survive to the final rounds of the initial game. But maybe they were too slow to get a chair in the next one and thus became victims of a system with dwindling places to rest. In the end, all the players had to worry about the threat of losing a place in future games.

In this sense, modern mass homelessness was not only a symptom, a consequence of the societal shifts of the New Gilded Age. Experiencing "literal" homelessness was only one form of displacement—losing jobs, neighborhoods, and even entire homelands. Modern mass homelessness was more than just a consequence of the housing crisis that emerged during the New Gilded Age. It was also a harbinger of wider forms of loss of place—a warning about the looming threat on the horizon.

Nonetheless, over more than two decades I saw repeatedly how homeless people, even while enduring the harshest circumstances, could create community, banding together to struggle against hopelessness and for something better. I was lucky enough to work alongside so many remarkable people who lived through homelessness and then worked to overcome it—not only for themselves, but for those who would come after them. They marched, rallied, and protested, standing up to brutal, right-wing policies and the leaders who crafted them. They organized to create and preserve genuinely affordable housing and for an end to mass homelessness. Or they helped individuals fight for their rights and seek better treatment in an often harsh, unjust system.

So many of them were lost along the way, joining the tens of thousands of Americans who died each year while homeless—and the innumerable people who went before them. Their legacy and memory shape the ongo-ing battle. In the end, the struggle against mass homelessness—against mass displacement—is not only a fight for a better and more just future, but also a way to honor those who have been lost.

ACKNOWLEDGMENTS

So many people helped with the writing of this book. There is simply no way I can adequately thank them all, but the following is a start.

More than anything, I owe an incalculable debt to the countless homeless and formerly homeless people I've known over the years. Some were mentioned in this book, some generously shared their stories, some I worked alongside as an advocate and organizer, and all of them taught me more than I could ever even begin to convey. Far too many have passed away, and I am forever grateful for what they left behind, especially James, Tyrone, and the extraordinary Carolyn Rodgers.

I'm so grateful to my colleagues at the Coalition for the Homeless, including Mary Brosnahan, Shelly Nortz, and my former Advocacy Department colleagues, including Tony Taylor, Lindsey Davis, Giselle Routhier, Gabriela Sandoval Requena, and many others. I'm forever indebted to the Coalition's founders: Ellen Baxter, Bob Hayes, and Kim Hopper.

My enormous thanks go to my colleagues at the Legal Aid Society's Homeless Rights Project, including Amanda Moretti, Joshua Goldfein, Jane Bock, and Steve Banks. I'm also grateful to colleagues at other New York City advocacy groups with whom I was fortunate to work on a host of campaigns and issues, including VOCAL-NY, New York Communities for Change, the Urban Justice Center, the Community Service Society, Housing Works, Tenants and Neighbors, Artists, Athletes, and Activists, and many others. I'm also incredibly thankful for what I learned from my fellow advocates at the National Coalition for the Homeless.

The team at Melville House has been amazing, in particular Carl

Bromley, who first helped bring the project to life, and Mike Lindgren and Nicholas Taylor, who saw it through to the end. Kirsten Reach provided invaluable support in getting the book into its final form. My thanks go as well to the teachers and students at the Sackett Street Writers Workshop, where I wrote early drafts of several chapters.

So many friends and family supported me—both in my advocacy work and throughout the process of writing this book—and I can't even begin to list them all. But I have to mention my late parents, Kathleen Hayes Markee and Robert Markee, and my brother Bob Markee; my friend Chris Storey, who gifted me the book's title and discussed some of its core ideas during a long walk through Paris; and my friend Kerrick Johnson, who generously listened and helped me shape some of the wider notions around cities and displacement.

Above all, though, my thanks and love go to Lizzy and Elias, who were there for me through it all.

NOTE ON DATA SOURCES

Throughout this book, data on New York City homelessness come primarily from nightly shelter census records kept by the municipal agencies overseeing the city's various shelter systems. The largest has long been the municipal homeless shelter system, which was operated in the 1980s and early 1990s by the New York City Department of Social Services, and afterwards by the Department of Homeless Services. Those agencies also tracked data on various aspects of the homeless shelter system, including length-of-stay, residents' previous episodes of homelessness, applications for shelter, and demographic information.

Various other city agencies have also run several smaller shelter systems serving specific homeless populations, including domestic violence survivors; people living with AIDS; runaway and homeless youth; individuals displaced by fires and other disasters, or by building condemnations; and, beginning in the 2020s, homeless immigrants. A relatively small network of privately operated, "faith-based shelters"—often located in churches, synagogues, and mosques —has also partnered with the city government to shelter some homeless adults. These faith-based shelters were usually linked to city-run "drop-in centers" that served homeless individuals and often let them sleep overnight in chairs.

Because historical records for these smaller shelter systems are often incomplete, throughout most of the book, I primarily cite nightly census data for the municipal homeless shelter system, whose records date to the early 1980s, ensuring historical consistency. But it is important to recognize that the main homeless shelter system's data excludes thousands of people residing in those other systems, and thus understates the true size of New York City's homeless population.

For the unsheltered homeless population, there has never been an accurate measurement. Since the mid-2000s, the city government has conducted estimates on a single winter night each year, which consistently underestimated the true scale of the unsheltered population.

Additional data on New York City homelessness and expenditures come from the New York City Independent Budget Office and the Mayor's Management Report, a mandated annual report produced by the Office of the Mayor.

For national homelessness data, I relied primarily on the Annual Homelessness Assessment Report (AHAR), a report to Congress produced by the US Department of Housing and Urban Development. The AHAR is a single-night, "point in time" estimate of people sleeping in shelters or public spaces, conducted since 2005 by local governments, such as cities or counties. As explained in the book, the AHAR is notorious for undercounting the size of local homeless populations. In general, data on sheltered homeless people are more reliable, though some localities omit shelters from their tallies. However, data on unsheltered homelessness are far less reliable, especially in large cities, and further limited by the single-night methodology. Nonetheless, the AHAR provides a "floor estimate" of the nightly US homeless population.

Additional US and New York homelessness data come from the US Department of Education, which publishes annual figures on homeless students using a broader definition of homelessness that includes not only sheltered and unsheltered people, but also "hidden homeless" people residing in doubled-up housing, as well as motels and hotels. Additional data on the "hidden homeless" population come from the US Bureau of the Census.

Data on population and housing come primarily from the US Bureau of the Census. In New York City, pursuant to rent-regulation laws, the census bureau has conducted the Housing Vacancy Survey (HVS) roughly every three years since the 1970s, providing a rich source of data on housing affordability and conditions over many decades. Housing data for the United States and other cities were taken both from US Census records and from reports and census data compiled and analyzed by the National Low Income Housing Coalition and the Joint Center for Housing Studies at Harvard University.

Economic and employment data come from the Federal Reserve Economic Data database maintained by the Federal Reserve Bank of St. Louis, a rich source of historical information that draws from the census bureau, the US Department of Labor, and other federal agencies.

ENDNOTES

INTRODUCTION

1   Kenneth L. Kusmer, *Down and Out, On the Road: The Homeless in American History* (Oxford University Press, 2002).

2   Patrick Markee, "State of the Homeless 2015: Turning the Tide—New York City Takes Steps to Combat Record Homelessness, but Albany Must Step Up," Coalition for the Homeless, March 19, 2015, available at coalitionforthehomeless.org.

3   Advocates for Children, "Student Homelessness in New York City, 2023–24," November 18, 2024, available at advocatesforchildren.org.

CHAPTER 1

1   Robert Caro, *The Power Broker: Robert Moses and the Fall of New York* (Vintage, 1975), 65–66.

2   Margaret Morton, *The Tunnel: The Underground Homeless of New York City* (Yale University Press, 1995).

3   Teun Voeten, *Tunnel People*, trans. Robert Hackney (PM Press, 2010).

4   Colum McCann, *This Side of Brightness* (Picador, 1998).

5   Jennifer Toth, *The Mole People: Life in the Tunnels Beneath New York City* (Chicago Review Press, 1993).

6   John Tierney, "In Tunnel, 'Mole People' Fight to Save Home," *New York Times*, June 13, 1990.

7   Melinda Henneberger, "U.S. to Offer Housing Vouchers to Lure Homeless from the Subways," *New York Times*, November 18, 1994.

8   Toth, *Mole People*, ix–x.

9   Kenneth L. Kusmer, *Down and Out, On the Road: The Homeless in American History* (Oxford University Press, 2002), 37.

10   Edwin G. Burrows and Mike Wallace, *Gotham: A History of New York City to 1898* (Oxford University Press, 1999), 1031.

11   Tim Cresswell, *The Tramp in America* (Reaktion Books, 2001), 111.

12 Cresswell, *Tramp in America*, 118.

13 Thomas Main, *Homelessness in New York City: Policymaking from Koch to de Blasio* (New York University Press, 2016), 89–93.

14 Michael Shnayerson, *The Contender: Andrew Cuomo, a Biography* (Twelve Books, 2015), 124.

15 Office of the Mayor, City of New York, New York City Commission on the Homeless, "The Way Home: A New Direction in Social Policy," February 1992.

16 Office of the Mayor, City of New York, New York City Commission on the Homeless, "The Way Home: A New Direction in Social Policy," February 1992, 7.

17 Celia Dugger, "Report to Dinkins Urges Overhaul in Shelter System for the Homeless," *New York Times*, January 31, 1992.

18 New York City Commission on the Homeless, "Way Home," 73; Main, *Homelessness in New York City*, 80–82; Michael Cragg and Brendan O'Flaherty, "Do Homeless Shelter Conditions Determine Shelter Population? The Case of the Dinkins Deluge," *Journal of Urban Economics* 46, no. 3 (November 1999): 377. The original version of the study was published by the Milken Institute in 1997 under the title "Does Subsidized Housing Increase Homelessness? Testing the Dinkins Deluge Hypothesis."

19 Shnayerson, *Contender*, 124.

20 Main, *Homelessness in New York City*, 95–96; Shnayerson, *Contender*, 125.

21 Main, *Homelessness in New York City*, 95.

22 Coalition for the Homeless, "Losing the Way Home: Privatization and the Municipal Shelter System," October 1997.

23 Foscarinis, Maria, *And Housing for All: The Fight to End Homelessness in America* (Prometheus Books, 2025), p. 121.

24 Dennis P. Culhane et al., "Public Service Reductions Associated with Placement of Homeless Persons with Severe Mental Illness in Supportive Housing," *Housing Policy Debate* 13, no. 1 (2002): 107–63.

25 Malcolm Gladwell, "Million-Dollar Murray," *New Yorker*, February 5, 2006.

26 Terrence McCoy, "Meet the Outsider Who Accidentally Solved Chronic Homelessness," *Washington Post*, May 6, 2015.

27 Michael Kimmelman, "How Houston Moved 25,000 People from the Streets into Homes of Their Own," *New York Times*, June 15, 2023.

28 Kelly McEvers, "Utah Reduced Chronic Homelessness by 91 Percent; Here's How," *All Things Considered* (National Public Radio), December 10, 2015.

CHAPTER 2

1   Kim Hopper, *Reckoning with Homelessness* (Cornell University Press, 2003), 60–116.

2   Edwin G. Burrows and Mike Wallace, *Gotham: A History of New York City to 1898* (Oxford University Press, 1999), 1020–38.

3   Neil Smith, "'A Riot Is Now in Progress in Tompkins Park,' 1874," in *Revolting New York: How 400 Years of Riot, Rebellion, Uprising, and Revolution Shaped a City*, ed. Neil Smith and Don Mitchell (University of Georgia Press, 2018), 105; Burrows and Wallace, *Gotham*, 1023.

4   Burrows and Wallace, *Gotham*, 1023.

5   Smith, "'Riot Is Now in Progress in Tompkins Park,'" 106.

6   Smith, "'Riot Is Now in Progress in Tompkins Park,'" 107–8.

7   Burrows and Wallace, *Gotham*, 1026.

8   Thomas Kessner, *Capital City: New York City and the Men Behind America's Rise to Economic Dominance, 1860–1900* (Simon and Schuster, 2003), 193.

9   Kerry Tobin and Joseph Murphy, "The New Demographics of Homelessness," in *Ending Homelessness: Why We Haven't, How We Can*, ed. Donald W. Burnes and David L. DiLeo (Lynne Rienner Publishers, 2016), 33.

10 Kenneth L. Kusmer, *Down and Out, On the Road: The Homeless in American History* (Oxford University Press, 2002), 230–31.

11 Kusmer, *Down and Out, On the Road*, 233.

12 Richard Plunz, *A History of Housing in New York City* (Columbia University Press, 1990), 30.

13 Plunz, *History of Housing in New York City*, 35–49.

14 David Madden and Peter Marcuse, *In Defense of Housing: The Politics of Crisis* (Verso Books, 2016), 154–55.

15 Robert M. Fogelson, *The Great Rent Wars: New York, 1917–1929* (Yale University Press, 2013), 84; Madden and Marcuse, *In Defense of Housing*, 156–58.

16 Richard Rothstein, *The Color of Law: A Forgotten History of How Our Government Segregated America* (Liveright Publishing Corporation, 2017), 17–38.

17 Doug Henwood, "A Very Useful Crisis," *LBO News*, May 15, 2024, available at lbo-news.com.

18 Kim Phillips-Fein, *Fear City: New York's Fiscal Crisis and the Rise of Austerity Politics* (Metropolitan Books, 2017).

19 John Hess, "Vagrants and Panhandlers Appearing in New Haunts," *New York Times*, August 6, 1976.

20 Ralph Blumenthal, "Four Days on Subway: A Fresh Look at Lingering Problems," *New York Times*, March 1, 1977.

21 Ellen Baxter and Kim Hopper, "Private Lives / Public Spaces: Homeless Adults on the Streets of New York City," Community Service Society, February 1981, available at coalitionforthehomeless.org.

22 Hopper, *Reckoning with Homelessness*.

23 David Stout, "Federal Welfare Shift Spotlights Unusual Amendment to State Constitution," *New York Times*, September 8, 1996.

24 Sarah Rimer, "The Other City: New York's Homeless," *New York Times*, January 30, 1984.

25 Ian Frazier, "Hidden City," *New Yorker*, October 28, 2013.

26 Robin Herman, "Pact Requires City to Shelter Homeless Men," *New York Times*, August 27, 1981.

27 Callahan v. Carey, New York State Supreme Court (consent decree, 1981).

28 Callahan v. Carey, New York State Supreme Court (consent decree, 1981).

29 Eldredge v. Koch, New York State Supreme Court (1982).

30 *New York State Statistical Yearbook* (Rockefeller Institute of Government, 1998).

31 Anthony J. Blackburn, "Single Room Occupancy in New York City," New York City Department of Housing Preservation and Development, January 1986, 1-1-1-8. SRO buildings were primarily converted old- and new-law tenement buildings, whose units were subdivided during the 1930s.

32 Blackburn, "Single Room Occupancy in New York City."

33 Blackburn, "Single Room Occupancy in New York City."

34 Patrick Markee, "Housing a Growing City: New York's Bust in Boom Times," Coalition for the Homeless, July 2002, 84–86, with data from the New York State Department of Social Services, available at coalitionforthehomeless.org.

35 Tim Sablik, "Recession of 1981–82," last updated November 22, 2013, Federal Reserve Bank, available at federalreservehistory.org.

36 Dennis Hevesi, "Yvonne McCain, Plaintiff in Suit on Shelter for Homeless Families, Dies at 63," *New York Times*, November 2, 2011.

37 Thomas Main, *Homelessness in New York City: Policymaking from Koch to de Blasio* (New York University Press, 2016), 48.

38 Hopper, *Reckoning with Homelessness*, 131–46; Kim Hopper, "Counting the

New York Homeless: An Ethnographic Perspective," *New England Journal of Public Policy* 8, no. 1 (72) (1992): 771–91; Mireya Navarro, "Census Peers into Corners to Count Homeless," *New York Times*, March 21, 1990; Dianne F. Barrett et al., "The 1990 Census Shelter and Street Night Enumeration," US Bureau of the Census, 1992.

39 Glenn Fowler, "Koch Pays Visit to New Shelter on Wards Island," *New York Times*, January 4, 1980.

40 Celia Dugger, "Decreases Ordered at 2 Big Shelters for the Homeless," *New York Times*, December 24, 1992.

41 Pitts v. Black, 608 F. Supp. 696 (S.D.N.Y. 1984); National Coalition for the Homeless, "Voting Rights Registration Manual: You Don't Need a Home to Vote," August 2012.

42 Mixon v. Grinker, New York State Supreme Court (1990).

43 Josh Barbanel, "City Has Fewer Rental Apartments, Survey Finds," *New York Times*, March 6, 1985.

44 Sarah Bartlett, "Federal Aid Cutbacks in '80's Hurt New York City," *New York Times*, May 26, 1991.

45 Oksana Mironova, "Closing the Door: Subsidized Housing at a Time of Federal Instability," Community Service Society, February 2018.

46 Martha Moscowitz, "Turn Up the Heat: It's Time to Raise New York's Shelter and Fuel Allowances," Empire Justice Center, 2012.

47 Markee, "Housing a Growing City."

48 Markee, "Housing a Growing City."

49 Jiggetts v. Grinker, New York State Supreme Court (1988).

50 Markee, "Housing a Growing City," 76.

51 Alex Schwartz, "New York City and Subsidized Housing: Impacts and Lessons of the City's $5 Billion Capital Budget Housing Plan," *Housing Policy Debate* 10, no. 4 (1999): 839–77.

52 Schwartz, "New York City and Subsidized Housing," 844–45.

53 Frazier, "Hidden City."

54 Ted Houghton, "A Description and History of The New York / New York Agreement to House Homeless Mentally Ill Individuals," Corporation for Supportive Housing, May 2001.

55 Michael Cragg and Brendan O'Flaherty, "Do Homeless Shelter Conditions Determine Shelter Population? The Case of the Dinkins Deluge," *Journal of Urban Economics* 46, no. 3 (November 1999): 377–415.

56 Neil Smith, "'Die Yuppie Scum!': Homelessness, Gentrification, and the Liberation of Tompkins Square Park, 1988," in Smith and Mitchell, *Revolting New York*, 230.

57 Smith, "'Die Yuppie Scum!,'" 225, 228–30.

58 Smith, "'Die Yuppie Scum!,'" 226–28; Seth Tobocman, *War in the Neighborhood* (Ad Astra Comix, 2016).

59 Smith, "'Die Yuppie Scum!,'" 232–35.

CHAPTER 3

1 George Blecher, "Murder, Politics and Architecture: The Making of Madison Square Park," *New York Times*, August 3, 2018.

2 Blecher, "Murder, Politics and Architecture."

3 Edwin G. Burrows and Mike Wallace, *Gotham: A History of New York City to 1898* (Oxford University Press, 1999), 945–46; Blecher, "Murder, Politics and Architecture."

4 Burrows and Wallace, *Gotham*, 1034.

5 Benjamin Holtzman, *The Long Crisis: New York City and the Path to Neoliberalism* (Oxford University Press, 2021), 212.

6 New York Police Department, "Quality of Life Enforcement Options: A Reference Guide," revised July 18, 1996.

7 Sarah Kershaw, "Police Remove Encampment of Homeless," *New York Times*, February 28, 1997.

8 City of New York, Office of the Mayor, "State of the City Address," January 13, 2000.

9 Ginia Bellafante, "Rudolph Giuliani's Outrage on Homelessness, and Richard Gere's," *New York Times*, August 28, 2015.

10 Willa Cather, *My Mortal Enemy* (Alfred A. Knopf, 1926), available at the Willa Cather Archive, University of Nebraska–Lincoln, https://cather.unl.edu.

11 Joseph Goldstein, "Judge Rejects New York's Stop-and-Frisk Policy," *New York Times*, August 12, 2013.

12 Larry Celona, "Kelly's Squeegee Squeeze," *New York Post*, January 9, 2002.

13 Bob Herbert, "Trumping Charity," *New York Times*, December 20, 2001.

14 Nina Bernstein, "Police Arrest 125 in Nighttime Raids on Homeless Shelters," *New York Times*, January 20, 2000.

15 Robert Worth, "Police File Charges Against Officer Who Refused to Arrest

Homeless Man Sleeping in Garage," *New York Times*, March 26, 2003; Robert Worth, "Police Officer Is Put on a Year's Probation for Refusing to Arrest a Homeless Man," *New York Times*, October 29, 2004.

16   Picture the Homeless v. City of New York, United States District Court, Southern District of New York (2002).

17   Richard Pérez-Peña, "Amtrak Is Ordered Not to Eject the Homeless from Penn Station," *New York Times*, February 22, 1995.

18   Nina Bernstein, "A Homeless Man Challenges New York City Crackdowns," *New York Times*, November 22, 1999.

19   Jim Dwyer, "Police Charged Panhandlers Under Unconstitutional Law," *New York Times*, June 10, 2005.

20   Sabrina Tavernise, "Lacking $2 Bus Fare to Shelter, Homeless Get a Free Ride, to Jail," *New York Times*, May 4, 2005.

21   Coalition for the Homeless, "Survey of Homeless New Yorkers About Encounters with the Police," 2013.

22   Benjamin Holtzman, "The Corporate Campaign to Save Madison Square Park," Gotham Center for New York City History, City University of New York, July 16, 2020.

23   Kim Phillips-Fein, *Fear City: New York's Fiscal Crisis and the Rise of Austerity Politics* (Metropolitan Books, 2017), 208.

24   Holtzman, "Corporate Campaign to Save Madison Square Park."

25   Holtzman, "Corporate Campaign to Save Madison Square Park."

26   Holtzman, "Corporate Campaign to Save Madison Square Park."

27   Nina Bernstein, "After 7-Year Fight, Homeless Get $816,000 in Back Wages," *New York Times*, October 25, 2000.

28   Amy Armstrong et al., "The Benefits of Business Improvement Districts: Evidence from New York City," Furman Center for Real Estate and Policy, New York University, July 2007.

29   Julie Bosman, "Times Square's Homeless Holdout, Not Budging," *New York Times*, March 29, 2010.

30   George Kelling and James Q. Wilson, "Broken Windows: The Police and Neighborhood Safety," *Atlantic*, March 1982.

31   Josh Getlin and Carla Rivera, "Bratton's Plans for Homeless Debated," *Los Angeles Times*, October 31, 2005.

32   New York Civil Liberties Union, "Stop-and-Frisk Data," May 2019, available at nyclu.org.

33 See, for example, Bernard E. Harcourt, *Illusion of Order: The False Promise of Broken Windows Policing* (Harvard University Press, 2001).

34 Alex Vitale, *City of Disorder: How the Quality of Life Campaign Transformed New York Politics* (New York University Press, 2008).

35 Clarence Taylor, *Fight the Power: African Americans and the Long History of Police Brutality in New York City* (New York University Press, 2019), 6.

36 Risa Goluboff, "The Forgotten Law That Gave Police Nearly Unlimited Power," *Time*, February 1, 2016.

37 Matt Taibbi, *I Can't Breathe: A Killing on Bay Street* (Siegel and Grau, 2017).

38 Hurubie Meko and Anusha Bayya, "Daniel Penny Is Acquitted in Death of Jordan Neely on Subway," *New York Times*, December 9, 2024.

39 City of New York, Office of the City Comptroller, "Safer for All: A Plan to End Street Homelessness for People with Serious Mental Illness in NYC," January 13, 2025.

40 Randall Kuhn and Dennis Culhane, "Applying Cluster Analysis to Test a Typology of Homelessness by Pattern of Shelter Utilization: Results from the Analysis of Administrative Data," *American Journal of Community Psychology* 26, no. 2 (April 1998): 207–32.

41 Stephen Metraux and Dennis P. Culhane, "Recent Incarceration History Among a Sheltered Homeless Population," *Crime and Delinquency* 52, no. 3 (July 2006): 504–17.

42 Stephen Metraux and Dennis P. Culhane, "Homeless Shelter Use and Reincarceration Following Prison Release: Assessing the Risk," *Criminology and Public Policy* 3, no. 2 (March 2004): 139–60.

43 Malcolm Gladwell, "Million-Dollar Murray," *New Yorker*, February 5, 2006.

44 City of New York, Mayor's Office of Criminal Justice, "Summons Warrants Fact Sheet," 2018.

45 Brad H. v. City of New York, New York State Supreme Court (2000).

46 Joan Didion, "Sentimental Journeys," in *We Tell Ourselves Stories in Order to Live: Collected Nonfiction* (Everyman's Library, 2006).

47 Christiane Bird, *A Block in Time: A New York City History at the Corner of Fifth Avenue and Twenty-Third Street* (Bloomsbury Publishing, 2022), 300.

CHAPTER 4

1 Michael Powell and Christine Haughney, "New York's Homeless Get Prison for Shelter," *Washington Post*, August 16, 2002.

2   Michael Cooper, "Jail Reopens as a Shelter for Families," *New York Times*, August 12, 2002.

3   Associated Press, "4 Officials Ordered to Spend Night with Homeless," November 21, 1992; Celia Dugger, "Court Rebukes New York City over Homeless," *New York Times*, July 30, 1993.

4   Cooper, "Jail Reopens as a Shelter for Families."

5   Sarah Kershaw, "Jail Closed as Shelter to Children After Report of Lead-Based Paint," *New York Times*, August 15, 2002.

6   Leslie Kaufman, "City Is Told to Rethink Shelter at Jail," *New York Times*, August 20, 2002.

7   Leslie Kaufman, "City to Pay Millions to Homeless Forced to Sleep in an Office," *New York Times*, September 20, 2002.

8   Wayne Barrett, *Rudy! An Investigative Biography of Rudolph Giuliani* (Basic Books, 2000), 190–92.

9   Barrett, *Rudy!*, 191.

10 Celia Dugger, "Giuliani Eases Stance on Plans for Homeless," *New York Times*, March 20, 1994.

11 State of New York, "New York Code of Rules and Regulations" (18 CRR-NY 352.35).

12 State of New York, "New York Code of Rules and Regulations" (18 CRR-NY 352.35).

13 Main, *Homelessness in New York City*, 127–29.

14 Main, *Homelessness in New York City*, 129–30; Nina Bernstein, "Giuliani to Order Homeless to Work for Their Shelter," *New York Times*, October 26, 1999.

15 Bernstein, "Giuliani to Order Homeless to Work for Their Shelter."

16 Coalition for the Homeless, "New Yorkers Critical of Giuliani Homeless Policy," survey conducted by Global Strategy Group, January 1999, available at coalitionforthehomeless.org.

17 Lynn Duke, "The Unsheltered in a Storm," *Washington Post*, December 10, 1999.

18 Nina Bernstein, "Giuliani's New Policy on Work for the Homeless Leaves Many Unanswered Questions," *New York Times*, October 27, 1999.

19 City of New York, New York Police Department, memo from the chief of patrol on homeless outreach and enforcement, November 23, 1999.

20 Elizabeth Bumiller, "In Wake of Attack, Giuliani Cracks Down on Homeless," *New York Times*, November 20, 1999.

21   Duke, "Unsheltered in a Storm."

22   David Herszenhorn, "1,000 in Park Denounce Giuliani on Homeless Arrest Policy," *New York Times*, December 6, 1999.

23   Elizabeth Bumiller, "Shelters Vow to Defy Mayor on Work Rule," *New York Times*, December 18, 1999.

24   Callahan v. Carey, New York State Supreme Court (2000).

25   Nina Bernstein, "Giuliani to Appeal Decision on a Work-for-Shelter Policy," *New York Times*, December 7, 2001.

26   Ted Houghton, "A Description and History of the New York / New York Agreement to House Homeless Mentally Ill Individuals," Corporation for Supportive Housing, May 2001.

27   New York City Department of Homeless Services, Residential Placement Management Services reports, 1992–2001. Cited in Coalition for the Homeless, "Supportive Housing as a Cost-Effective Way to Reduce Homeless Shelter Capacity," April 16, 2002.

28   Houghton, "Description and History of the New York / New York Agreement," 6–7; Ray Hernandez, "Pataki and Giuliani Agree on Housing for the Mentally Ill," *New York Times*, April 22, 1999.

29   New York City Independent Budget Office, "Fiscal History: Housing Preservation and Development," available at ibo.nyc.ny.us. Data covers city fiscal years 1991–98, which span July 1 of the previous calendar year through June 30.

30   New York City Independent Budget Office, "Fiscal History: New York Police Department," available at ibo.nyc.ny.us. Data covers city fiscal years 1994–2002, which span July 1 of the previous calendar year through June 30.

31   New York City Department of Homeless Services, shelter census reports. Cited in Markee, "Housing a Growing City," 116.

32   City of New York, "Mayor's Management Report." Data covers city fiscal years 1994–98, which span July 1 of the previous calendar year through June 30. Cited in Markee, "Housing a Growing City," 117.

33   Nina Bernstein, "Homeless Shelters in New York Fill to Highest Level Since 80's," *New York Times*, February 8, 2001.

34   Data from the US Bureau of the Census, Housing and Vacancy Surveys, 1991–99. Cited in Markee, "Housing a Growing City," 14, 39–61.

35   Derek Rose, "Mayor Eyes Putting Cop in Each Shelter," *New York Daily News*, January 7, 2002.

36   Jacob Fries, "In Making Crowded Homeless Shelters Safer, Some View the

Issue with a Sense of Security," *New York Times*, January 10, 2002.

37 Adam Nagourney, "Quality of Life Is High Priority for Bloomberg," *New York Times*, December 27, 2001.

38 Diane Cardwell, "City to Clear Homeless Encampments," *New York Times*, July 18, 2006.

39 Nina Bernstein, "Bloomberg to Fight Ban on Shelter Evictions," *New York Times*, June 19, 2002.

40 Bernstein, "Bloomberg to Fight Ban on Shelter Evictions."

41 Leslie Kaufman, "Shelters Seek to Oust Families Who Keep Rejecting Housing," *New York Times*, September 16, 2002.

42 Bernstein, "Bloomberg to Fight Ban on Shelter Evictions," *New York Times*, June 19, 2002.

43 "Mayors Come and Go, This Judge Is Forever," *New York Daily News*, October 23, 2002.

44 Leslie Kaufman, "One Constant in Homeless Litigation: New York v. the Judge," *New York Times*, November 12, 2002.

45 Leslie Kaufman, "New York Reaches Deal to End 20-Year Legal Fight on Homeless," *New York Times*, January 18, 2003; Main, *Homelessness in New York City*, 148–49.

46 David Saltonstall, "Lift Bar on Using Jail as Shelter, Says Mike," *New York Daily News*, November 23, 2002; Joanne Wasserman, "Mike Says Ex-Jail OK as Shelter," *New York Daily News*, May 8, 2003.

47 Leslie Kaufman, "Officials Tour Cruise Ships in a Search for Shelter Space," *New York Times*, November 21, 2002; David Seifman, "Homeless May Take Cruise," *New York Post*, November 23, 2002.

48 Elizabeth Brown, "The Rising Number of Homeless Families in NYC, 2002–2012: A Look at Why Families Were Granted Shelter, the Housing They Had Lived in and Where They Came From," New York City Independent Budget Office, November 2014, 3, available at ibo.nyc.ny.us. The report utilizes data from the New York City Department of Homeless Services.

49 Dan Barry, "About New York: War Veteran's Homecoming Is Spent in Homeless Shelters," *New York Times*, April 24, 2004.

50 Dennis Hamill, "Forgotten Valor: Once-Passionate Iraq War Veteran's Experience with Homelessness, Info That Led to Invasion Alter Her Perspective," *New York Daily News*, March 20, 2013; Mika Basson, "War Cries of a New Yorker—Nicole Goodwin," *Amsterdam News*, October 13, 2016.

51 Barry, "About New York."

CHAPTER 5

1   Alison Gregor, "Bedford-Stuyvesant: Diverse and Changing," *New York Times*, July 9, 2014.

2   Gregor, "Bedford-Stuyvesant."

3   Michael Woodsworth, *Battle for Bed-Stuy: The Long War on Poverty in New York City* (Harvard University Press, 2016), 144–47.

4   Nancy Smith et al., "Understanding Family Homelessness in New York City: An In-Depth Study of Families' Experiences Before and After Shelter," Vera Institute of Justice, September 2005.

5   Leslie Kaufman, "City Shifts View on Homelessness," *New York Times*, June 16, 2004.

6   Leslie Kaufman, "Homeless Families Blocked from Seeking US Housing Aid," *New York Times*, October 20, 2004.

7   Figures from City of New York, Office of the Mayor, *Mayor's Management Reports*; and the New York City Department of Homeless Services. Data covers city fiscal years 1990–2013, which span July 1 of the previous calendar year through June 30.

8   Figures from City of New York, Office of the Mayor, *Mayor's Management Reports*; and the New York City Department of Homeless Services. Data covers city fiscal years 1990–2013, which span July 1 of the previous calendar year through June 30.

9   Figures from City of New York, Office of the Mayor, *Mayor's Management Reports*; and the New York City Department of Homeless Services. Data covers city fiscal years 1990–2013, which span July 1 of the previous calendar year through June 30.

10   Maggie Haberman, "City Housing Proposal Aims at Working Poor," *New York Daily News*, October 20, 2004.

11   Kaufman, "Homeless Families Blocked from Seeking US Housing Aid."

12   Michael Cragg and Brendan O'Flaherty, "Do Homeless Shelter Conditions Determine Shelter Population? The Case of the Dinkins Deluge," *Journal of Urban Economics* 46, no. 3 (November 1999): 377–415.

13   Cragg and O'Flaherty, "Do Homeless Shelter Conditions Determine Shelter Population?"

14   Brendan O'Flaherty and Ting Wu, "Fewer Subsidized Exits and a Recession: How New York City's Family Homeless Shelter Population Became Immense," *Journal of Housing Economics* 15, no. 2 (June 2006): 99–125.

15   Smith et al., "Understanding Family Homelessness in New York City."

16 Jennifer Steinhauer, "Bloomberg Plans More Housing Aid for the Homeless," *New York Times*, June 18, 2002.

17 Nina Bernstein, "Once Again, Trying Housing as a Cure for Homelessness: Mothers with Children Are Getting Preference in City Assignments for Subsidized Apartments," *New York Times*, June 23, 2002.

18 City of New York, Office of the Mayor, "Uniting for Solutions Beyond Shelter," June 23, 2004, available at nyc.gov.

19 Kaufman, "City Shifts View on Homelessness."

20 Leslie Kaufman, "Mayor Urges Major Overhaul for Homeless," *New York Times*, June 24, 2004; Leslie Kaufman, "City Is Gambling on an Old Program to Cure Homelessness," *New York Times*, July 19, 2004.

21 State of New York and City of New York, "New York / New York III Supportive Housing Agreement," November 3, 2005, available at health.ny.gov; Patrick Markee, "The 'New York / New York III Agreement': A Significant First Step in Expanding Supportive Housing Resources for Homeless New Yorkers," Coalition for the Homeless, January 31, 2016, available at coalitionforthehomeless.org.

22 Leslie Kaufman, "State Revamps Assistance Plan for Homeless," *New York Times*, December 11, 2004.

23 Lindsey Davis, "Homeless Families at Risk: Hazardous Conditions in the Housing Stability Plus Program," Coalition for the Homeless, February 2007, available at coalitionforthehomeless.org.

24 Tina Moore, "How City Is Poisoning Kids: Many Families Placed in Lead-Tainted Apts.," *New York Daily News*, January 14, 2007.

25 New York City Department of Homeless Services, "Client Responsibility Procedure," November 17, 2003.

26 Patrick Markee, "Losing Shelter: New York's Harmful Policy of Ejecting Homeless Adults Living with Mental Illness and Disabilities from Shelter to the Streets," Coalition for the Homeless, June 24, 2009, available at coalitionforthehomeless.org.

27 Sewell Chan, "City Settles Lawsuit Over Homeless Families," *New York Times*, September 17, 2008.

28 John Mollenkopf, "The Evolution of New York City's Black Neighborhoods," *Metropolitics*, May 9, 2017, available at metropolitics.org.

29 Mollenkopf, "Evolution of New York City's Black Neighborhoods."

30 Woodsworth, *Battle for Bed-Stuy*, 319.

CHAPTER 6

1   Patrick Markee, "State of the Homeless 2015: Turning the Tide—New York City Takes Steps to Combat Record Homelessness, but Albany Must Step Up," Coalition for the Homeless, March 19, 2015, available at coalitionforthehomeless.org.

2   Main, *Homelessness in New York City*, 107–8.

3   Main, *Homelessness in New York City*, 123–24.

4   City of New York, "Mayor's Management Report." Data covers city fiscal years 1995–98, which span July 1 of the previous calendar year through June 30. Cited in Patrick Markee, "Housing a Growing City: New York's Bust in Boom Times," Coalition for the Homeless, July 2002, 98, available at coalitionforthehomeless.org.

5   Bob Herbert, "We're Human Beings," *New York Times*, January 3, 1997.

6   "Clergy Opens Refuge, Hits City's Rules," *New York Daily News*, January 1, 1997.

7   Affidavit of Sanford Friedman, MD, Albert Einstein College of Medicine, quoted in Thomas Main, *Homelessness in New York City: Policymaking from Koch to de Blasio* (New York University Press, 2016), 120.

8   Jennifer Egan, "To Be Young and Homeless," *New York Times Magazine*, March 24, 2002.

9   Nina Bernstein, "Homeless Shelters in New York Fill to Highest Level Since 80's," *New York Times*, February 8, 2001.

10 Elizabeth Brown, "The Rising Number of Homeless Families in NYC, 2002–2012: A Look at Why Families Were Granted Shelter, the Housing They Had Lived in, and Where They Came From," New York City Independent Budget Office, November 2014.

11 Leslie Kaufman, "For Some Homeless Couples, Shelter Is an Office Floor Provided by the City," *New York Times*, January 8, 2005.

12 Nina Bernstein, "Mentally Ill Boy Kills Himself in Shelter Hotel," *New York Times*, August 8, 2002.

CHAPTER 7

1   David Oshinsky, *Bellevue: Three Centuries of Medicine and Mayhem at America's Most Storied Hospital* (Doubleday, 2016), 172–75.

2   Miguel A. Faria Jr., "Violence, Mental Illness, and the Brain: A Brief History of Psychosurgery: Part 1—From Trephination to Lobotomy," *Surgical Neurology International*, April 2013.

3   Oshinsky, *Bellevue*, 227–37.

4   Centers for Disease Control and Prevention, "Mental Patient Data for Fiscal Year 1955," *Public Health Reports* 71, no. 3 (March 1956): 214–15.

5   *New York State Statistical Yearbook* (Rockefeller Institute of Government, 1998).

6   Oshinsky, *Bellevue*, 215–16.

7   Oshinsky, *Bellevue*, 216–17.

8   Oshinsky, *Bellevue*, 217.

9   Oshinsky, *Bellevue*, 217.

10   Ian Frazier, "Hidden City," in *Hogs Wild: Selected Reporting Pieces* (Farrar, Straus and Giroux, 2016), 272–301, originally published in *The New Yorker*, October 28, 2013.

11   Leslie Kaufman, "For Some Homeless Couples, Shelter Is an Office Floor Provided by the City," *New York Times*, January 8, 2005.

12   Kaufman, "For Some Homeless Couples, Shelter Is an Office Floor Provided by the City."

13   Oshinsky, *Bellevue*, 287.

14   Andrea Elliott, *Invisible Child: Poverty, Survival, and Hope in an American City* (Random House, 2021).

15   Laura Nahmias, "Cuomo Plan to Shelter Homeless at Creedmoor Nixed, Senior Official Says," *Politico*, December 29, 2015.

16   Randall Kuhn and Dennis Culhane, "Applying Cluster Analysis to Test a Typology of Homelessness by Pattern of Shelter Utilization: Results from the Analysis of Administrative Data," *American Journal of Community Psychology* 26, no. 2 (April 1998): 207–32.

CHAPTER 8

1   Patrick Markee and Judith Goldiner, "The City of New York's Use of Apartments as Temporary Shelter Through the Scatter-Site / Cluster-Site Shelter Program," testimony of the Coalition for the Homeless and the Legal Aid Society before the New York City Council, Committee on General Welfare, October 10, 2013.

2   Urban Institute, "State and Local Expenditures," 2024, available at urban.org.

3   Abby Goodnough, "Giuliani Abandons Plan to Evict Five Community Programs," *New York Times*, February 19, 1999.

4   David M. Herzenhorn, "US Wresting Homeless Fund from Giuliani," *New York Times*, December 12, 1999.

5   Michael Powell and Russ Buettner, "In Matters Big and Small, Crossing Giuliani Had Price," *New York Times*, January 22, 2008.

6   Demetra Smith Nightingale et al., "Work and Welfare Reform in New York City During the Giuliani Administration: A Study of Program Implementation," Urban Institute Labor and Social Policy Center, July 2002, available at urban.org; Wayne Barrett, *Rudy! An Investigative Biography of Rudolph Giuliani* (Basic Books, 2000), 318.

7   Jason DeParle, "What Welfare-to-Work Really Means," *New York Times Magazine*, December 20, 1998.

8   Carl Vogel and Neil DeMause, "Jason's Brain Trust," *City Limits*, December 1, 1998.

9   Vogel and DeMause, "Jason's Brain Trust."

10 Vogel and DeMause, "Jason's Brain Trust."

11 Jennifer Ehrle et al., "Recent Changes in Wisconsin Welfare and Work, Child Care, and Child Welfare Systems," Urban Institute, September 2001.

12 Kimberly McLarin, "City Sued over Program to Curb Welfare Fraud," *New York Times*, December 30, 1995.

13 Leslie Kaufman, "City Vows to Improve Aid to Homeless Families," *New York Times*, March 19, 2007.

14 Nina Bernstein, "New York City Plans to Extend Workfare to Homeless Shelters," *New York Times*, February 20, 1999.

15 Alex Traub, "George McDonald, Power Broker for the Powerless, Dies at 76," *New York Times*, February 4, 2021.

16 John Tierney, "The Big City; Helping Hand Holds Out a Broom," *New York Times*, December 22, 1999.

17 Serge F. Kovaleski, "Charity Backing Bloomberg 3rd Term Got Millions," *New York Times*, August 6, 2010.

18 Elizabeth Benjamin, "Doe, a Dear for Bloomberg?," *New York Daily News*, October 4, 2008.

19 Michael Barbaro and David W. Chen, "Bloomberg Enlists His Charities in Bid to Stay," *New York Times*, October 17, 2008.

20 Tom Topousis, "The 'Dough' Fund," *New York Post*, June 29, 2009; "Doing Good—Quite Comfortably," *New York Post*, June 30, 2009.

21 Tina Moore, "Doe Fund Nonprofit Head George McDonald Pocketed $100,000 Prize Given to the Charity," *New York Daily News*, November 5, 2010.

22 Celeste Katz, "Mayor Bloomberg and 2013 Hopeful George McDonald: A

Right to Shelter for Homeless?," *New York Daily News*, March 8, 2013.

23 Dana Rubinstein, "Founder of Vaunted City Charity Accused of Creating a 'Hostile' Work Environment," *Politico*, November 7, 2019.

24 Julian Brash, *Bloomberg's New York: Class and Governance in the Luxury City* (University of Georgia Press, 2011), 58–59.

25 Michael Cooper, "At $92.60 a Vote, Bloomberg Shatters an Election Record," *New York Times*, December 4, 2001.

26 Edward-Isaac Dovere, "The Real Power of Bloomberg's Money," *Atlantic*, January 7, 2020.

27 Barbaro and Chen, "Bloomberg Enlists His Charities in Bid to Stay."

28 Leslie Kaufman, "Billionaire Mayor Takes Up the Cause of the Homeless," *New York Times*, April 28, 2005.

29 Diane Cardwell, "City to Clear Homeless Encampments," *New York Times*, July 18, 2006.

30 Alexander Kaufman, "Michael Bloomberg Has a Toxic Legacy on Lead," *Mother Jones*, December 22, 2019.

31 Ian Frazier, "Hidden City," *The New Yorker*, October 28, 2013.

32 Linda Gibbs et al., *How Ten Global Cities Take on Homelessness: Innovations That Work* (University of California Press, 2021).

33 Gibbs et al., *How Ten Global Cities Take on Homelessness*, 16–17.

34 Cindy Rodriguez, "To Create Housing for Homeless, Landlords Evict Paying Tenants," *WNYC News*, August 12, 2013.

35 Andrew Rice, "Why Run a Slum If You Can Make More Money Housing the Homeless?," *New York Magazine*, November 30, 2013.

36 Patrick Markee, "State of the Homeless 2014: Turning Point," Coalition for the Homeless, March 12, 2014, 13.

CHAPTER 9

1 Jeffrey C. Mays, "De Blasio Rebuffs Question on Homelessness: 'I'm in the Middle of a Workout,'" *New York Times*, October 6, 2018.

2 Celia Dugger, "Decreases Ordered at 2 Big Shelters for the Homeless," *New York Times*, December 24, 1992.

3 Nancy Todd, *New York's Historic Armories: An Illustrated History* (State University of New York Press, 2006), 131-132.

4 Todd, *New York's Historic Armories*, 101–19.

5   Kim Phillips-Fein, "Conspicuous Destruction," *New York Review of Books*, October 19, 2023.

6   Todd, *New York's Historic Armories*, 128.

7   Nina Bernstein, "Storm Bared a Lack of Options for the Homeless in New York," *New York Times*, November 20, 2012.

8   Phillips-Fein, "Conspicuous Destruction."

9   Todd, *New York's Historic Armories*, 30.

10 Edwin G. Burrows and Mike Wallace, *Gotham: A History of New York City to 1898* (Oxford University Press, 1999), 1036.

11 Todd, *New York's Historic Armories*, 30–31.

12 Don Mitchell, "A New Urban Order: Transit Strikes, 1886-1895," in *Revolting New York: How 400 Years of Riot, Rebellion, Uprising, and Revolution Shaped a City*, ed. Neil Smith and Don Mitchell (University of Georgia Press, 2018), 120.

13 Todd, *New York's Historic Armories*, 32.

14 Burrows and Wallace, *Gotham*, 1037.

15 Burrows and Wallace, *Gotham*, 1037.

16 Todd, *New York's Historic Armories*, 32.

17 Patrick Markee, "War and Homelessness: How American Wars Create Homelessness Among United States Armed Forces Veterans," Coalition for the Homeless, March 27, 2003, available at coalitionforthehomeless.org.

18 Steven Greenhouse, "Strong Voice in 'Fight for 15' Fast-Food Wage Campaign," *New York Times*, December 4, 2014.

19 Kim Hopper, *Reckoning with Homelessness* (Cornell University Press, 2003).

CHAPTER 10

1   Leslie Kaufman, "Inspectors Find Home for Men Full and Filthy," *New York Times*, September 26, 2006.

2   Roxanne Daniel and Wendy Sawyer, "What You Should Know About Halfway Houses," Prison Policy Initiative, September 3, 2020, available at prisonpolicy. org.

3   A three-part June 2012 *New York Times* investigation by Sam Dolnick of private halfway houses in New Jersey finding corruption and mistreatment of residents: "As Escapees Stream Out, a Penal Business Thrives," June 16, 2012; "At a Halfway House, Bedlam Reigns," June 17, 2012; and "At Penal Unit, a Volatile Mix Fuels a Murder," June 18, 2012.

4   Lindsey Davis, "Warehousing the Homeless: The Rising Use of Illegal Boarding Houses to Shelter Homeless New Yorkers," Coalition for the Homeless, January 2008, available at coalitionforthehomeless.org.

5   Davis, "Warehousing the Homeless," 14.

6   Davis, "Warehousing the Homeless," 14.

7   Kaufman, "Inspectors Find Home for Men Full and Filthy."

8   Patrick Markee, "State of the Homeless 2006," Coalition for the Homeless, January 24, 2006, utilizing data from the New York City Department of Homeless Services, available at coalitionforthehomeless.org.

9   Leslie Kaufman, "Billionaire Mayor Takes Up the Cause of the Homeless," *New York Times*, April 28, 2005.

10 Frank Mauro, "State of Working New York 2004," Fiscal Policy Institute, September 6, 2004, available at fiscalpolicy.org.

11 Melanie Lefkowitz, "For Some Under City's Revised Plan to End Homelessness, Landing a Job Could Mean They Would Lose Their Home," *Newsday*, December 19, 2005.

12 Sewell Chen, "Critics See Flaws in a Program to Help the Homeless Pay Rent," *New York Times*, May 8, 2006.

13 Alan Feuer, "The Neediest Cases Fund: Nearly Evicted in Error, and Left with Nothing," *New York Times*, November 16, 2008.

14 Leslie Kaufman, "City Vows to Improve Aid to Homeless Families," *New York Times*, March 19, 2007.

15 Trymaine Lee, "Homeless Families in City Shelters Hit Record, Despite the Mayor's Efforts," *New York Times*, March 8, 2007.

16 Kaufman, "City Vows to Improve Aid to Homeless Families."

17 Giselle Routhier, "Revolving Door: How the Bloomberg Administration is Putting Thousands of Formerly-Homeless Families at Risk of Returning to Homelessness," Coalition for the Homeless, July 20, 2010, available at coalitionforthehomeless.org.

18 Patrick Markee, "The Revolving Door Keeps Spinning: New Data Shows that Half of 'Advantage' Families Have Returned to the NYC Homeless Shelter System," Coalition for the Homeless, December 28, 2013, available at coalitionforthehomeless.org.

19 Mosi Secret, "Clock Ticks for a Key Homeless Program," *New York Times*, May 31, 2011.

20 Patrick Markee, "Housing a Growing City: New York's Bust in Boom Times," Coalition for the Homeless, July 2002, 14, available at coalitionforthehomeless.org.

21   Alex Schwartz, "New York City's Affordable Housing Plans and the Limits of Local Initiative," *Cityscape* 21, no. 3 (2019): 365.

22   Schwartz, "New York City's Affordable Housing Plans and the Limits of Local Initiative."

23   Samuel Stein, *Capital City: Gentrification and the Real Estate State* (Verso Books, 2019), 93–100.

24   Neil DeMause, "'Landlords Just Went Wild': A Brief History of Vacancy Deregulation in New York," *Hellgate*, March 20, 2024, available at hellgatenyc. com.

25   Alex Schwartz, *Housing Policy in the United States*, 4th ed. (Routledge, 2021), 48.

26   Schwartz, *Housing Policy in the United States*, 144–45.

27   Schwartz, *Housing Policy in the United States*, 190–91.

28   Jonathan Mahler and Steven Eder, "'No Vacancies' for Blacks: How Donald Trump Got His Start, and Was First Accused of Bias," *New York Times*, August 27, 2016.

29   Mahler and Eder, "'No Vacancies' for Blacks."

30   Samuel Stein, "The Art of the Rent Gap," *n+1*, October 25, 2024.

31   Charles V. Bagli, "A Trump Empire Built on Inside Connections and $885 Million in Tax Breaks," *New York Times*, September 17, 2016.

32   David Madden and Peter Marcuse, *In Defense of Housing: The Politics of Crisis* (Verso Books, 2016), 69.

33   Michael Stone, *Shelter Poverty: New Ideas on Housing Affordability* (Temple University Press, 1993).

34   Madden and Marcuse, *In Defense of Housing*, 25.

35   Richard Rothstein, *The Color of Law: A Forgotten History of How Our Government Segregated America* (Liveright Publishing Corporation, 2017), 190.

36   Henri Lefebvre, *The Urban Revolution*, trans. Robert Bononno (University of Minnesota Press, 2003), 160.

37   Madden and Marcuse, *In Defense of Housing*, 34.

38   Association for Neighborhood and Housing Development, "The Sub-Prime Loan Crisis in New York Apartment Housing: How Collapsing Predatory Equity Deals Will Harm Communities and Investors in New York City," October 2008, 3, available at anhd.org.

39   C. J. Hughes, "Kushner Cos.' East Village Breakup Continues with Two More Building Sales," *Crain's New York*, November 22, 2024.

40 City of New York, Department of Finance, Division of Tax Policy and Data Analytics, "Annual Report of the New York City Real Property Tax, Fiscal Year 2022," May 2022, available at nyc.gov.

41 Matthew Desmond, *Evicted: Poverty and Profit in the American City* (Crown Publishers, 2016), 296.

42 The Eviction Lab, "Key Findings," July 10, 2023, available at evictionlab.org.

CHAPTER 11

1   National Center for Homeless Education, "Student Homelessness in America: School Years 2019–20 to 2021–22," 2023, available at nche.ed.gov.

2   National Low Income Housing Coalition, "Out of Reach 2024," 2024, available at nlihc.org.

3   National Low Income Housing Coalition, "The Gap: A Shortage of Affordable Homes" (2024), available at nlihc.org.

4   David Van Tassel and John J. Grabowski, eds., *The Encyclopedia of Cleveland History*, 2nd ed. (Indiana University Press, 1996).

5   Daniel Kerr, *Derelict Paradise: Homelessness and Urban Development in Cleveland, Ohio* (University of Massachusetts Press, 2011), 200–202.

6   Mark Arsenault and Rebecca Ostriker, "Beyond the Gilded Gate: A Boston Building, Scattered Souls, and Rent Control Revisited," *Boston Globe*, December 17, 2023; David H. Autor et al., "Housing Market Spillovers: Evidence from the End of Rent Control in Cambridge, Massachusetts," National Bureau of Economic Research Working Paper 18125, June 2012.

7   National Low Income Housing Coalition, "Out of Reach 2024."

8   Marjorie Hernandez, "San Diego Homeless Ban 'Doomed to Fail' Unless Town Enacts Zero Tolerance: Ex-Mayor," *New York Post*, June 23, 2023.

9   National Low Income Housing Coalition, "Out of Reach 2024."

10 National Low Income Housing Coalition, "The Gap."

11 Ending Community Homelessness Coalition, "State of the HRS: A Report on the State of the Homelessness Response System in Austin / Travis County," August 2024, available at austinecho.org.

12 Audrey Duff, "This Ain't No KOA," *Austin Chronicle*, February 16, 1996.

13 Duke Helfand and Richard Winton, "Bratton Admits Skid Row Displacement," *Los Angeles Times*, October 4, 2007.

14 Jonathan Ben-Menachem, "Media Frame: Stop Quoting Bill Bratton," *The Appeal*, July 22, 2019, available at theappeal.org.

15   National Law Center on Homelessness and Poverty, "Housing Not Handcuffs 2019: Ending the Criminalization of Homelessness in US Cities," National Homelessness Law Center, December 2019, 12–15, available at homelesslaw. org.

16   Human Rights Watch, "'You Have to Move!': The Cruel and Ineffective Criminalization of Unhoused People in Los Angeles," August 14, 2024, available at hrw.org.

17   Tyler Walicek, "Homeless Sweeps Are Expensive, Useless and Cruel, Human Rights Watch Charges," *Truthout*, August 25, 2024, available at truthout.org.

18   National Law Center on Homelessness and Poverty, "Tent City, USA: The Growth of America's Homeless Encampments and How Communities Are Responding," National Homelessness Law Center, 2017, available at homelesslaw.org.

19   National Law Center on Homelessness and Poverty, "Tent City, USA," 8.

20   National Law Center on Homelessness and Poverty, "Tent City, USA," 9.

21   National Law Center on Homelessness and Poverty, "Housing Not Handcuffs 2019," 16.

22   Ryan Autullo and Laura Morales, "Tourism, Safety Concerns Spurred Austin's Elite to Support Camping Ban PAC in Prop B Race," *Austin American-Statesman*, May 17, 2021.

23   Rebecca Burns, "How the Right Made Homelessness a Crime," *Rolling Stone*, August 13, 2024, originally published in *In These Times*.

24   Burns, "How the Right Made Homelessness a Crime."

25   Reis Thebault and Ann E. Marimow, "Supreme Court Says Cities Can Ban Homeless from Sleeping Outside," *Washington Post*, June 28, 2024.

26   Veera Korhonen, "Turnover Rate in Emergency Shelter and Transitional Housing Programs in the United States From 2007 to 2017," Statista, August 24, 2024, available at statista.com.

27   National Center for Homeless Education, "Student Homelessness in America," 2023, available at nche.ed.gov.

28   Molly K. Richard et al., "Quantifying Doubled-Up Homelessness: Presenting a New Measure Using US Census Microdata," *Housing Policy Debate* 34, no. 1 (2022): 3–24.

29   National Low Income Housing Coalition, "Out of Reach 2024."

30   National Low Income Housing Coalition, "Out of Reach 2024."

31   National Low Income Housing Coalition, "The Gap."

32 Joint Center for Housing Studies of Harvard University, "America's Rental Housing 2024," 2024, available at jchs.harvard.edu.

33 Sophia Wedeen, "Low-Cost Rentals Have Decreased in Every State," Joint Center for Housing Studies of Harvard University, July 6, 2023, available at jchs.harvard.edu.

34 US Bureau of the Census, "Current Population Survey, Annual Social and Economic Supplement," various years.

35 Pew Research Center, "Most Americans Say There Is Too Much Economic Inequality in the US, but Fewer Than Half Call It a Top Priority," January 9, 2020, available at pewresearch.org.

36 Angela Hanks et al., "Systematic Inequality: How America's Structural Racism Helped Create the Black-White Wealth Gap," Center for American Progress, February 21, 2018, available at americanprogress.org.

37 Federal Reserve Economic Data, Federal Reserve Bank of St. Louis, "Share of Total Net Worth Held by the Top 1% (99th to 100th Wealth Percentiles)," available at fred.stlouisfed.org.

38 David Harvey, *Rebel Cities: From the Right to the City to the Urban Revolution* (Verso Books, 2012), 35, 42.

39 Harvey, *Rebel Cities*, 31.

40 Ingrid Gould Ellen and Samuel Dastrup, "Housing and the Great Recession," Russell Sage Foundation and Stanford Center on Poverty and Inequality, October 2012, available at furmancenter.org.

41 See Brett Christophers, *Rentier Capitalism* (Verso Books, 2022).

42 National Low Income Housing Coalition, "The Gap."

43 Benny Docter and Martha Galvez, "The Future of Public Housing: Public Housing Fact Sheet," Urban Institute, October 2019, available at urban.org.

44 Hugo Priemus et al., "Housing Vouchers in the United States, Great Britain, and the Netherlands: Current Issues and Future Perspectives," *Housing Policy Debate*, 16, no. 3 (2005): 575–609.

45 New York City Department of Health and Mental Hygiene, "Annual Report on Deaths Among Persons Experiencing Homelessness," various years.

46 City of Los Angeles, Office of the Controller, "Deaths of Unhoused People in the City of LA, 2023," available at controller.lacity.gov; Sam Levin and Will Craft, "Revealed: 300% Surge in Deaths of Unhoused People in LA Amid Fentanyl and Housing Crises," *Guardian*, February 22, 2024.

47 Barry Zevin et al., "Homeless Mortality in San Francisco: 2019–2020, 2021, January Through June Only," City of San Francisco, available at the National

Health Care for the Homeless Council, nhchc.org.

48 National Health Care for the Homeless Council, "Homeless Mortality: The Facts," available at nhchc.org.

49 Caroline Bologna, "Why the Phrase 'Pull Yourself Up by Your Bootstraps' Is Nonsense," *HuffPost*, August 9, 2018, available at huffpost.com.

50 Richard White, *The Republic for Which It Stands: The United States During Reconstruction and the Gilded Age, 1865–1896* (Oxford University Press, 2017), 159–60.

51 White, *Republic for Which It Stands*, 159–60.

52 Lisa Camner McKay, "How the Racial Wealth Gap Has Evolved—and Why It Persists," Federal Reserve Bank of Minneapolis, October 3, 2022, available at minneapolisfed.org.

53 Luis Ferré-Sadurní et al., "Landmark Deal Reached on Rent Protections for Tenants in N.Y.," *New York Times*, June 11, 2019.

54 Cassidy Pearson and Jenny Schuetz, "Where Pro-Housing Groups Are Emerging," Brookings Institution, March 31, 2022, available at brookings.edu.

55 Mark Fisher, "The Slow Cancellation of the Future," in *Ghosts of My Life: Writings on Depression, Hauntology, and Lost Futures* (Zero Books, 2014).

CHAPTER 12

1 Doug Henwood, "A Very Useful Crisis," *LBO News*, May 15, 2024, available at lbo-news.com.

2 Henwood, "Very Useful Crisis."

3 Andrew Heritage, "Job Loss by Metro Area Shows Devastation from China Shock," Coalition for a Prosperous America," September 20, 2023, available at prosperousamerica.org.

4 Gerald Taylor, "Unmade in America: Industrial Flight and the Decline of Black Communities," Alliance for American Manufacturing, October 2016.

5 Andy Merrifield, "Two-Fold Urbanism: A Negative Dialectic of the City," in *Dialectical Urbanism: Social Struggles in the Capitalist City* (Monthly Review Press, 2002), 165.

6 Ruth Milkman and Joseph van der Naald, "The State of the Unions 2024: A Profile of Organized Labor in New York City, New York State, and the United States," City University of New York, School of Labor and Urban Studies, 2024.

7 Ruth Glass, *London: Aspects of Change* (MacGibbon and Kee, 1964).

8   Samuel Stein, *Capital City: Gentrification and the Real Estate State* (Verso Books, 2019), 49.

9   Stein, *Capital City*, 45.

10 John Mollenkopf, "The Evolution of New York City's Black Neighborhoods," *Metropolitics*, May 9, 2017, available at metropolitics.org.

11 Christopher Mele, *Selling the Lower East Side: Culture, Real Estate and Resistance in New York City* (University of Minnesota Press, 2000), 195–97.

12 Neil Smith, *The New Urban Frontier: Gentrification and the Revanchist City* (Routledge, 1996), 190–209.

13 Nina Bernstein, "As Students Move Back In, Some Evacuees Are Set Adrift Again," *New York Times*, November 6, 2012.

14 NYC Department of Homeless Services, letter from Seth Diamond, March 26, 2013.

15 Benjamin H. Strauss et al., "Economic Damages from Hurricane Sandy Attributable to Sea Level Rise Caused by Anthropogenic Climate Change," *Nature*, May 18, 2021.

16 Casey Crownhart, "Here's What We Know About Hurricanes and Climate Change," *MIT Technology Review*, August 20, 2023.

17 Joint Center for Housing Studies of Harvard University, "State of the Nation's Housing 2024," 2024, available at jchs.harvard.edu, based on data from the National Oceanic and Atmospheric Administration and the Federal Emergency Management Agency.

18 New York City Mayor's Office of Immigrant Affairs, "State of Our Immigrant City: Annual Report," March 2018.

19 Office of the Texas Governor, "Texas Transports Over 100,000 Migrants to Sanctuary Cities," news release, January 12, 2024; Sergio Martínez-Beltrán, "Texas Has Spent More Than $148 Million Busing Migrants to Other Parts of the Country," *Texas Tribune*, February 21, 2024.

20 Luis Ferré-Sadurní, "What to Know About the Migrant Crisis in New York City," *New York Times*, August 19, 2024; J. David Goodman et al., "Bus by Bus, Texas' Governor Changed Migration Across the US," *New York Times*, July 23, 2024.

21 Coalition for the Homeless, using data from NYC Mayor's Office of Operations, NYC Open Data, "Local Law 37/2011—Temporary Housing Assistance Usage Statistics," available at coalitionforthehomeless.org.

22 Coalition for the Homeless, "State of the Homeless 2024: Rights Under Attack,

Leadership in Retreat," July 2024, available at coalitionforthehomeless.org.

23 Arya Sundaram, "On Randall's Island, a Growing Divide Between Sheltered Migrants and Neighbors," *Gothamist*, September 2, 2024, available at gothamist.com.

24 Arya Sundaram, "Heavy Rainfall Causes Randall's Island Tent Facility for Migrants to Leak Like a Sieve," *Gothamist*, September 29, 2023, available at gothamist.com.

25 Luis Ferré-Sadurní, "New York City to Impose Stricter Limits on Migrant Adults in Shelters," *New York Times*, March 15, 2024.

26 Saskia Sassen, *Expulsions: Brutality and Complexity in the Global Economy* (Harvard University Press, 2014).

27 Mike Davis, *Planet of Slums* (Verso Books, 2017).

28 Karl Marx, *Capital: A Critique of Political Economy, Volume 1*, trans. Ben Fowkes (Penguin Books, 1990).

29 Søren Mau, *Mute Compulsion: A Marxist Theory of the Economic Power of Capital*, trans. Jonas Holst (Verso Books, 2023), 297–98.

30 Davis, *Planet of Slums*; Manuel Castells, *La cuestión urbana*, 12th ed. (Siglo Ventiuno Editores, 1988).

31 Ashley Nellis, "Mass Incarceration Trends," Sentencing Project, May 21, 2024, available at sentencingproject.org.

32 Nellis, "Mass Incarceration Trends."

CONCLUSION

1 White, Richard, *The Republic for Which It Stands: The United States during Reconstruction and the Gilded Age, 1865-1896* (Oxford University Press, 2017), p. 2.

2 Markee, Patrick, "State of the Homeless 2015: Turning the Tide," Coalition for the Homeless, March 19, 2015, pp. 2–3, available at coalitionforthehomeless.org.

3 James Baldwin, "Fifth Avenue, Uptown," in *The Price of the Ticket: Collected Nonfiction, 1948–1985* (St. Martin's Press, 1985).

4 Slee, Gillian and Matthew Desmond, "Eviction and Voter Turnout: The Political Consequences of Housing Instability," *Politics & Society* (Volume 51, 2023,, pp. 3–29), pp. 3–5.

For a complete list of sources for this book, please see
www.mhpbooks.com/books/placeless